Other books in The Princeton Review Series

Cracking the SAT and PSAT
Cracking the New SAT and PSAT
Cracking the New SAT and PSAT with Diagnostic Tests on Disk
Cracking the ACT
Cracking the LSAT
Cracking the LSAT with Diagnostic Tests on Disk
Cracking the GRE
Cracking the GRE with Diagnostic Tests on Disk
Cracking the GMAT
Cracking the MCAT
Cracking the Biology Achievement
Cracking the Chemistry Achievement
Cracking the English Achievements
Cracking the French Achievement
Cracking the History Achievements
Cracking the Math Achievements
Cracking the Physics Achievement
Cracking the Spanish Achievement
Cracking the TOEFL with audiocassette
How to Survive Without Your Parents' Money
Grammar Smart
Math Smart
Study Smart
Student Access Guide to America's Top 100 Internships
Student Access Guide to College Admissions
Student Access Guide to the Best Business Schools
Student Access Guide to the Best Law Schools
Student Access Guide to the Best Medical Schools
Student Access Guide to Paying for College
Student Access Guide to The Best 286 Colleges
Word Smart: Building a Better Vocabulary
Word Smart II: How to Build a More Educated Vocabulary

Also available on cassette from Living Language

Grammar Smart
Word Smart

THE **PRINCETON** REVIEW

CRACKING
THE GMAT®
with Diagnostic Tests on Disk

1994 EDITION

THE **PRINCETON** REVIEW

CRACKING
THE GMAT®
with Diagnostic Tests on Disk

1994 EDITION

GEOFF MARTZ,
JOHN KATZMAN,
AND ADAM ROBINSON

VILLARD BOOKS NEW YORK 1993

ISSN: 1062-5550
ISBN: 0-679-74888-1

Manufactured in the United States of America

9 8 7 6 5 4 3 2

Second Revised Edition

FOREWORD

In 1981 I founded The Princeton Review in order to help prepare high school students for the SAT (Scholastic Aptitude Test). My first course had nineteen students, and it was held in my parents' apartment. A year later, I began working with Adam Robinson, a highly regarded tutor. Within five years we had become the largest SAT course in the country.

Our SAT techniques are based in part on what we feel to be essential flaws in the design of the test—flaws that could cause students to score well below their true potential. When we looked at the GMAT (Graduate Management Admissions Test), we realized that it contains many of the same flaws as the SAT. (Both tests are written by the Educational Testing Service.) We felt that our techniques for tackling the SAT could be equally useful in tackling the GMAT. So, along with Geoff Martz, one of our veteran teachers and development experts, we designed a course specifically geared for the GMAT. For the past seven years, this course has been taught across the country. It has helped GMAT students attain the same phenomenal score improvements as our SAT students.

How do we do it?

First, unlike many coaches, we do not insist that the student learn dozens of math theorems or memorize all rules of written grammar. Our extensive examination of the GMAT has shown that the information needed to do well on this test is surprisingly limited. Thus, we concentrate on a small number of crucial concepts.

Those who have sweated through the GMAT and who have felt that the scores did not reflect their college grades or their business acumen probably suspect that there is more to mastering a standardized test than just reviewing rusty math and verbal skills. So we take our preparation a step further and teach techniques specifically designed to master multiple-choice standardized tests.

Finally, The Princeton Review offers even more than a thorough review and great techniques. Our classes are small (eight to twelve students) and are grouped according to ability. For students who require extra help, we provide smaller group work sessions and even one-on-one tutoring. In addition, we administer several diagnostic GMATs under actual exam conditions.

Unfortunately, many students can't get to our courses. So for you we have written this book. Although the book explains our strongest techniques, it cannot substitute for small classes and great teaching. Still, careful study and practice of the techniques will provide you with the means to boost your score significantly.

To get the maximum effect of our approach, you must practice on actual GMATs. The only source of real GMAT questions is a book published by the Educational Testing Service called *The Official Guide for GMAT Review*. Available in bookstores, it contains three complete GMATs plus sample sections of each question type. Applying our techniques to the questions in *The Official Guide for GMAT Review* will prove to you that they work. Make the techniques an integral part of the way you think about tests and you will be comfortable and confident using them when it counts—on the day of your actual GMAT.

When our first book, *Cracking the System: The SAT*, was published in 1986, many people asked us when we'd be coming out with books on other tests and other subjects. Since then we've published not only the book you are reading but also *College Admissions: Cracking the System, Word Smart* (a vocabulary book that will help you prepare for the GMAT, by the way), and guides to the GRE, LSAT, and MCAT.

If you have any questions about our course, or about academic matters in general, give us a call at 1-800-995-5585.

Good luck on your GMAT!

—John Katzman

ACKNOWLEDGMENTS

Our GMAT course is much more than clever techniques and powerful computer score reports; the reason our results are great is that our teachers care so much about their students. We would like to thank all the teachers who have made the GMAT course so successful, but in particular the core group of teachers and development people who helped get it off the ground: Alicia Ernst, Tom Meltzer, Paul Foglino, John Sheehan, Mark Sawula, Nell Goddin, Teresa Connelly, and Phillip Yee. We would also like thank Diane Reverand along with everyone at Villard Books and our agent, Julia Coopersmith.

Finally, we would like to thank the people who truly have taught us everything we know about the GMAT: our students.

CONTENTS

PART ONE

ORIENTATION

CHAPTER ONE

Orientation

What Is the Graduate Management Admission Test?

The Graduate Management Admission Test (GMAT) is a three-and-a-half-hour standardized multiple-choice test divided into seven sections:

1. a 20-question problem-solving math section.
2. a second 20-question problem-solving math section.
3. a 25-question math section called Data Sufficiency.
4. a 23-question Reading Comprehension section.
5. a 27-question grammar section called Sentence Correction.
6. a 20-question Critical Reasoning section.
7. an Experimental section.

Each of these sections lasts thirty minutes, and sections can appear in any order. The Experimental section is not used in the scoring process. The test publisher uses it to try out new questions for future tests and to gauge the relative difficulty of your GMAT. The Experimental section will look just like a regular section and can be from any of the section types. For example, on the test you take you might find that there are two Sentence Correction sections (one real, one Experimental). We will have more to say about the Experimental section later.

Where Does the GMAT Come From?

The GMAT is published by the Educational Testing Service (ETS) under the sponsorship of the Graduate Management Admission Council (GMAC). The council is supposed to oversee ETS. Both ETS and GMAC are private companies. We'll tell you more about them in this chapter.

How Is the GMAT Scored?

Four or five weeks after you've taken the GMAT, you will receive a report from ETS containing three scores:

1. Your total score
   This is reported on a scale that runs from 200 to 800, much like the SAT.

2. Your verbal score
   This is reported on a scale that runs from 0 to 60.

3. Your math score
   This is also reported on a scale that runs from 0 to 60.

Business schools tend to focus on the total score, which means that you can make up for your weakness in one area by being strong in another. For example, if your quantitative skills are better than your verbal skills, they will help pull up your total score. Total scores go up or down in ten-point increments. In other words, you might receive 490 or 500 on the GMAT, never 494 or 495.

You will also see a percentile ranking next to each score. For example, if you saw a percentile of 72 next to your verbal score, it would mean that 72 percent of the people who took this test scored lower than you did in verbal skills.

Are GMAT Scores Equivalent to SAT Scores?

No. Even though they both use the same 200–800 scale, GMAT scores are not the same as SAT scores. For one thing, the pool of applicants to business schools is much more select than the pool of applicants to colleges. People who take the GMAT have already graduated from college. In addition, most have several years of business experience.

The GMAT itself is more complex than the SAT. GMAT questions cover a broader range of topics and have a greater degree of difficulty.

Most people find that their GMAT score is somewhat lower than the score they received on the verbal or math SAT. According to ETS, two thirds of the people who take the GMAT score between 380 and 590.

What Is The Princeton Review?

The Princeton Review is a coaching school based in New York City. It has branches in over fifty cities across the country and several branches abroad. The Princeton Review's techniques are unique and powerful. We developed them after studying dozens of real ETS exams, analyzing them with computers, and proving our theories with our students. They work because they are based on the same principles that ETS uses in writing the test.

The Princeton Review's techniques for beating the GMAT will help you improve your scores by teaching you to:

1. think like the test-writers at ETS
2. take full advantage of the limited time allowed
3. find the answers to questions you don't understand by using our unique process-of-elimination techniques
4. avoid the traps that ETS has set for you (and use those traps to your advantage)

A Warning

Many of our techniques for beating the GMAT are counterintuitive. Some of them seem to violate "common sense." To get the full benefit of our techniques, you must trust them. The only way to develop this trust is to practice the techniques and convince yourself that they work.

But you have to practice them *properly*. If you try our techniques on the practice problems in most popular GMAT coaching books, you will probably decide that they don't work.

Why?

Because the practice questions in those books are very different from the questions on real GMATs. These books may have Data Sufficiency questions and Sentence Correction questions and Reading Comprehension questions, but if you compare them with the questions on real GMATs you'll find that the resemblance is only superficial. In fact, studying the practice questions and techniques in some of the other books could actually hurt your GMAT score.

One reason these coaching books do not use real GMAT questions is that the Graduate Management Admission Council won't let them. So far, the council has refused to let anyone (including us) license actual questions from old tests. The council says it is in the process of figuring out an equitable licensing system, but we aren't holding our breath. For one thing, the council has its *own* review book (published jointly with ETS) called *The Official Guide for GMAT Review*. The cover of the book boasts that it has 900 *authentic* GMAT test questions. ETS is apparently not in any hurry to let anyone else have access to real questions.

For this reason, we strongly recommend that you purchase the current edition of *The Official Guide for GMAT Review*. Ignore the suggested methods for answering the questions—they are too time-consuming to be of any use during a real test—and concentrate on the real GMAT sections.

The book can be found in many bookstores, or you can order it by sending a check for $11.95 (within the United States) to:

Graduate Management Admission Test
Educational Testing Service
P.O. Box 6108
Princeton, NJ 08541-6108

By practicing our techniques on real GMATs, you will be able to prove to yourself that the techniques work and increase your confidence when you actually take the test.

CHAPTER TWO

How to Think About the GMAT

Are You a Genius or an Idiot?

If you're like most people, you think standardized tests measure how smart you are. If you score 800 on the GMAT, you may think of yourself as a genius (and the future manager of a corporate empire). If you score 200, you may think of yourself as an idiot (and the future manager of a convenience store). You may think that the GMAT measures your math and verbal abilities. At the very least, you probably believe that the GMAT is an accurate predictor of how you'll do in business school.

One reason you might believe this is because ETS encourages you to think that it's so.

What Is ETS?

If you went to ETS to interview for a job, you would be impressed with the working conditions: a beautiful 400-acre estate just outside Princeton, New Jersey. The estate used to be a hunting club, and it boasts a swimming pool, a goose pond, a baseball diamond, lighted tennis courts, jogging trails, an expensive house for the company president, and a chauffeured motor pool.

You would also be impressed with the company's financial structure. ETS is a large private company, and it makes a lot of money. (It's also tax-exempt.) It sells the GMAT and the SAT of course, but it also sells about 500 other tests—including those for CIA agents, golf pros, travel agents, firemen, and barbers.

However, what would probably impress you the most, businesswise, is the fact that ETS has pulled off a deal that would in any other field have rendered it liable to antitrust action: ETS has a monopoly.

To Get into Business School You Can

A) take the GMAT
B) take the GMAT

If you don't like *Time*, you can read *Newsweek*. If you don't like AT&T, there are a host of competitors to choose from. But if you don't like the GMAT . . .well, you might as well consider going into social work.

ETS won't mind. They write that test, too.

It might strike you that a company could get fat and lazy without any competition to keep it honest, but you can't really blame ETS for trying to hold on to a deal that's as sweet as this one. And in order to do that, ETS must convince both you and the business schools you are applying to that the GMAT actually measures something.

There's just one hitch. It doesn't.

What Does the GMAT Measure?

The GMAT is not a test of how smart you are. Nor is it a test of your business ability. **It's simply a test of how good you are at taking ETS tests.** ETS says that "the GMAT is not a test of knowledge in specific subjects." This is also untrue. In fact, you will learn that by studying the very specific knowledge outlined in this book, you can substantially improve your score.

The GMAT as Job Interview

The first axiom of any how-to book on job interviewing is that you must always tell your interviewer what he or she wants to hear. Whether or not this is a good job-hunting advice, it happens to be a very useful strategy on the GMAT. The test-writers at ETS think in very predictable ways. You can improve your score by learning to think the way they do and by learning to anticipate the kinds of answers they think are correct.

How Not to Get a Job at ETS

Whatever you do, don't mention Harvard Business School. ETS is kind of sensitive about that. A few years ago, Harvard decided to try an experiment. They admitted part of their entering class according to the standard criteria (grade point average, GMAT, etc). One fifth of the class, however, were admitted without reference to their GMAT scores.

When the students finished their first year, the admissions officers at Harvard sat down and compared the two groups. After analyzing the results, Harvard decided to stop using the GMAT. If you send Harvard your GMAT results, they won't even open the envelope.

Who Writes the GMAT?

Many people believe that GMAT questions are written by university professors or successful executives. This is not true. Virtually all questions are written by ordinary company employees or by college students and other people who are hired part-time from outside ETS. Sometimes the questions are even written by teenagers. The daughter of one ETS vice president spent the summer after she graduated from high school writing questions for ETS tests.

ETS "examiners" try to write each question so that it can be used in as many as four different tests. Some of the questions from the GMAT have turned up on the SAT. As you struggle with a difficult question on the GMAT, it may console you to know that somewhere in America a hapless barber is having even more trouble with it than you are.

How Much Does the GMAT Change from Test to Test?

Not very much. Imagine that you're one of ETS's test-writers struggling to produce tests that will be taken by over 7 million students each year. Not only must your test question be suitable for the test you are now writing, but it must also be good enough to be included in a file from which future test questions for other tests may be chosen. Under these circumstances, what is needed is a kind of generic question written according to established formulas. While ETS has tried several different question types over the years, the essential philosophy of the GMAT hasn't changed much since the test was first administered in 1954.

Will ETS Change the Test in Response to The Princeton Review?

To make a significant change in the GMAT, ETS would have to alter its most fundamental notions of standardized testing. Until ETS is willing to give up its essential philosophy, the GMAT will remain a flawed test, and our techniques (which are based on those flaws) will continue to work just fine.

However, we are not asleep. We monitor each new GMAT very closely. Each year, we will publish a new edition of this book to reflect the subtle shifts that happen over time, as well as any changes in question type.

Forget About the "Best" Answer

The instructions for the GMAT tell you to select the "best" answer to every question. What does "best" answer mean? **It means the answer ETS believes to be correct.**

Is the GMAT Just Like the SAT?

The GMAT and the SAT are both prepared by the same organization, so they share the same philosophy. But there are substantial differences between the two tests. The GMAT is a much tougher test, and it contains question types not found on the SAT. Many of the techniques developed by The Princeton Review for the SAT are useful on some sections of the GMAT, but we have also developed new techniques and expanded on some of the old ones.

Is This Book Just Like the Princeton Review Course?

No. You won't have the benefit of taking four proctored GMATs that are analyzed and scored by our computers. You won't get to sit in small classes with ten other highly motivated students who will spur you on. You won't get to work with two expert instructors who can assess your strengths and pinpoint your weaknesses. There is no way to put these things in a book.

What you *will* find in this book are some of the techniques and methods that have enabled our students to crack the system—plus a review of the essentials you cannot afford not to know.

If at all possible, you should take our course. If that is impossible, then there is this book.

How to Crack the System

In the following chapters we're going to teach you our method for cracking the GMAT. Read each chapter carefully. Some of our ideas may seem strange at first. For example, when we tell you that it is sometimes easier to answer hard GMAT questions without actually working out the entire problem, you may think, "This isn't the way I conduct business."

The GMAT Isn't About Business

We're not going to teach you business skills. We're not going to teach you math and English. We're going to teach you the GMAT.

CHAPTER THREE

Cracking the System: Basic Principles

How to Score Higher (Instantly) on the GMAT

Nothing else we're going to suggest in this book will be as easy to accomplish as what we're about to tell you. In the following pages we will show you many powerful techniques to raise your score, and give you many insights into the way this test is designed, but none will be as simple to make use of as this first basic concept:

Don't Answer All the Questions!

Most people take the GMAT as if it were a race with points awarded for completing the course. Answering 135 questions hastily somehow seems preferable to answering, say, 115 questions carefully. Nothing could be further from the truth.

It turns out that you can score extremely well on the GMAT by completely skipping some of the questions. While the scoring formula varies slightly from test to test, here are some general guidelines:

• **You can score well above 550 (which is itself well above the national average) by getting 20 questions wrong *and* completely ignoring 25 questions.** That works out to skipping an average of 4 questions on *every* section.

Don't believe us? Look in the back of the current edition of *The Official Guide for GMAT Review,* which includes three full-length GMATs. On those tests someone who got 20 questions wrong and skipped 25 additional questions scored 570 or 580.

• **You can score well above 500 on the GMAT by getting 25 questions wrong and completely ignoring 30 questions.** That works out to skipping an average of 5 questions on *every* section.

On the GMATs in the back of the *Official Guide,* someone who got 25 questions wrong and skipped 30 questions scored 530 or 540.

You May Think You Already Skip Questions

Most students end up skipping a few questions. Of course, they're not really "skipping" these questions. They look at a question, spend three minutes trying to figure it out and then end up leaving it blank. In other words, they "skip" problems because they don't know the answer.

Don't You Dare Skip a Question Just Because You Don't Know the Correct Answer

This may sound a little loony, but it turns out that you don't always have to know the correct answer to get a question right.

Try answering the following question:

What is the unit of currency in Yugoslavia?

What? You don't know? You'd better skip it then.

Unless you work for an international bank or have traveled in Eastern Europe, there is no reason why you should know the unit of currency in Yugoslavia. (By the way, the GMAT doesn't ask such factual questions. We're using this one to make a point.) As it stands now, since you don't know the answer you would have to skip this question, right?

Not necessarily. GMAT questions are written in multiple-choice format. One of the five choices has to be the answer. How do you find it?

By Looking for Wrong Answers Instead of Right Ones

Let's put this question into a multiple-choice format—the only format you'll ever find on the GMAT—and see if you still want to skip it.

> What is the unit of currency in Yugoslavia?
>
> (A) the dollar (B) the franc (C) the pound sterling
> (D) the yen (E) the dinar

How to Score Higher (Almost Instantly) on the GMAT

Suddenly this question isn't difficult anymore. You may not have known the right answer, but you certainly knew enough to eliminate the wrong answers. Wrong answers are often easier to spot than right answers. Sometimes they just sound weird. At other times they're logically impossible. While it is rare to be able to eliminate all four of the incorrect answer choices on the GMAT, you will almost always be able to eliminate at least one of them—and frequently two or more—by using Process of Elimination. Process of Elimination (POE for short) will enable you to answer questions that you don't have the time or the inclination to figure out exactly. We will refer to POE in every single chapter of this book. It is one of the most fundamental tools you will use to increase your score.

Try another example:

> Which of the following countries uses the peso as its
> unit of currency?
>
> (A) Russia (B) Canada (C) Venezuela (D) England (E) Chile

This time you can probably only get rid of three of the five answer choices using POE. The answer is clearly *not* Russia, Canada or England, but most people probably don't know for sure whether the answer is Venezuela or Chile.

You've got the question down to two possibilities. Should you guess, or just leave the question blank?

Heads or Tails

A Chilean might flip a peso. You have a fifty-fifty chance of getting this question right—heads you win, tails you lose.

But how much do you stand to win or lose?

ETS figures out your score by adding up all the questions you get right and then subtracting a quarter of all the questions you get wrong. (Blank answers are completely ignored—they don't cost you any points and they don't add any points.) The sum of correct answers minus a quarter of incorrect answers is your raw score. Using a "scoring formula," this is then converted into the number somewhere between 200 and 800 that will be sent to the business schools you're applying to.

For every correct answer, you get one raw point.

For every blank answer, you get nothing.

For every wrong answer, ETS subtracts one fourth of a raw point.

In other words, four mistakes will erase one correct answer. ETS does this to prevent you from guessing randomly, but let's see how this really works.

Guessing Is Good

Raw points and scaled scores are confusing. Let's put this in terms of something we deal with every day: money.

For every answer you get right, ETS will give you a dollar. For every question you leave blank, ETS will give you nothing. For every answer you get wrong, ETS will take away twenty-five cents.

If you guessed completely at random on five questions, what would happen? There are five answer choices for each question, so you would have a one-in-five chance of getting the right answer on each of the questions. According to the laws of probability, you should get one out of the five questions correct.

So ETS gives you a dollar.

In the meantime, you got four questions wrong. So ETS takes away a quarter for each of the four questions.

What just happened? By guessing completely at random, you ended up with exactly the same score as if you had left all five questions blank. In other words, guessing didn't hurt you. Guessing *never* hurts you.

Heads You Win a Dollar, Tails You Lose a Quarter

Let's go back to the peso problem. We were down to a fifty-fifty guess. The answer was Chile or Venezuela. In this case we're no longer guessing at random. We've eliminated three of the answer choices—the odds are much better now. Heads you win a dollar, tails you lose a quarter.

Suppose there were two problems you didn't know how to solve on the GMAT but POE allowed you to eliminate three answer choices on each of them. This leaves you with two fifty-fifty guesses. The odds say you'll get one of these two questions correct. So ETS gives you a dollar. The odds say you'll get the other one wrong. So ETS takes away twenty-five cents.

You're seventy-five cents ahead.

You Can Increase Your Score by Guessing

In the chapters that follow, we'll show you specific ways to make use of POE to increase your score. You may feel uncomfortable about using these techniques at first, but the sooner you make them your own, the sooner you'll start to improve your score.

Is This Fair?

If you took any math courses in college you probably remember that the correct answer to a problem, while important, wasn't the only thing you were graded on. Your professor was surely more interested in *how* you got the answer, whether you wrote an elegant equation or used the right formula.

If your equation was correct but you messed up your addition at the end, did you get the entire question wrong? Most college professors give partial credit for an answer like that. After all, what's most important is the mental process that goes into getting the answer, not the answer alone.

On the GMAT, if you don't pencil in the right oval on your answer sheet, you're wrong. It doesn't matter that you knew *how* to do the problem, or that you marked the wrong answer on your answer sheet *by mistake*. You're just wrong.

This really isn't fair. It seems only fitting that you should be able to benefit from the flip side of this situation. If you fill in the correct oval, ETS doesn't care how you got that answer either.

When you leave a question blank on the GMAT, the impression you give is that you knew nothing about the question. But consider the peso question. While it's true that you probably weren't sure of the exact answer, you did know several things about that problem: You knew three answers that were definitely wrong. Didn't you deserve partial credit for knowing that?

You won't get it unless you guess.

If Guessing Is So Great, Why Leave ANY Questions Blank?

First of all, on some questions you really may not know anything. If there are no answer choices you can eliminate, there is no sense in guessing. Second, POE takes time. Rushing to finish all the questions in a section will cause you to make careless mistakes, and may cause you to fall into the traps ETS has set for you. On problems where you have to guess, take the time to make sure you guess well.

So Which Questions Should You Skip?

There are two types of questions you should skip.

The ones you don't like. Let's imagine that you're in the middle of a 20-question problem-solving section. If you're shooting for a score of 550, you know that you can safely skip four problems and still have room to make a few mistakes.

This means that all you have to do on this section is find sixteen problems that you like.

If you take one look at problem number 12 and develop an instant, unreasoning hatred for it, skip it and never give it a second thought.

The ones you know absolutely nothing about. If there is absolutely nothing you can think of to do on a problem, then it makes no sense to spend any time on it. Skip it and move on.

CRACKING THE SYSTEM: BASIC PRINCIPLES

Summary

1. You don't need to answer every question on the GMAT in order to get an extremely good score. By skipping some questions, you save time and improve your accuracy on the ones you choose to do.

2. Not knowing the exact answer to a question, however, is not a good reason to leave it blank.

3. When you don't know the right answer to a question, look for wrong answers instead. This is called POE.

4. Guessing blindly will not hurt your score. Guessing well will *raise* your score.

CHAPTER FOUR

Cracking the System: Advanced Principles

Putting the Basic Principles to Work

In the last chapter we reviewed some basic principles about cracking the GMAT. We showed you that it is possible to:

1. find correct answers by using POE, the Process of Elimination, to get rid of incorrect answer choices
2. earn partial credit for partial information

In this chapter we'll show you which choices to eliminate, when you should guess and when it makes sense to skip a question entirely.

You'll also learn how to

1. take advantage of question order, particularly on the math sections
2. make better use of your time by scoring the easy points first
3. use the Joe Bloggs principle to eliminate obviously incorrect choices
4. find the traps ETS has set for you
5. turn these traps into points

Order of Difficulty

If you've seen an actual GMAT, you probably noticed that the questions in the math sections got harder as you went along. You probably didn't think much of it at the time, but this is always true on the GMAT. Every math section starts out easy and gets progressively harder. In the verbal sections the same principles apply, although you'll see as you get to the chapters that cover these sections that the verbal strategies we will be showing you will make the order of difficulty irrelevant.

Easy, Medium, Hard

In general it's a good idea to think of each math section of the GMAT as having three parts:

1. The easy third: Questions in the first third of a section are easy.
2. The medium third: Questions in the middle third are medium.
3. The difficult third: Questions in the last third are difficult.

For example, in a 20-question math section, questions 1–7 are easy, 8–14 are medium, and 15–20 are hard. If you keep this in mind, you'll have a big advantage on the GMAT. You'll know that it's silly to spend a lot of time trying to answer the 20th (and therefore hardest) question of a math section before you've answered all the easy questions.

All questions on the GMAT are worth the same number of points. Why not do the easy ones first? Smart test-takers save the hard questions for last, after they've racked up all the easy points.

Lies, Damned Lies, and Statistics

Why does ETS construct the GMAT this way? ETS is obsessed with statistics. One statistic ETS thinks is important is the accuracy of its tests in measuring low-scoring as well as high-scoring students. The GMAT is supposed to measure "general developed abilities" over a wide spectrum. In other words, it is supposed to be just as fair in assessing the ability of someone who scores 200 as it is in assessing the abilities of someone who scores 800.

If ETS put the difficult questions first, many people would never get to the easier questions that they could answer correctly. So ETS puts the easiest questions first and gradually increases the level of difficulty. It is not much different from a high jump contest in which the bar is raised a notch on each round. The theory is that a student will answer questions correctly until he or she reaches his or her level of ability, and then will get everything else wrong. This is supposed to ensure that each student receives every point he or she "deserves."

The people at ETS are very pleased with the GMAT. After all they write it, and it makes a lot of money for them every year. In fact, they think this test is so good it can make a meaningful distinction between someone who scores 420 and someone who scores 450. They're especially proud of their statistics. Just about every article we've ever seen about education in America uses statistics compiled by ETS. But ETS has this little problem.

ETS's Problem

The GMAT is a multiple-choice test.

That may not seem like a problem to you, but consider the following situation. Suppose an average student takes the GMAT and answers all the questions he understands. The student is all set to put down his pencil when one last difficult question catches his eye. One of the answer choices just "seems" right. So he picks it.

And gets it right.

ETS gets nightmares just thinking about this situation. That average student was supposed to get 500. He "deserved" 500. But by guessing the correct answer to one extra problem, he may have gotten 510.

Ten points more than he "deserved."

ETS's Solution

ETS's statistics wouldn't be worth much if students could routinely guess the correct answer to difficult questions by picking answers that *seemed* right.

So ETS came up with a wonderful solution:

On difficult questions, answer choices that *seem* right to the average student are always wrong.

Choosing Answers that *Seem* Right

When we take the GMAT, most of us don't have time to work out every problem completely, or to check and double-check our answers. We just go as far as we can on each problem and then choose the answer that seems correct based on what we've been able to figure out. Sometimes we're completely sure of our answer. At other times we simply do what we can and then follow our hunch. We may pick an answer because it "just looks right," or because something about it seems to go naturally with the question.

Whether you're a high scorer or a low scorer, this is almost certainly the way you approach the GMAT. You figure out as much of each problem as you can and then choose the answer that seems right, all things considered. Sometimes you're fairly positive that your answer is correct. But at other times—on hard problems—all you can do is follow your hunch and hope you're right.

Which Answers Seem Right?

That all depends on how high your score is.

Suppose you took the GMAT and scored 800. That means every answer that *seemed* right to you actually *was* right. You picked the answer that seemed right on every question, and every one of those answers was correct.

Now suppose your friend took the GMAT and scored 200. That means every answer that *seemed* right to your friend actually was *wrong*.

Of course, most people who take the GMAT don't score 800 or 200. The average person scores somewhere in between.

What Happens When the Average Person Takes the GMAT?

The average person isn't right all the time. But the average person isn't wrong all the time, either. Like everybody else, the average person picks the answer that *seems* right on every problem. Sometimes these hunches are correct; sometimes they are not.

To be specific:

- **On the easy questions in each section, the average person tends to pick the correct answer. The answers that *seem* right to the average person actually *are* right on these questions.**
- **On the medium questions in each section, the average person's hunches are right only some of the time. Sometimes the answers that *seem* right to the average person really *are* right; sometimes they are wrong.**
- **Finally, on the difficult third, the average person's hunches are *always* wrong. The answers that *seem* right to the average person on these questions invariably turn out to be wrong.**

Meet Joe Bloggs

We're going to talk a lot about "the average person" from now on. For the sake of convenience, let's give him a name: Joe Bloggs. Joe Bloggs is just the average American prospective business-school student. He has average grades from college, and will get an average grade on the GMAT. There's a little bit of him in everyone, and there's a little bit of everyone in him. He isn't brilliant. He isn't dumb. He's exactly average.

How Does Joe Bloggs Approach the GMAT?

Joe Bloggs, the average person, approaches the GMAT just as everybody else does. Whether the question is hard or easy, he always chooses the answer that *seems* to be correct.

Here's an example of what a difficult problem might look like on a GMAT problem-solving section:

18. The output of a factory was increased by 10% to keep up with rising demand. To handle the Christmas rush, this new output was increased by 20%. By approximately what percent would the output now have to be decreased in order to restore the original output?

(A) 20%   (B) 24%   (C) 30%   (D) 32%   (E) 79%

This is the 18th question in a 20-question section. Therefore, according to the order of difficulty, it is one of the hardest problems in that section. Don't bother trying to work the problem out now. You will learn how to do this type of problem (percentage decrease) in the first math chapter.

How Did Joe Bloggs Do on This Question?

He got it wrong.
  Why?
  Because ETS set a trap for him.

Which Answer Did Joe Bloggs Pick on This Question?

Joe didn't think this was a hard problem. The answer *seemed* perfectly obvious. Joe Bloggs picked choice (C). Joe assumed that if you increase production first by 10% and then by 20%, you have to take away 30% to get back to where you started. Joe chose choice (C) as his answer.

ETS led Joe away from the correct answer, and actually may have encouraged him to guess, by giving him an answer that *seemed* right. In fact, the correct answer is choice (B). Here's the same problem with slightly different answer choices. We've changed the choices to make a point:

18. The output of a factory was increased by 10% to keep up with rising demand. To handle the Christmas rush, this new output was raised by 20%. By approximately what percent would the output now have to be decreased in order to restore the original output?

(A) 21%   (B) 24%   (C) 34.2%   (D) 37%   (E) 71.5%

If Joe had seen this version, he wouldn't have thought it was an easy question anymore. Now none of the answers would *seem* right to

Joe. He might have left it blank, or he might have guessed. This would have made the question fairer, but ETS didn't want to take the chance that an *average* person might get this question right by mistake.

Could ETS Have Made This an Easy Question Instead?

Sure, by writing different answer choices.

Here's the same question with choices we've substituted to make the correct answer choice obvious:

18.   The output of a factory was increased by 10% to keep up with rising demand. To handle the Christmas rush, this new output was raised by 20%. By approximately what percent would the output now have to be decreased in order to restore the original output?

(A) a million %   (B) 24%   (C) a billion %
(D) a trillion %   (E) a zillion %

When the problem is written this way, Joe Bloggs can see that the answer has to be choice (B). It seems right to Joe because all the other answers seem obviously wrong.

Profiting from Other People's Bankruptcy

Everyone knows about a company that is a textbook example of how *not* to run a company.

Suppose you started your own company, with three partners: Freddie Laker, John Delorean, and Ivan Boesky. You have an important business decision to make, and each of your partners gives you his advice. Laker says, "Sell your product for less than it cost you to make it. It always worked for me." Delorean says, "I have a great investment opportunity for you. Get together $200,000 in cash and call this number in Bolivia." Boesky says, "Listen, what you need is good inside information."

Are you going to make use of the advice of these losers? Sure, you now know three things you're not going to do.

Joe Bloggs is a textbook example of how *not* to take a test.

Your Partner on the Test: Joe Bloggs

When you take the GMAT a few weeks or months from now, you'll have to take it on your own, of course. But suppose for a moment that ETS allowed you to take it with Joe Bloggs as your partner. Would Joe be any help to you on the GMAT?

You Probably Don't Think So

After all, Joe is wrong as often as he's right. He knows the answers to the easy questions, but so do you. You'd like to do better than average on the GMAT, and Joe earns only an average score (he's the average person, remember). All things considered, you'd probably prefer to have someone else for your partner.

But Joe might turn out to be a pretty helpful partner, after all. Since his hunches on difficult questions are *always* wrong, couldn't you improve your chances on those questions simply by finding out what Joe wanted to pick, and then picking something else?

If you could use what you know about Joe Bloggs to eliminate one, two, or even three obviously incorrect choices on a hard problem, wouldn't you improve your score by guessing among the remaining choices?

The Joe Bloggs Principle

We're going to teach you how to use Joe Bloggs on the GMAT. When you come to difficult questions on the test, you're going to stop and ask yourself, "How would Joe Bloggs answer this question?" And when you see what he would do, you're going to do something else. Why? Because you know that on hard questions, Joe Bloggs is *always* wrong.

What If Joe Bloggs Is Right?

Remember what we said about Joe Bloggs at the beginning. He's the average person. He thinks the way most people do. If the right answer to a hard question seemed right to most people, the question wouldn't be hard, would it?

Joe Bloggs is right on some questions: the easy ones. But he's always wrong on the hard questions.

Should You Always Just Eliminate Any Answer That Seems to Be Correct?

No!

Remember what we said about Joe Bloggs:

1. His hunches are often correct on easy questions.
2. His hunches are sometimes correct and sometimes incorrect on medium questions.
3. His hunches are always wrong on difficult questions.

Putting Joe Bloggs to Work for You

In the following chapters, we'll be teaching you many specific problem-solving techniques based on the Joe Bloggs principle. The Joe Bloggs principle will help you:

1. use POE to eliminate incorrect answer choices.
2. make up your mind when you have to guess.
3. avoid careless mistakes.

Summary

1. The questions in each of the three math sections start out easy and gradually get harder. Most people are supposed to get the first question correct. Almost no one is expected to get the last one correct.

2. The questions in the verbal sections generally follow the same pattern, but you will find that our techniques will make ETS's order of difficulty irrelevant.

3. Since you know where the easy questions are located, you should never waste time trying to figure out the answer to a hard question if there are still easy questions you haven't tried. All questions are worth the same number of points. Why not do the easy ones first?

4. Except for Sentence Correction questions, every section of the GMAT can be divided into thirds by degree of difficulty as follows:

- On the easy third of each section, the average person gets most of the answers right. The answers that *seem* right to the average person actually *are* right on these questions.
- On the medium third of each section, though, the average person's hunches are right only some of the time. Sometimes the answers that *seem* right to the average person really *are* right; sometimes they are wrong.
- Finally, on the difficult third, the average person's hunches are *always* wrong. The average person picks the correct answer on the hardest questions only by accident. The answers that *seem* right to the average person on these questions invariably turn out to be wrong.

5. Almost everyone approaches the GMAT by choosing the answer that *seems* correct, all things considered.

6. Joe Bloggs is the average person. He earns an average score on the GMAT. On easy GMAT questions, the answers that *seem* correct to him are usually correct. On medium questions, they're sometimes correct and sometimes not. On hard questions, they're *always* wrong.

7. The correct answer on a hard question could never seem right to most people. If it did, the question would be easy, not hard.

CHAPTER FIVE

Taking the GMAT

Tick, Tick, Tick . . .

If you've read the first three chapters of this book, you've already begun to see that while doing well on this test involves proper utilization of time, the GMAT isn't quite the race against time you may have thought it to be.

Using the pacing guide on page 14, you can begin to map out a strategy of how many questions you actually need to answer in order to get the score you're looking for. There will be many problems you can afford to skip completely.

We're going to show you some powerful techniques in the chapters ahead. To take full advantage of these techniques, it's important that you practice on real GMATs. The practice tests in most other GMAT preparation books won't help you; they aren't sufficiently like real GMATs. The only available source of real GMAT questions is a book we've already mentioned in the first chapter: *The Official Guide for GMAT Review*, which is published by ETS.

Periodically, as you work through this book, you should time yourself while taking real GMAT sections. This will give you practice in using our techniques, and get you used to taking the test under timed conditions.

The Princeton Review Diagnostic Test

At the back of this book you will find a complete GMAT diagnostic test designed by The Princeton Review. While not a real ETS exam, our diagnostic offers one important advantage the real ones do not: our answer key (found at the end of the test) not only provides you with the correct answers and a scoring chart but also tells you which Princeton Review techniques can help to answer each question. We recommend that you take this exam about halfway through your preparation.

On the Day of the Real Test

Get up early, have breakfast, and do a couple of GMAT questions you've already seen in order to get your mind working. You don't want to have to warm up on the test itself. Bring a snack to the test center. You'll get one break during the test. Some people spend the break comparing answers in the hallway and getting upset because their answers don't match. Ignore the people around you. Why assume that they know any more than you do? Use the break to eat the food you've brought.

At the test site you'll be asked for some form of picture ID. Your driver's license, passport, or employee ID will do. Bring four sharpened No. 2 pencils and a reliable watch, preferably digital. Obviously no calculators are permitted.

Before the test starts, make sure you're comfortable. Is there enough light; is your desk sturdy? Don't be afraid to speak up; you're going to be spending three and a half hours at that desk.

As you begin each new section, put the last one behind you. Don't get rattled if you think you've done poorly on a particular section. Most people find that their impression of how they did on a section is often worse than the reality. More important, you should remember that one of the seven sections you'll be taking doesn't count. The Experimental section is often harder and weirder than the rest of the test. If you feel you've blown a particular section, there's a good chance it was Experimental.

However, even if you're sure you've spotted the Experimental section, never just blow it off. Take each section as if it counts. You don't want to be wrong about something so important.

At the End of the Test

When you finish the test, there will be some time while the proctor reads you final thank-you-for-flying-ETS instructions and collects test booklets. Use this time to darken the responses on your answer sheet and to erase any stray marks you may have made. The machine that scans your answer sheet may miss a response if it is too faint or record a stray mark as a wrong answer.

One oval you should *not* darken is the one that allows you to cancel your scores then and there. If you choose to cancel at the test site, you will not be able to change your mind later. Even if you're unhappy with the way the test went, you should certainly go home and sleep on it before making a decision. If you still want to cancel, you can do so later by mail. ETS must receive your written request to cancel within seven days of the test.

Do *not* assume that your test has been scored correctly. Send away for ETS's Test Disclosure Service. For $10, ETS will send you a copy of the test you took (minus the Experimental section) and a photocopy of your answer sheet. It is possible that one or more of your responses was too faint to be picked up by the scanning machine but is perfectly visible to the eye. By the same token, an erased answer may have been scored as an incorrect response. Check your answers against the key and complain if you think you've been misscored.

One Final Thought Before You Begin

No matter how high or low you score on this test, and no matter how much you improve your performance with this book, you should *never* accept the score ETS sends you as an accurate assessment of your abilities. The temptation to see a high score as evidence that you're a genius, or a low score as evidence that you're an idiot, can be very powerful.

When you've read this book and practiced our techniques on real GMAT questions, you'll be able to judge for yourself whether the GMAT actually measures much besides how well you do on the GMAT.

Think of this as a kind of game—a game you can get good at.

PART TWO

HOW
TO CRACK
THE
VERBAL
GMAT

CHAPTER SIX

Sentence Correction

The Sentence Correction section of the GMAT is composed of 27 sentences, each of which is partly underlined. You must decide whether a sentence is grammatically correct the way it is written or, if it needs a correction, which of the answer choices best replaces the underlined portion.

Before we begin, take a moment to read the following instructions. They are a close approximation of instructions you will see on the real GMAT. Be sure you know and understand these instructions before you take the GMAT. If you learn them ahead of time, you won't have to waste valuable seconds reading them on the day you take the test.

The Bad News

It is important to understand the fine print of the instructions you have
just read. The test-writers at ETS ask you to choose the "best" answer,
by which they mean the answer they think is right. The bad news is
that some of the "correct" answer choices in this section will probably
not sound correct to you. The rules of English as interpreted by ETS
are very different from the rules of English that govern what we read
in newspapers or hear on television or speak in our everyday lives.

How many times have you heard your boss, or a television
anchorperson, or a president of the United States, make the following
statement?

> "Hopefully, we will know the answer to that
> question tomorrow."

While you probably don't want to make a habit of correcting
people's grammar, you should know that this sentence is not techni-
cally correct. According to ETS, the president was supposed to say,
"It is hoped that we will know the answer to that question tomorrow."
It may be of some comfort to you that your boss, the television
anchorperson, and the president of the United States would all get a
question like this wrong if they took the GMAT.

GMAT English

GMAT English should be studied the same way you would approach
any other foreign language. It has its own rules and its own internal
logic. GMAT English has much in common with American English,
but if you rely solely on your ear, you may get into trouble.

Confronted with a badly constructed sentence, most of us could find *a* way to fix that sentence. Most of the time we would probably break the sentence into two separate sentences (GMAT sentences are often too long and unwieldy). Unfortunately, on this test we are forced to find *the* way to fix the sentence; that is to say, ETS's way to fix it.

To do well on this section of the test, you will have to learn GMAT English.

The Good News

ETS test-writers try to stick to the basics. If they tested a controversial point of grammar, they might be proven wrong. They don't want to have to change their minds after a test is given and mail 20,000 letters explaining why they're changing the answer key (something that has happened from time to time in the past). The easiest way to avoid trouble is to test a handful of the rules of standard written English that are commonly agreed upon.

There are huge books devoted exclusively to the correct use of English. You could spend the next six weeks just studying grammar and never even scratch the surface. The good news is that this won't be necessary. Although there are hundreds of rules of standard written English that could be tested, the GMAT concentrates on only a few.

In other words, GMAT English is fairly easy to learn.

Sentence Correction: Cracking the System

In this chapter we'll show you the most common types of errors tested in GMAT sentences, and how to spot them. We'll show you how ETS chooses the four incorrect choices for each question, and we'll show you how to use Process of Elimination to make your life a lot easier.

To forestall the objections of the expert grammarians out there, let us say at the outset that this discussion is not designed to be an all-inclusive discussion of English grammar. You are reading this chapter to do well on sentence correction *as it appears on the GMAT*. Thus, if we seem to oversimplify a point, or ignore an arcane exception to a rule, it is because we do not feel that any more detail is warranted. Remember, this isn't English; it's GMAT English.

Order of Difficulty

According to ETS, the Sentence Correction section usually starts with easy sentences, gets progressively more difficult, and then finishes with a couple of easy sentences. Most of our students find that they can't tell the difference; the first question often seems as poorly worded as the last. You will find that our Sentence Correction techniques make the order of difficulty in this section irrelevant.

Process of Elimination

Most people approach Sentence Correction questions the same way. They read the original sentence and then read the entire sentence again, substituting answer choice (B) for the underlined part. Then they go back and do the same thing for answer choices (C), (D), and (E). This approach is both laborious and confusing. It's hard to keep five different versions of the same sentence straight, especially when all five of them are awkward.

The Princeton Review approach will utilize Process of Elimination to narrow down your choices before you have to start reading the answer choices carefully.

Since there are relatively few types of errors that appear on the Sentence Correction section, we will focus on teaching you how to spot these errors. Once you've spotted the error in a sentence you'll be able to go through the answer choices and eliminate any that also contain that error. Then you can decide among the remaining choices.

Basic Principles

Let's look at a Sentence Correction question written in a way that you will unfortunately never see on the real GMAT—with only the correct answer listed:

Registered brokerage firms have been required to record details of all computerized program trades made in the past year so that government agencies will be able to decide if they should be banned.

(A)
(B)
(C)
(D)
(E) will be able to decide if program trades should be banned

Piece of cake, right? It gets a little harder when they throw in the other four answer choices. Don't worry if you aren't sure why answer choice (E) is better than the original sentence. We will cover how to spot this type of error (pronoun reference) a little later in the chapter. For now, it's enough to know that the "they" in the underlined portion of the sentence was ambiguous. It wasn't clear whether "they" referred to "registered brokerage firms," "details," or the "computerized program trades."

Don't bother saying it was perfectly obvious that "they" referred to the program trades. This is GMAT English, remember? It doesn't matter if *you* knew what the sentence meant. The sentence had to be clear to the ETS test-writer who wrote it.

Zen and the Art of Test Writing

Let's put ourselves in the place of the GMAT test-writer who wrote this question. He has just finished his sentence and he has his correct answer, but he isn't finished yet. He still has to write four other answer choices. It's actually kind of difficult to come up with four answer choices that seem plausible but are wrong. If the test-writer makes the incorrect choices too obviously wrong, Joe Bloggs might be able to pick the correct answer without having really understood the rule of English involved. If the test-writer makes the incorrect answer choices too subtle, Joe Bloggs won't find one that seems right to him, and therefore might guess at random. The test-writer does *not* want Joe to guess at random. If Joe guesses at random, he might actually pick the right answer.

One Down, Four to Go

Selecting the correct answer was easy for our test-writer—after all, *he* wrote the question. He will probably spend much more time on the incorrect answer choices.

Answer Choice (A)

Coming up with the first wrong answer choice also is easy for our test-writer; answer choice (A) always repeats the underlined part of the original sentence. This is the choice to select if you think the sentence is correct as written. Two down, three to go.

If You Can't Sell a Lemon, Repackage It

To see whether Joe has spotted the error of the sentence, the ETS test-writer will include the *same error* in at least one, usually two, of the other answer choices. If Joe didn't like the error in the original sentence, maybe he'll like it better surrounded by different words. Look at the same sentence again, this time with two incorrect answer choices that both include the same error found in the original sentence:

> Registered brokerage firms have been required to record details of all computerized program trades made in the past year so that government agencies <u>will be able to decide if they should be banned</u>.
>
> (A)
> (B) should be able to decide if they should be banned
> (C) should be able to decide if they can be banned
> (D)
> (E)

Joe Bloggs has no idea what point of grammar is being tested in this question. He picks answers because they sound good. Our test-writer is hoping that one of these answer choices will sound better to Joe than the correct answer. Both choices change the sentence in different ways, but both still contain the ambiguous "they," and both are still wrong.

Almost Right

Our test-writer has one more kind of trap to insert into his question. This time the trap isn't for Joe Bloggs; it's for the person who has spotted the error in the sentence but is in too big a hurry to make fine distinctions.

Usually one of the incorrect answer choices will actually fix the original error—*but will create some new error in the process.*

Spotting the original error is all well and good, but our test-writer wants to make sure you really "deserve" to get this one right. So he'll include an answer choice that's almost right. It will be a close variation of the "best" answer; it will correct the mistake in the original sentence; it will be *wrong.*

Here's the same sentence with an answer choice that fixes the original mistake but creates a new one:

Registered brokerage firms have been required to
record details of all computerized program trades
made in the past year so that government agencies
<u>will be able to decide if they should be banned</u>.

(A)
(B)
(C)
(D) will be able to decide if program trades should
     be able to be banned
(E)

Answer choice (D) fixes the original problem; there is no longer an
ambiguous "they" in the sentence. Our test-writer is hoping that
anyone who has spotted the original error will read just far enough to
see that answer choice (D) fixes it, but not far enough to see that there
is something else wrong. What's wrong? On the GMAT, only animate
objects are "able" to do anything.

Three Down, Two to Go

Let's look at the entire problem, now that our test-writer has finished
it, and count our blessings.

Registered brokerage firms have been required to
record details of all computerized program trades
made in the past year so that government agencies
<u>will be able to decide if they should be banned</u>.

(A) will be able to decide if they should be banned
(B) should be able to decide if they should be
     banned
(C) should be able to decide if they can be banned
(D) will be able to decide if program trades should
     be able to be banned
(E) will be able to decide if program trades should
     be banned

Here's how to crack it: By spotting what was wrong in the original
sentence, we could have eliminated three of the five answer choices.
Choice (A) merely repeated the original sentence word for word.
Choices (B) and (C) contained the same error found in the original
sentence.

We're down to choice (D) or (E). Both fix the original error.
What's the difference between them? Three words. If you don't see
it, don't soul-search. Just pick one and move on. The correct answer
is choice (E).

Our Basic Approach

To use POE, you must be able to spot the errors in the original sentences. Fortunately, ETS leans heavily on only a few major types of errors. Just recognizing these errors should enable you to answer many of the twenty-seven problems in a Sentence Correction section—once you've learned one other important concept:

The Most Common Error Is *No* Error

About one fifth of the Sentence Correction sentences are fine just the way they are. If a sentence is correct as is, the "best" answer is answer choice (A), which repeats the original sentence. There are usually about five (A)s in every Sentence Correction section.

How do you tell when there is nothing wrong with a sentence?

You can tell that a sentence is correct by the *absence* of any of the other types of errors that we are going to show you how to look for. Try not to use your ear—at least not at first. As you read each sentence, you'll be marking off a mental checklist of likely ETS errors. If you come to the end of the list without having found an error in the sentence, chances are very good that there was none.

When in doubt, leave the question blank and come back to it after you've finished the other questions. Now count the number of (A)s you've already chosen. If you've marked down fewer than five (A)s, the odds are even greater that there was nothing wrong with the original sentence. If you've already chosen more than five (A)s, you haven't scoured carefully enough. Go back over this question, and any other (A)s you weren't completely sure about, and take a harder look.

We'll come back to (A)s later in the chapter, after you've learned how to spot the major errors.

Before We Start, Some Basic Terminology

You won't be asked to *name* the parts of speech on the GMAT. However, an acquaintance with some of these terms is necessary to understand the techniques we're about to show you.

- A *noun* is a word used to name a person, place, thing, or idea.
- A *verb* is a word that expresses action.

Here is a very basic sentence:

Sue opened the box.

In this sentence, *Sue* and *box* are both nouns, and *opened* is a verb. *Sue* is considered the subject of this sentence because it is the person, place, or thing about which something is being said. *Box* is considered the object of the sentence because it receives the action of the verb.

- An *adverb* is a word that modifies a verb.
- An *adjective* is a word that modifies a noun.
- A *preposition* is a word that notes the relation of a noun to an action or a thing.
- A *phrase* is a group of words acting as a single part of speech. A phrase is missing either a subject or a verb or both.
- A *prepositional phrase* is a group of words beginning with a preposition. Like any *phrase*, a prepositional phrase does not contain both a subject and a verb.

Here's a more complicated version of the same sentence.

Sue quickly opened the big box of chocolates.

In this sentence, *quickly* is an adverb modifying the verb *opened*. *Big* is an adjective modifying the noun *box*. *Of* is a preposition because it shows a relation between *box* and *chocolates*. *Of chocolates* is a prepositional phrase that acts like an adjective by modifying *box*.

- A *pronoun* is a word that takes the place of a noun.
- A *clause* is a group of words containing a subject and a verb.

Here's an even more complicated version of the same sentence:

Because she was famished, Sue quickly opened the big box of chocolates.

There are two clauses in this sentence. *Sue quickly opened the big box of chocolates* is considered an independent clause because it contains the main idea of the sentence, and could stand by itself. *Because she was famished* is also a clause (it contains a subject and a verb) but it cannot stand by itself. This is known as a dependent clause. The word *she* is a pronoun referring to the noun *Sue*.

The Major Errors of GMAT English

1. Pronoun Errors

There are two main types of pronoun errors. The first is called *pronoun reference*. You saw an example of this in the sentence about program trading above. Take a look at a simple example:

> *Samantha and Jane went shopping, but she couldn't find anything she liked.*

This type of mistake used to drive Harold Ross, the founding editor of *The New Yorker*, crazy. He was famous for his scrawled "Who he?" in the margins of writers' manuscripts. It is supposed to be absolutely clear who is being referred to by a pronoun. In the example above, the pronoun "she" could refer to either Samantha or Jane. The pronoun is ambiguous and must be fixed. You can do this in three different ways:

> Samantha and Jane went shopping, but *Samantha* couldn't find anything she liked.

> Samantha and Jane went shopping, but *Jane* couldn't find anything she liked.

> Samantha and Jane went shopping, but *they* couldn't find anything *they* liked.

The second type of pronoun error is called *pronoun case*. Here is a simple example:

> *The average male moviegoer expects to see at least one scene of violence per film, and they are seldom disappointed.*

In this case, the pronoun "they" clearly refers to the average male moviegoer, so there is no ambiguity of reference. However, "the average male moviegoer" is *singular*. "They" cannot be used to take the place of a singular noun. There is really only one way to fix this sentence.

> The average male moviegoer expects to see at least one scene of violence per film, and *he* is seldom disappointed.

ETS is very fond of both of these types of errors, and routinely makes use of them several times during a test. By the way, as we mentioned earlier, you don't have to memorize any of the terminology we use. You simply have to recognize a GMAT English error when you see it.

How Do You Spot a Pronoun Error?

That's easy. Look for pronouns.

A pronoun is a word that replaces a noun. Here's a list of common pronouns. (You don't need to memorize these—just be able to recognize them.)

Singular	Plural	Can Be Singular or Plural
I, me	we, us	none
he, him	they, them	any
she, her	both	you
you	some	who
it	these	which
each	those	what
another	that	theirs
either		
neither		
one		
other		
such		
mine		
yours		
his, hers		
ours		
this		
that		

Every single time you spot a pronoun, you should immediately ask yourself the following two questions:

- Is it completely clear, not just to me but to a pedantic ETS test-writer, who or what the pronoun is referring to?
- Does the pronoun agree in number with the noun it is referring to?

Let's look at an example:

> While Brussels has smashed all Western European tourism revenue records <u>this year, they still lag well behind in exports</u>.
>
> (A) this year, they still lag well behind in exports
> (B) in the past year, they still lag well behind in exports
> (C) in the past year, it lags still well behind in exports
> (D) this year, they lag still well behind in exports
> (E) this year, it still lags well behind in exports

Here's how to crack it: As you read the sentence for the first time, look to see if there is a pronoun. There is: "they." Let's make sure the pronoun is being used correctly. Who is the "they" supposed to refer to? Brussels. Is Brussels plural? No, place names are always singular. We have a pronoun case problem here.

Now that you've spotted the problem, go through the answer choices. Any answer choice with the pronoun "they" in it has to be wrong. You can cross off answer choices (A), (B), and (D). You're down to answer choices (C) or (E).

Both of the remaining answer choices fix the original problem. Read them both carefully. If you aren't sure, take a fifty-fifty guess. If you said answer choice (E), you were right. The adverb "still" in answer choice (C) must go in front of the verb.

2. Misplaced Modifiers
Misplaced modifiers come in several forms, but ETS's favorite looks like this:

> *Coming out of the department store, John's wallet was stolen.*

When a sentence begins with a participial phrase (just a fancy term for a phrase that starts with a verb ending in *ing*), that phrase is supposed to modify the noun or pronoun immediately following it.

Was the "wallet" coming out of the department store? No.

There are two ways to fix this sentence.

First, we could change the second half of the sentence so that the noun or pronoun that comes after the participial phrase is actually what the phrase is supposed to refer to:

> Coming out of the department store, *John was robbed of his wallet.*

Or, we could change the first half of the sentence into an adverbial clause (which contains its own subject) so that it is no longer necessary for the first half of the sentence to modify the noun that follows it:

> *As John was* coming out of the department store, his wallet was stolen.

Other forms of misplaced modifiers:

A. *Participial phrases preceded by a preposition:*

> *On leaving the department store, John's wallet was stolen.*

(<u>Corrected version</u>: On leaving the department store, John was robbed of his wallet.)

B. *Adjectives:*

> *Frail and weak, the heavy wagon could not be budged by the old horse.*

(<u>Corrected version</u>: Frail and weak, the old horse could not budge the heavy wagon.)

C. *Adjectival phrases:*

> *An organization long devoted to the cause of justice, the mayor awarded a medal to the American Civil Liberties Union.*

(<u>Corrected version</u>: An organization long devoted to the cause of justice, the American Civil Liberties Union was awarded a medal by the mayor.)

In each of these examples, the modifying phrase modified the wrong noun or pronoun.

How Do You Spot a Misplaced Modifier?

That's easy. *Whenever a sentence begins with a modifying phrase followed by a comma, the noun or pronoun right after the comma should be what the phrase is talking about.* Every single time you see a sentence that begins with a modifying phrase, check to make sure it modifies the right noun or pronoun. If it doesn't, you've spotted the error in the sentence.

The correct answer choice will either change the noun that follows the modifying phrase (the preferred method) or change the phrase itself into an adverbial clause so that it no longer needs to modify the noun.

Let's look at two examples:

> <u>Originally written in 1961, Joseph Heller scored a literary hit with his comedic first novel, *Catch-22.*</u>
>
> (A) Originally written in 1961, Joseph Heller scored a literary hit with his comedic first novel, *Catch-22.*
> (B) Originally written in 1961, Joseph Heller scored a literary hit with *Catch-22*, his comedic first novel.
> (C) Originally written in 1961, *Catch-22*, the comedic first novel by Joseph Heller, was a literary hit.
> (D) *Catch-22*, which was originally written in 1961 by Joseph Heller, scored a literary hit with his comedic first novel.
> (E) *Catch-22*, the comedic first novel, scored a literary hit for Joseph Heller by its being written in 1961.

Here's how to crack it: As you read the sentence for the first time, go through your checklist. Is there a pronoun error in the sentence? No. Does the sentence begin with a modifying phrase? Yes. Now we're getting somewhere. Let's check to see if the modifying phrase actually modifies what it is *supposed to*. Does it? No. "Joseph Heller" is not what was written in 1961. This is a misplaced modifier.

Now that you've spotted the error, look through the other answer choices and eliminate any that contain the same error. Choice (B) contained the same error. Get rid of it. You're down to choices (C), (D), or (E).

Now, there are really only two ways to fix this kind of error, as you know. Do any of the answer choices change the noun that follows the modifying phrase? Yes. Answer choice (C). This is probably the right answer. Read through the other two choices just to make sure there's nothing better. Choices (D) and (E) contain awkward constructions. Choice (C) is the "best" answer.

> <u>Although not quite as liquid an investment as</u> a money-market account, financial experts recommend a certificate of deposit for its high yield.
>
> (A) Although not quite as liquid an investment as
> (B) Although it is not quite as liquid an investment as
> (C) While not being quite as liquid an investment as
> (D) While it is not quite as liquid as an investment
> (E) Although not quite liquid an investment as

Here's how to crack it: Go through your checklist. Is there a pronoun in this sentence? Yes, the third from last word of the sentence is a pronoun, but it clearly refers back to the certificate of deposit. False alarm. Does the sentence begin with a modifying phrase? Yes. Now we're getting warmer. Check to see whether the modifying phrase modifies what it's supposed to modify. Does "although not quite as liquid an investment . . ." refer to financial experts? No. This is a misplaced modifier.

The clearest way to fix this sentence would be to change the noun that follows the modifying phrase:

> *Although not quite as liquid an investment as a money-market account, a certificate of deposit is recommended by financial experts for its high yield.*

However, you can't fix *this* sentence that way for the very good reason that only the first phrase of the sentence was underlined. This time, you'll have to find a way to fix the modifying phrase itself. Look for an answer choice that changes the modifying phrase into an adverbial clause with its own subject and verb.

Choices (A), (C), and (E) do not have subjects and can therefore be eliminated immediately. Choices (B) and (D) each have a subject—in both cases, the word "it"—turning the modifying phrases into adverbial clauses. However choice (D) contains a new error: the word "as" has been moved, leaving "money-market" stranded in the middle of the sentence with no function. While it sounds atrocious, choice (B) is the "best" answer.

A close relative of a misplaced modifier is a *dangling modifier*. You can spot both errors in exactly the same way. Here's a simple example:

> *Before designing a park, the public must be con-*
> *sidered.*

Again, this sentence starts with a modifying phrase followed by a comma. The noun following the comma is what the modifying phrase is supposed to modify. Is it? No! "The public" didn't design the park. A dangling modifier differs from a misplaced modifier in that a dangling modifier doesn't just modify the wrong word. There *is* no word for it to modify.

To fix this sentence, we would have to insert whoever is designing the park into the sentence:

> *Before designing a park, the architect must con-*
> *sider the public.*

3. Parallel Construction

There are two kinds of ETS sentences that test parallel construction. The first is a sentence that contains a list, or has a series of actions set off from one another by commas. Here's an example:

> *Among the reasons cited for the city*
> *councilwoman's decision not to run for reelection*
> *were the high cost of a campaign, the lack of*
> *support from her party, and desiring to spend*
> *more time with her family.*

When a main verb controls several phrases that follow it, each of those phrases has to be set up in the same way. In the sentence above, three reasons were listed. The three reasons *were* (main verb):

> the high cost of a campaign
> the lack of support from her party
> > and
> desiring to spend more time with her family

The construction for each of the three reasons is supposed to be parallel. The first two items on the list are phrases that are essentially functioning as nouns: the high *cost* (of a campaign); the *lack* (of support from her party). However, the third item on the list seems more like a verb than a noun. How could we change the word "desiring" to a more noun-like state? If you said, "the desire," you were absolutely correct. It should read:

> the high cost of a campaign
> the lack of support from her party
> > and
> *the desire* to spend more time with her family.

The second kind of ETS sentence that tests parallel construction is a sentence that is divided into two parts. Here's an example:

> *To say that the song patterns of the common robin*
> *are less complex than those of the indigo bunting*
> *is doing a great disservice to both birds.*

If the first half of a sentence is constructed in a particular way, the second half must be constructed in the same way. The first half of this sentence begins, "To. . . ," therefore the second half has to begin the same way:

> *To say that the song patterns of the common robin*
> *are less complex than those of the indigo bunting*
> *is to do a great disservice to both birds.*

How Do You Spot Parallel Construction?

That's easy. Every time you read a Sentence Correction problem, look to see if you can find a series of actions, a list of three things, or a sentence that is divided into two parts.

Here's an example:

In a recent survey, the Gallup poll discovered that the average American speaks 1.3 languages, buys a new car every 5.2 years, <u>drinks 14 gallons of alcoholic beverages every year, and forgot to pay at least one bill per quarter.</u>

(A) drinks 14 gallons of alcoholic beverages every year, and forgot to pay at least one bill per quarter
(B) drinks 14 gallons of alcoholic beverages every year, and forgets to pay at least one bill per quarter
(C) can drink 14 gallons of alcoholic beverages every quarter and forgot to pay at least one bill per quarter
(D) drinks 14 gallons of alcoholic beverages every year, and forgets at least to pay one bill per quarter
(E) drank 14 gallons of alcoholic beverages every year, and forgets to pay at least one bill per quarter

Here's how to crack it: As you read the sentence for the first time, run through your checklist. Is there a pronoun? No. Does the sentence begin with a modifying phrase? Yes, but the word after the phrase is what is supposed to be modified, so this is not a misplaced modifier. Is there a list of three things or a series of actions? Yes. Let's see if all the actions are parallel. The average American . . .

speaks (1.3 languages)
buys (a new car . . .)
drinks (14 gallons . . .)
and
forgot (to pay . . .)

The first three verbs are all in the same tense, but the fourth one isn't. The problem in this sentence is a lack of parallel construction.

Now that you know what the error is, go through the answer choices. Any choice that contains the word "forgot" is wrong. We can eliminate choices (A) and (C). Choice (E), even though it fixes the parallel construction of the fourth verb, changes the parallel construction of the third verb. Eliminate.

Choices (B) and (D) have perfect parallel construction. If you aren't sure which one is correct, guess and move on. If you picked choice (B), you were right. In choice (D), the adjectival phrase "at least" had to be in front of "one bill."

4. Tense

On the GMAT, tense problems are often just a matter of parallel construction. In general, if a sentence starts out in one tense, it should probably stay there. Let's look at an example:

When he was younger he walked three miles every day and *has lifted* weights too.

The clause "when he was younger" puts the entire sentence firmly in the past. Thus the two verbs that follow should be in the past tense as well. You may not have known the technical term for "has lifted" (the present perfect tense) but you probably noticed that it was inconsistent with "walked" (the simple past tense). The sentence should read:

When he was younger he walked three miles every day and *lifted* weights too.

Here are the tenses that come up on the GMAT:

tense	example
present	He *walks* three miles a day.
simple past	When he was younger, he *walked* three miles a day.
present perfect	He *has walked* three miles a day for the last several years.
past perfect	He *had walked* three miles a day until he bought his motorcycle.
future	He will walk three miles a day, starting tomorrow.

It isn't important that you know the names of these tenses, as long as you understand how they're used. As we said before, a sentence that begins in one tense should generally stay in the same tense. For example, a sentence that begins in the present perfect (which describes an action that has happened in the past, but is still potentially going on in the present as well) should stay in the present perfect.

He has walked three miles a day for the last several years, and has never complained.

One exception to this rule is a sentence containing the past perfect (in which one action in the past happens before another action in the past). By definition, any action set in the past perfect must have another action coming after it set in the simple past.

> *He had ridden his motorcycle for two hours when*
> *it ran out of gas.*

The only other exceptions to this rule come up when one action in a sentence clearly precedes another:

> *The dinosaurs are extinct now, but they were once*
> *present on the earth in large numbers.*

In this case, the sentence is clearly referring to two different time periods: "now," which requires the present tense, and a period long ago, which requires the past tense.

How Do You Spot Tense Errors?

That's easy. Look for changes in verb tense *in the answer choices*. If the answer choices give you several versions of a particular verb, then you should be looking to see which one is correct. Here's an example.

> A doctor at the Amsterdam clinic maintains that if children eat a diet high in vitamins and <u>took vitamin supplements, they will be less likely to catch</u> the common cold.
>
> (A) took vitamin supplements, they will be less likely to catch
> (B) took vitamin supplements, they are less likely to catch
> (C) take vitamin supplements, they were less likely of catching
> (D) take vitamin supplements, they will be less likely of catching
> (E) take vitamin supplements, they are less likely to catch

Here's how to crack it: As you read the sentence, go through your checklist. There is one pronoun ("they") in the sentence, but in this case it clearly refers only to the children. Is there a modifying phrase? No. Is there a list of things or a series of actions? Not really. Are the verb tenses consistent? Look at the answer choices. Aha! (A) and (B) offer us "took" while (C), (D), and (E) offer us "take." Let's see which is correct.

Look at the dependent clause that is partially underlined.

> ...that if children *eat* a diet high in vitamins and
> <u>took</u> vitamin supplements...

Obviously, one of these verbs is inconsistent with the other, and since only one of them is underlined, that's the one that must be wrong. The correct sentence must have a "take" in it, so we can eliminate choices (A) and (B). Choice (C) puts the rest of the sentence in the past tense, so scratch (C). Choice (D) puts the rest of the sentence in the future tense. This *might* be acceptable, but the choice also uses the incorrect idiomatic expression "likely of catching." The correct answer to this question is Choice (E), which keeps the entire sentence in the present tense.

5. Subject-Verb Agreement Errors

A verb is supposed to agree with its subject. Let's look at an example:

> *The number of arrests of drunken drivers are
> increasing every year.*

ETS likes to separate the subject of a sentence from its verb with several prepositional phrases, so that by the time you get to the verb you've forgotten whether the subject was singular or plural.

The subject of the sentence above is "number," which is singular. The phrase "of arrests of drunken drivers" modifies the subject. The verb of this sentence is "are," which is plural. If we set off the prepositional phrases with parentheses, this is what the sentence looks like:

> The number (of arrests of drunken drivers) are . . .

To fix this sentence we need to make the verb agree with the subject:

> The number (of arrests of drunken drivers) *is*
> increasing every year.

How to Spot Subject-Verb Agreement Errors

Cover up the prepositional phrases between the subject and the verb of each clause of the sentence so you can see whether there is an agreement problem. You should also be on the lookout for nouns that sound plural but are in fact singular:

<u>Some nouns that are generally singular</u>:

The Netherlands	(the name of any city, state, or country).
Tom or John	(any two singular nouns connected by an "or")
the family	
the audience	
politics	
measles	
the number	
the amount	

You are already on the lookout for pronouns since they're first on your checklist. Sometimes pronouns can be the subject of a sentence, in which case the verb has to agree with the pronoun. There are some pronouns that people tend to think are plural when they are in fact singular:

<u>Singular pronouns</u>
either
neither
each
everyone
everybody
nobody

Let's look at an example of a subject-verb error as it might appear on the GMAT:

> Many political insiders now believe that the dissension in Congress over health issues <u>decrease the likelihood for significant action being</u> taken this year to combat the rising costs of healthcare.
>
> (A) decrease the likelihood for significant action being
> (B) decrease the likelihood that significant action will be
> (C) decrease the likelihood of significant action to be
> (D) decreases the likelihood for significant action being
> (E) decreases the likelihood that significant action will be

Here's how to crack it: As you read the sentence for the first time, run through your mental checklist. Is there a pronoun, or a modifying phrase, or a list of several things, or a series of parallel actions, or a change in tense? Not this time. Let's check for subject-verb agreement. The subject of the independent clause is "insiders" and the correct verb, "believe," follows almost immediately, so there's no problem in the main clause.

However, let's look at the dependent clause that follows: "That the dissension over health issues decrease the likelihood..."

In this clause, the subject is "dissension." To find the verb, put parentheses around any prepositional phrases. It should look like this:

...the dissension (over health issues) decrease...

Is this correct? No, the singular "dissension" needs the singular verb "decreases." Looking at the answers, we can immediately eliminate choices (A), (B), and (C). Now let's examine choices (D) and (E). Both fix the subject-verb error, but choice (D) uses the unidiomatic expression "likelihood for." The correct answer is choice (E).

6. Apples and Oranges

Another error that ETS likes to include is what we call apples and oranges. Here's a simple example:

The people in my office are smarter than other offices.

Taken literally, this sentence compares "the people in my office" with "other offices." This is what we call an apples-and-oranges sentence. It compares two dissimilar things (in this case, "people" and "offices.") To fix this sentence, we need to make the comparison clear. There are two ways to do this:

> The people in my office are smarter than *the people* in other offices.

> or

> The people in my office are smarter than *those* in other offices.

We hope that you recognized "those" as a pronoun taking the place of "the people." The correct answer to an apples-and-oranges question on the GMAT almost invariably uses a pronoun ("that" or "those") rather than a repetition of the noun.

Apples-and-oranges problems also come up when you compare two actions:

> *Synthetic oils burn less efficiently than natural oils.*

In this case, what is being compared is not the two types of oil, but how well each type of oil *burns*. You could fix this by changing the sentence to read,

> Synthetic oils burn less efficiently than natural oils *burn*.

However, ETS would rather that you fix it by replacing the second verb (in this case, "burn") with a replacement verb ("do" or "does.") Here is how ETS would like to see this sentence rewritten:

> Synthetic oils burn less efficiently than *do* natural oils.

How Do You Spot Apples and Oranges?

Look for sentences that make comparisons. These sentences often include words such as "than", "as", "similar to" and "like". When you find one of these comparison words, check to see whether the two things being compared are really comparable.

Let's look at an example.

> Doctors sometimes have difficulty diagnosing viral pneumonia because the early symptoms of this potentially deadly illness <u>are often quite similar to the common cold</u>.
>
> (A) are often quite similar to the common cold
> (B) often resemble that of the common cold
> (C) are often quite similar to those of the common cold
> (D) are often quite similar to the common cold's symptom
> (E) quite often are, like the common cold, similar

Here's how to crack it: Go through your checklist; do you see any suspicious pronouns, misplaced modifiers, unparallel constructions, needless shifts in tense, or subject-verb problems? Good. There aren't any. Do you see any comparison words? Yes, the sentence uses "are similar to." Let's see exactly what is being compared. The symptoms of one illness are being compared directly to . . . another illness. Aha! This is an apples and oranges error. To make this sentence correct, we need to compare the *symptoms* of one illness to the *symptoms* of the other, and the way ETS would prefer that we do it is to use a replacement pronoun.

If we look at the answer choices, we can eliminate choices (A) and (E) because neither makes any attempt to compare symptoms to symptoms. Choice (B) looks promising because it uses the replacement pronoun "that;" however, "symptoms" is plural, and therefore can't be replaced by the singular "that." Choice (D) seems promising because it seems to be trying to compare symptoms to symptoms—but if you look closer, you'll notice that the last word of choice (D) is "symptom," which is singular. The correct answer is choice (C).

7. Quantity Words
ETS likes to see if you know how to indicate quantity. Here's an example.

> On the flight to Los Angeles, Nancy had to choose *among* two dinner entrees.

If there were more than two items being compared, then "among" would be correct. However, if there are only two choices available, the correct quantity word should be "between."

On the flight to Los Angeles, Nancy had to choose *between* two dinner entrees.

Here are the comparison quantity words that come up on the GMAT most frequently:

if two items	if more than two items
between	among
more	most
better	best
less	least

Another type of quantity word that shows up on the GMAT from time to time involves things that can be counted as opposed to things that can't. For example, if you were standing in line at a buffet, and you didn't want as big a serving of soup as the person in front of you received, which of the following would be correct?

Could I have *fewer* soup, please?

or

Could I have *less* soup, please?

If an item can't be counted, the correct adjective would be "less." However, if we were talking about french fries (which can be counted) the correct adjective would be "fewer."

countable	not countable
fewer	less
number	amount, quantity
many	much

How Do You Spot Quantity Word Errors?

That's easy. Look for quantity words. Whenever you see a "between," check to see if there are only two items being discussed in the sentence. (If there are more, you'll need an "among.") Whenever you see an "amount," make sure that whatever is being discussed cannot be counted. (If the sentence is talking about the "amount" of people, then you'll need to change it to "number.")

Here's what a quantity word error might look like on the GMAT:

Of the many decisions facing the energy
commission as it meets to decide on new directions
for the next century, the question of the future of
nuclear energy <u>is for certain the more perplexing</u>.

(A) is for certain the more perplexing
(B) is certainly the most perplexing
(C) it seems certain, is the most perplexed
(D) is certainly the more perplexing
(E) it seems certain, is perplexing the most

Here's how to crack it: If your checklist includes quantity words, the word "more" will set off red flags as you read the sentence. If there were two decisions facing the energy commission, then "the more perplexing" would be correct. However, the sentence says there are "many" decisions. Therefore the sentence must read, "the most perplexing."

This lets us eliminate choices (A) and (D) immediately. Choice (C) gives the impression that it is the *question* that is perplexed. Eliminate. Choice (E) incorrectly positions "the most" after the word it is supposed to modify. The correct answer is choice (B).

8. Idiom
ETS likes to test certain idiomatic expressions. Here's an easy example:

There is little doubt that large corporations are indebted for the small companies that broke new ground in laser optics.

It is incorrect to say you are indebted *for* someone.

There is little doubt that large corporations are indebted to the small companies that broke new ground in laser optics.

Idiomatic errors are difficult to spot in that there is no single rule to look for. In fact, there are really no rules. Each idiom has its own particular usage. There is no real reason why an idiomatic expression is correct. It is simply a matter of custom.

However, you haven't been speaking English for the past twenty years for nothing. The main similarity between GMAT English and

American English is that they both use the same idiomatic expressions.

You already know them.

How Do You Spot Idiomatic Errors?

If you've gone through the first seven items on your checklist—pronouns, misplaced modifiers, parallel construction, tense, subject-verb agreement, apples and oranges, and quantity words—and still haven't found an error, try pulling idiomatic expressions out of the sentence so you can see whether they're correct.

Then make up your own sentence using the suspect idiom:

> I am indebted *for* my parents for offering to help
> pay for graduate school.

Does that sound right? Of course not. I am indebted *to* my parents. Usually if you take the expression out of the long and awkward sentence and use it in an everyday sentence, the error (if there is one) will be obvious. Here's what an idiom question might look like on the GMAT:

> The administration of a small daily dose of aspirin
> has not only been shown to lower the risk of heart
> attack, <u>and it has also been shown to help</u> relieve
> the suffering of arthritis.
>
> (A) and it has also been shown to help
> (B) and it has also been shown helpful to
> (C) but it has also been shown to help
> (D) but it has been shown helpful in addition for
> (E) in addition it has also been shown helping

Here's how to crack it: As always, run through your checklist. Is there a pronoun in the sentence? Yes, but if you check the answer choices, you'll discover that the same pronoun appears in each one. Obviously, pronoun error is *not* what is being tested this time. Is there a modifying phrase? No. So much for misplaced modifiers. Is there a list of things or a series of actions? No. To be sure that there really is no parallel construction problem we should look at the two halves of the sentence as well. The first half "...has been shown," matches the second half, "...has also been shown," and both are in the same tense, so there is no problem with either parallel construction or tense. There are no comparison words either, so we don't have to worry about apples and oranges. Could there be something wrong with an idiomatic expression in the original sentence? Let's try a sentence of our own.

Not only is he nasty...

How would you finish this sentence? If you said something like "*. . . but he is also disgusting*," you would be absolutely correct. In GMAT English, "not only. . ." is always followed somewhere in the same sentence by "but . . . also." Let's look at the answer choices to see which can be eliminated. (A), (B) and (E) all use some other conjunction instead of "but," which means that the only possible answers are (C) and (D). Choice (D) uses "in addition" instead of "also." This *might* not be fatal, but then keep reading after the underlining: "helpful in addition for relieve the suffering of arthritis." If the word "for" seems to stick out, it is because we need to form the infinitive case of "relieve" by using "to." Thus, the correct answer is (C).

One Last Example:

The foresight that was evident in the court's selection of an independent trustee to oversee the provisions of the agreement will probably go unremarked by the press.

(A) that was evident in the court's selection of an independent trustee
(B) that was evident by the court's selection of an independent trustee
(C) evidenced with the court's selection of an independent trustee
(D) evidenced of the court's selection of an independent trustee
(E) that was evident of the court's selection of an independent trustee

Here's how to crack it: As you read the sentence, go through your checklist. Is there a pronoun? No. Does the sentence begin with a modifying phrase? No. Is there a list of three things or a series of actions? No. Is there a tense error? No. Is there a subject-verb problem? No. Is there a comparison word such as "similar" or "than"? No. Are there any quantity words to check? No. Do any expressions in the sentence seem suspicious? No.

We have checked off all the items on our list. Maybe nothing is wrong with this sentence. Mark down choice (A) provisionally. When you've finished with the entire section, count the (A)s you've chosen. If you have too many, go back to this problem and take a closer look.

If you have five or fewer, however, you were probably right in the first place. The "best" answer to this question is choice (A).

If You're Really Gung-Ho

You can expand your checklist to include as many types of errors as you like. Obviously the more types of errors you can identify, the more prepared you'll be to take the test. But you should bear in mind that while there are other types of errors that we haven't discussed, these errors don't come up very often on the GMAT. For example, a sentence with redundant words has appeared on the test from time to time, but not even as often as once per test. If you're seriously gunning to get every Sentence Correction question correct, you should dig out your old grammar book from high school and study it carefully. You should also take as many of the real ETS Sentence Correction sections in the *Official Guide for GMAT Review* as you can; pay special attention to the idiomatic expressions that come up in these sections since these are sometimes repeated.

What Happens If I Know There's Something Wrong But I Can't Figure Out What It Is?

You've just finished reading a sentence and there's obviously something wrong with it. You go through your checklist, but either this is an error that isn't on your list or you just aren't seeing it. What should you do?

Go straight to the answer choices to look for clues. Here's a set of answer choices from one of the previous examples:

> (A) decrease the likelihood for significant action being
> (B) decrease the likelihood that significant action will be
> (C) decrease the likelihood of significant action to be
> (D) decreases the likelihood for significant action being
> (E) decreases the likelihood that significant action will be

Forget about the original sentence entirely for a moment. Just looking at these answer choices, do you see anything that strikes you?

By examining the first few words of each of the answer choices, you will often find an excellent hint as to what kind of error you might be looking for in the original sentence. For example, in the answers above, ETS is offering you a choice of "decrease" or "decreases." What kind of error might this mean? Bingo: subject-verb agreement.

Even if the first few words of the answer choices do not provide a clue, all is not lost. Remember how our ETS test-writer constructs wrong answer choices: The test-writer likes to throw in one or more answer choices that fix the original error but create new errors in the process. You may not have been able to spot the original error, but you'll probably see the *new* errors in the bogus answer choices.

As you read the remaining answer choices, look for differences. Sometimes the realization that one answer choice is exactly the same as another with the exception of a couple of words will enable you to choose between them.

When you've eliminated everything you can, guess and move on. Remember: If you can eliminate one or more answer choices, you'll be most likely to gain points by guessing.

Summary

1. GMAT English is different from American English. You have to learn the rules.

2. Fortunately, the Sentence Correction section tests only a handful of rules. Once you learn them, you will be able to score quite well on this section.

3. Make a checklist of errors to look for when you read a Sentence Correction section. The major errors you should look for in a Sentence Correction problem are:

   A. *Pronouns*: If a sentence contains a pronoun, check to see whether the pronoun clearly refers to the noun it is replacing; also check to see whether the pronoun agrees in number with the noun to which it refers.

   B. *Misplaced modifiers:* If the sentence begins with a modifying phrase, check to make sure the noun it modifies comes directly after the modifying phrase.

C. *Parallel construction:* If a sentence contains a list of three things, or a series of actions, or is broken up into two halves, check to make sure the parts of the sentence are parallel.

D. *Tense:* If the answer choices contain different verb tenses, make sure the tense of the verb or verbs in the original sentence is correct. For the most part, verb tense should stay consistent throughout a sentence.

E. *Subject-verb agreement:* ETS sometimes puts extraneous prepositional phrases between the subject and the verb. Cover up these phrases so you can see whether the subject and the verb of each clause in the sentence agree with each other.

F. *Apples and oranges:* When a sentence makes a comparison, check to see whether the two things being compared are comparable.

G. *Quantity Words:* Whenever you see a quantity word (countable vs. uncountable; two vs. three or more) check to see if it is being used correctly.

H. *Idiom:* If a sentence contains an idiomatic expression that seems wrong to you, try taking the expression out of the sentence and creating a sentence of your own with the suspect expression.

4. If you've spotted the error, go through the answer choices, and eliminate any that contain the same error. Then look at the remaining answer choices and find the one that fixes the sentence.

5. If you can't find the error, first look to the answer choices for clues. Then consider the possibility that there might not be an error.

6. About one fifth of the sentences are correct as they are. When a sentence is correct, the answer is choice (A), which simply repeats the sentence word for word.

7. Once you've gained confidence in your ability to spot the major errors, you should expand your checklist to include other types of errors.

CHAPTER SEVEN

Reading Comprehension

The Reading Comprehension section of the GMAT contains three reading passages of about 500 words each. Each passage is followed by 7 or 8 questions, for a total of 23 questions.

Before we begin, take a moment to read the following set of instructions, which is a close approximation of the instructions you will find on the real GMAT.

> <u>Directions</u>: In this section, there are three reading passages, each followed by questions about the content of the passages. You should answer the questions based on your knowledge of what has been directly said in the passage or what can be inferred from it. Answer each question by choosing the best response.

Be sure you know and understand these instructions before you take the GMAT. If you learn them ahead of time, you won't have to waste valuable seconds reading them on the day you take the test.

GMAT Reading Comprehension: Cracking the System

It's important to know the instructions printed before each group of Reading Comprehension passages on the GMAT, but it's much more important to understand what these instructions mean. ETS's instructions don't tell you everything you need to know about GMAT Reading Comprehension passages. The rest of the chapter will teach you what you do need to know.

Our techniques will enable you to

1. gain points on the test by skipping (in some cases) one of the reading passages entirely
2. read quickly in a way that will allow you to understand the *structure* of the passage
3. eliminate answer choices that could not possibly be correct
4. take advantage of outside knowledge
5. take advantage of inside information (about the way ETSs test-writers think)
6. find answers in some cases *without reading the passages*

Basic Passage Types

There are only three types of reading passages on the GMAT:

1. *Social science passages*: These are passages about economics, history, or social issues. For example, you might see a passage about world food shortages or the free enterprise system.

2. *Science passages*: These are passages that describe scientific phenomena, such as gravitation or plate tectonics.

3. *Humanities passages*: These are passages that deal with the arts. For example, you might see a passage about a modern poet, or about the effect of women writers on the Victorian novel. While humanities passages have been a regular feature of the GMAT since 1954, ETS now seems to be phasing them out.

Which Passage-Types Will Appear on Your GMAT?

For the past year, the reading comprehension section has contained no humanities passage at all. If the present trend continues, the test you take will contain:

> 2 social science passages
> 1 science passage.

The three passages can appear in any order.

Order of Difficulty

In the Reading Comprehension section, the questions are not presented in order of difficulty, but the *passages* generally are. The first passage is supposed to be the easiest to understand. The last passage is supposed to be the most difficult. However, the ordering of passages is obviously a somewhat subjective decision made by ETS test-writers who rely on the experimental results of average test-takers. The test-writers have no idea which topic is going to prove most difficult for *you*. Thus, in the Reading Comprehension section it is important to figure out your *own* order of difficulty.

Choosing the Order in which You Do the Passages

When the proctor tells you to begin the Reading Comprehension section, your first impulse will be to launch straight into the first passage, but you will be infinitely better off if you pause for a moment to reconnoiter. Take a few seconds to look at the first few words of each of the three passages.

There are several factors to bear in mind in making your decision:

- *Familiarity with the subject matter*: You may have just finished reading a newspaper article about the number of women CEOs in the United States, or perhaps in college you wrote a paper on continental drift. If the topic is at all familiar to you, you will feel much more comfortable answering questions about it.

- *Which type of passage you generally prefer*: Don't laugh. After they've done a few timed sections, most people find that they have a favorite type of passage. Don't be surprised if your favorite runs counter to your normal choice of reading matter. Even if you never read science articles in real life, you may find that on the GMAT you do best with science passages.

- *Which of the three passages is the "minority passage:"* Invariably, the subject matter for one of the passages on each test will concern a minority group. There can sometimes be certain advantages to doing this passage. We'll tell you more about this later in the chapter.

- *The structure of the passage*: Many of the passages on the GMAT fall into a few key structure types. We will be showing you in detail how to recognize these later in the chapter, but here are two quick examples: if a passage begins, "The new economic climate provides opportunities as well as risks . . . " it is pretty clear how the rest of the passage will be organized (first, some examples of the opportunities, and then some examples of the risks;) if a passage begins, "There are three main classes of stars," again, the organization of the passage should be fairly clear right away.

Deciding on your own order in which to do the passages should take no more than a few seconds. Start with the passage that is easiest for you. Then do the second easiest. If you are going to run out of time, it might as well be on the passage you find the most difficult.

It May Even Make Sense for You to Skip One Reading Comprehension Passage Entirely— If You Read Normally

Some people find that by the time they have finished reading a passage carefully, there is little time left to answer the questions. If you insist on reading GMAT passages the way you *normally* read— carefully, word-by-word— you may be able to increase your score by skipping one entire passage and the questions based on that passage. Rather than invest the time to read three passages and answer all the questions hastily, you may be better off concentrating on two of the passages and the questions related to those passages. Skipping an entire passage and its questions is in some ways more efficient than skipping a few questions on each passage, because you spend less time reading.

On the Other Hand, Normal Reading Doesn't Make Any Sense on the GMAT

GMAT reading has nothing to do with normal reading. For one thing, no one in his right mind would ever read one of these passages of his own free will. They are excruciatingly boring, and full of dense blocks of facts, many of which are not needed in order to answer the questions.

GMAT reading has even less to do with business reading.

How to Succeed in Business

If your boss asked you to analyze a quarterly report and make a presentation of all the points it raised, you would go home and spend hours going over it. You would look for important information, anticipate questions, and memorize statistics.

Business reading is a careful, painstaking process.

How to Succeed on the GMAT

If you try to read GMAT passages the way you read quarterly reports, you'll never have time for the questions. Worse, you'll have spent a lot of time absorbing information that you don't need to know.

Reading Comprehension Questions Cover Only One Third of the Material in the Passage

Each reading passage is followed by 7 or 8 questions. You've probably assumed that to answer these questions correctly you'll need to know all the information contained in the passage. But this isn't true. The questions cover only a small portion of the passage. We're going to teach you how to identify the important part and ignore most of the rest. The less time you spend reading the passage, the more time you'll have for earning points.

Don't Get Bogged Down

If you read too carefully, underlining every other word and trying to understand every detail, at the end of the passage you'll discover that you've understood nothing. Did you ever finish a passage only to look up and ask yourself, "What did I just read?" Since the questions test only a small fraction of what you've read, you don't want to waste a lot of time memorizing unnecessary details.

There are two types of questions in Reading Comprehension, and neither requires you to memorize specific information:

1. *General questions*: To answer these, you need to have an understanding of the main idea and the *structure* of the passage.

2. *Specific questions*: Since you'll be asked about only a few specific pieces of information, it's silly to try to remember all the specific information contained in a passage. It makes much more sense to have a vague idea of where specific information is located in the passage. That way you'll know where to look for it if you need it.

Here's Our Step-by-Step Game Plan for "Reading" GMAT Reading Passages

We have a step-by-step game plan for attacking GMAT reading passages and answering the questions about them. We'll outline the plan first and then discuss each step in detail. Here's the outline:

Step 1: Find the main idea of the first paragraph. We'll show you how very shortly. Often the main idea of the first paragraph is also the main idea of the entire passage.

Step 2: Find the main idea of the second paragraph and see how its main idea fits into the *structure* of the entire passage. What does the second paragraph do in relation to the first paragraph?

Step 3: As you skim, look for structural signposts. (We'll explain these in just a minute.)

Step 4: Don't worry about details at this point. Move quickly from paragraph to paragraph, summarizing the main ideas and skimming over the rest. You'll come back for details later, when you know which ones you need. (You won't be able to remember the details anyway; why waste time trying to memorize them now?)

Step 5: Attack the questions.

Step 1: Find the Main Idea of the First Paragraph

Think of a GMAT reading passage as a house. The main idea of the passage is like the overall plan of the house; the main idea of each paragraph is like the plan of each room. Reading the passage is like walking through the house. As you walk, you don't want to waste time memorizing every detail of every room; you want to develop a general sense of the layout of the rooms and the structure of the house as a whole. If you tried to memorize every detail, you'd never get through the house. Later, when ETS asks you what was sitting on the table beside the chair in the master bedroom, you won't know the answer off the top of your head, but you will know exactly where to look for it. And you'll be able to answer more questions in less time than someone who has tried to memorize every detail.

Take a look at the first paragraph of a sample GMAT passage:

> Biologists have long known that some types of electromagnetic radiation such as X rays and gamma rays, can be dangerous to human beings. Operating at a frequency of 10^{18} through 10^{22} these rays, which are
> (05) well above the visible light spectrum, were first detected in the early years of the 20th century.

Here's how to crack it: The first sentence of a paragraph should always be read extremely carefully since it is so often the key to understanding the entire paragraph. This first sentence was no exception: the paragraph is about two types of radiation and their danger to humans. Many students find that it helps to jot down a couple of key words in the margin next to the paragraph to encapsulate the main idea.

However, once you've got that main idea, it isn't necessary to pay a lot of attention to the other sentences in the paragraph. For example, if you've already read the second sentence of this paragraph, you probably noticed that while the sentence included some specific facts, it added nothing to our understanding of the main point of the paragraph. Later, if ETS asks you a specific question about line 5, you can go back and find out the answer; it will still be there.

Think of This as *Variable* Speed Reading

Until you know what the main idea of a paragraph is, you want to read very carefully. However, as soon as you've got a handle on what is going on, you can speed up. Let your eyes glaze over when you get to the small details. Until ETS asks you about them, who cares?

The goal is to spend no more than two minutes "reading" the passage. Impossible? Sure, if you're going to insist on reading the way you normally do. Just remember that you don't get any points for reading the passages; when you take the real GMAT the proctor will *not* be walking around the test room awarding extra points for great reading technique. You get points for *answering questions*.

Step 2: Read the Second Paragraph and See How the Main Idea Fits into the Structure of the Entire Passage

Before you read the second paragraph, take a moment to decide what you would do now if you were writing this passage. The reading passages on the GMAT are deadly dull. Deciding what you would do if you were writing this piece will help you to remember the important ideas and understand the *structure* of the passage.

So far the author has said that it has long been known that X rays and gamma rays are harmful to humans.

If *you* were writing the next paragraph, what would you write now?

List three directions the passage might take:

1._____

2._____

3._____

Supporting the Main Idea

Perhaps you suggested giving an example or a description of how these rays can be harmful, or an example of how the harmful effect of these rays was first discovered. These are good answers. When the first paragraph gives the main idea of the passage, the next paragraph often gives *evidence in support of that idea*.

Here's the beginning of a second paragraph that did just that:

> The first studies about the ill-effects of X rays were conducted in 1925, in Vienna, and although they proved inconclusive, they led to more complete tests several years later . . .

Going off on a Tangent Thought

You might also have suggested discussing the danger of X rays and gamma rays to *other* life forms, or the dangers of *other* types of radiation. These are acceptable answers, too. Sometimes the second paragraph will *go off on a tangent thought*. Here's the beginning of an alternate second paragraph that does just that:

However, until now, no one has ever suggested that microwave radiation might also be harmful. In preliminary laboratory results, Cleary and Milham have found elevated growth rates in cancer cells exposed to low doses of microwaves . . .

Contradicting the First Paragraph

Another possibility would be to dispute the idea that X rays and gamma rays are harmful. Sometimes the author introduces an idea in the first paragraph in order to *contradict* it in the second. Here's how that might look:

However, recent work by scientists working in Russia, suggests a fascinating new possibility: that the harmful effects attributed to X rays and gamma rays are in fact the result of ionizing fields often found in close proximity with high frequency radiation . . .

There are really only three things any paragraph following the opening paragraph of a passage can do:

1. support the first paragraph by giving evidence or examples
2. go off on a tangent thought
3. contradict the paragraph before it

As you "read" the second paragraph, try to figure out which of the three it is going to be this time. Just as you did in the first paragraph, you will be looking for the main idea of the paragraph (often found in the first sentence). And again, as soon as you've found the main idea, you can speed up and ignore the details of the rest of the paragraph.

Here is the real second paragraph:

However, until now, no one has ever suggested that microwave radiation might also be harmful. In preliminary laboratory results, Cleary and Milham
(10) have found elevated growth rates in cancer cells exposed to low doses of microwaves. Cleary exposed cancer cells to levels of radiation that are commonly found in microwave ovens and found that the abnormal cells grew 30 percent faster than did
(15) unexposed cells. Milham's study focused on ham radio operators who are commonly exposed to levels of radiation slightly higher than those emitted by cellular telephones. He discovered elevated levels of myeloid leukemia.

Here's how to crack it: Reading the first sentence carefully, we realize that this paragraph is going off on a tangent thought. In fact, the passage is *not* going to be about the dangers of X rays or gamma rays; it is going to be about the possible dangers of microwaves. Now that we have the main idea, we can afford to skim or skip over the rest of the paragraph. If ETS asks us later about Cleary or Milham, we'll know where to find them, but until then, we can let this part of the passage pass in a blur.

If we were to write an outline of the second paragraph, it might look like this:

The second paragraph *goes off on a tangent*
— proposes that microwaves may also be dangerous.
  Based on studies by Cleary and Milham.
  Cleary says, "blah blah blah."
  Milham says, "blah blah blah."

It isn't necessary for you to write an outline as you read a passage as long as you think the outline. If you're like most of us, though, it helps to make a couple of notes in the margin.

Step 3: Look for Structural Signposts

Certain words instantly tell you a lot about the structure of a passage. For example, if you were reading a paragraph that began, "There are three reasons why the Grand Canyon should be strip-mined," at some point in the paragraph you would expect to find three reasons listed. If a sentence begins, "on the one hand," you would expect to find an "on the other hand" later in the sentence. These structural signposts show an alert reader what's going to happen later in a passage. Let's begin with one of the most frequently occurring structural signposts on the GMAT: the trigger word.

Trigger Words

The second paragraph from the GMAT passage you just read began with a word which probably automatically clued you in that a change was on the way: the word was "however."

Trigger words (such as "however" and "but") always signal a change in the direction of a passage. Here's a simple example:

First paragraph: Most economists believe that the budget deficit will take years to remedy. . .

Second paragraph: HOWEVER (trigger word), some economists believe there may a fast solution to the problem.

In this example the trigger word signals that the second paragraph will modify or qualify what has gone before. A trigger word at the beginning of any paragraph is a sure sign that this paragraph will disagree with what was stated in the preceding one.

Trigger words are important even if they do not appear at the beginning of a paragraph; they always signal a change of meaning, even if it is only within a sentence. Here's a simple example:

Small companies can be devastated by the loss of a major client, but they can usually survive a few smaller defections.

Which of the following statements is true?

(A) Small companies can be devastated by the loss of any client.
(B) The loss of some types of clients will not necessarily endanger a small company.

Analysis: When Joe Bloggs goes searching through this sentence for an answer, he doesn't read past the "but." He sees, "Small companies can be devastated by the loss of a major client," and picks choice (A). This is incorrect. The trigger word in this sentence (*but*) changes the meaning of the first part of the sentence so much that the answer can only be choice (B).

ETS likes to ask questions that appear to have one answer but actually have another. In creating such questions, test-writers look for places in the passage where the meaning changes. Then they trap Joe Bloggs by writing an incorrect choice that restates the first half of one of these sentences.

You can avoid these traps by circling trigger words and paying attention to where you find your answers.

Here are the trigger words that appear on the GMAT. You must memorize this list:

> but
> although (even though)
> however
> yet
> despite (in spite of)
> nevertheless
> nonetheless
> notwithstanding
> except
> while
> unless
> on the other hand

Continuing-The-Same-Train-of-Thought Words

Some structural signposts let you know that there will be no contradiction, no change in path. If you see a "first of all" it stands to reason that there will be a "second of all" and perhaps a "third." Other signs of continuation:

> in addition
> by the same token
> likewise
> similarly
> this (implies a reference to preceding sentence)

One other continuing structural element that appears on the GMAT is not a word. Sentences that appear inside parentheses often contain information you'll need to answer a question. You should circle any sentence that is enclosed within parentheses.

Yin-Yang Words

One of ETS's all-time favorite types of passage contrasts two opposing viewpoints—and certain words immediately give this away. See if you can supply the second half of the following sentences:

> The *traditional view* of the causes of global warm-
> ing focuses on the burning of fossil fuel . . .

(Second half: However, the *new* view is that there is some other cause.)

> *Until recently*, it was thought that the Mayan civilization was destroyed as a result of drought . . .

(Second half: however, *now* we believe that they were destroyed by space invaders.)

> The *classical* model of laissez-faire capitalism does not even admit the possibility of government intervention . . .

(Second half: but the *rock and roll* version of laissez-faire capitalism says, "Let me just get my check book.")

> *Before 1960*, it was commonly assumed that the atom was the smallest particle in the universe . . .

(Second half: however, after 1960 scientists began to suspect that there was something even smaller.)

Whenever you spot a "yin" word, you should realize that there is a "yang" on the way. Some other yin-yang words:

Yin	Yang
generally	(however, this time . . .)
the old view	(however, the new view . . .)
the widespread belief	(but the in-crowd believes . . .)
most scientists think	(but Doctor Spleegle thinks . . .)
on the one hand	(on the other hand . . .)

Structural elements can help you to understand a passage faster, with less "reading" and less wear and tear on your brain. Whenever you spot one of these signposts, circle it. A structural signpost is much more important to your understanding of a passage than is any individual fact within that passage.

Step 4: Skim Over Examples and Details

With each new paragraph, take a second before reading to decide what you would do now if you were writing the passage.

Then read the paragraph to see whether you're right. It doesn't matter if you aren't. You're just using this technique to stay involved with the passage. If the author of the passage does something unexpected, so much the better; you'll remember it even more clearly.

In each paragraph, read as much as you need to understand how the paragraph fits structurally into the passage, and keep your eyes open for structural signposts. Once you're able to see the direction of a paragraph, you can ignore the details. You won't be able to remember them anyway, so why waste time reading them carefully now?

In the second paragraph, the author went off on a tangent thought which was actually the main idea of the passage: Microwaves may also be dangerous. This was supported by two scientists' studies.

If *you* were writing the next paragraph, what would you write now?

List three possibilities:

1._____

2._____

3._____

If you wrote down the same alternatives we found in the second paragraph, you would be right on track. There might be examples or reasons in support of the main idea, there might be another tangent thought, or there might be a contradiction.

Let's see what the author did:

(20) The methodology of both Cleary and Milham has been questioned by other scientists in the field. Their first concern is whether Cleary's test-tube results can be extrapolated to human users of microwave ovens. So far, there has been no
(25) controlled study of the effects of microwave ovens on humans. Their second concern is that Milham's results did not take into account other characteristics of ham radio operators that might make them more susceptible to cancer. A third, more general concern
(30) is that all of the studies of microwave radiation conducted so far have been of short duration, raising the possibility that the dangers of long-term exposure have not yet been assessed.

Here's how to crack it: After setting up the main idea that microwaves may be hazardous to humans, and backing up this theory with studies by two scientists, the author now *qualifies* the theory by discussing problems in the methodology of the two scientists. That's right: the third paragraph is a kind of *contradicting* paragraph. Notice again how the first sentence let us know what was going on, and how the rest of the paragraph was organized by the signposts "first," "second," and "third." It is more important at this point to know that there are three reasons to doubt the studies, than to know exactly what those doubts are. If ETS asks about them, we know where to look.

If we were to write an outline of the third paragraph, it might look like this:

The third paragraph
— qualifies the theory that microwaves are dangerous by discussing shortcomings of the methodology of
    1) Cleary
    2) Milham
    3) and everybody else

Before you read the last paragraph, take a moment to decide what you would write now.
List three possibilities:

1._____

2._____

3._____

If you suggested writing a conclusion, that was a possibility. Usually when the main idea is given in the first paragraph, and the middle paragraphs are made up of examples, the last paragraph restates the main idea. If you suggested giving more examples in support of the main idea, that was a good answer as well. Sometimes ETS passages don't conclude, they just stop. If you suggested yet another contradiction, that was possible too; the third paragraph contradicted the main idea of the passage. Maybe the author will now contradict the contradiction and reaffirm the main point.

Let's see what the author did:

However, no one seriously disputes that the
(35) preliminary findings of Cleary and Milham must be
taken seriously or that new studies should be set up
to try to duplicate their results. Although federal
guidelines for how much electromagnetic energy can
be allowed to enter the work and home environment
(40) have been made more stringent since they were first
implemented in 1982, the recent studies pose
troubling questions about the safety of microwaves.

Here's how to crack it: The first word ("however") let us know that the author was going to come back to the original point: microwaves may be dangerous. Was this a conclusion? You bet.

In retrospect, the organization of the passage is pretty clear.

The first paragraph states the dangers of other types of waves.

The second paragraph talks about the dangers of microwaves as shown by two studies.

The third qualifies the two studies.

The fourth decides that, on balance, microwaves may indeed be dangerous.

More About Structure

Reading passages on the GMAT have only a few possible structures. The most common one:

Paragraph 1: main idea
Paragraph 2: examples of main idea
Paragraph 3: more examples
Paragraph 4: conclusion, restating main idea

A Yin-Yang structure might go like this:

Paragraph 1: An idea is proposed.
Paragraph 2: That idea is supported.
Paragraph 3: BUT (trigger word) the author
thinks that idea is wrong and advances another
idea (the main idea).

For example, a recent GMAT reading passage went like this:

Paragraph 1: Labeling a particular author as a
member of the Harlem Renaissance seems wrong.
Paragraph 2: Writers are too complex to have
just one label.

Paragraph 3: BUT (trigger word) this particular author really does seem to be best categorized as a member of the Harlem Renaissance.

Another variation of this structure:

Paragraph 1: An accepted idea is proposed.
Paragraph 2: BUT (trigger word) the author thinks that idea is wrong and advances another idea (the main idea).
Paragraph 3: The author's idea is supported.

For example, a recent GMAT reading passage went like this:

Paragraph 1: Marxists think the fate of women and that of socialism are linked.
Paragraph 2: HOWEVER (trigger word), the author disagrees.
Paragraph 3: Women, the author says, do not want revolution, just a few changes.

Another structure goes like this:

Paragraph 1: An idea is proposed.
Paragraph 2: That idea is supported.
Paragraph 3: The idea is qualified (i.e. negative aspects are explored).
Paragraph 4: BUT (trigger word), on balance the author still thinks the idea is correct.

This most resembles the passage you've just read. A recent GMAT passage went like this:

Paragraph 1: An explanation of a scientific phenomenon is advanced.
Paragraph 2: The explanation is supported.
Paragraph 3: Reasons to doubt the explanation are given.
Paragraph 4: BUT, in the end, most people have come to accept the explanation.

Step 5: Attack the Questions

Once you have grasped the main ideas of the paragraphs and the overall structure of the passage, you can attack the questions aggressively. As we noted earlier, each passage is followed by 7 or 8 questions of varying levels of difficulty. These questions *generally* follow the organization of the passage. In other words, a question about the first paragraph will probably come before a question about the second paragraph.

Some people believe it's a good idea to look at the questions before reading the passage. According to their reasoning, reading the questions first allows you to determine what's important in the passage. We might agree if there weren't as many as eight of them. It's impossible to keep eight questions in your head and read a complicated passage at the same time. By approaching the passages the way we've suggested, you'll get the general questions through an understanding of the structure, and you'll know just where to look to find the answers to specific questions.

POE

In the chapter on Sentence Correction, you learned that it's often easier to eliminate incorrect answers than to select the correct answers. The Process of Elimination is just as useful on Reading Comprehension questions as it was on Sentence Correction questions. How can you use POE in the Reading Comprehension section?

General Questions

- "What is the primary purpose of this passage?"
- "What is the author's tone?"
- "Which of the following best describes the structure of the passage?"

Each of the questions above is a general question. General questions have general answers, which you'll find if you understand the main ideas of each of the paragraphs and the structure that holds them all together. Thus, we can eliminate any answer to a general question that focuses on only one part of the passage or is too specific. For example:

The main topic of the passage is

    (A) the health hazards of X rays and gamma rays
        on humans
    (B) the overly-severe federal guidelines on
        radiation
    (C) the potential dangers of microwaves
    (D) a comparison of the work of Cleary and
        Milham
    (E) the limits of study methodology in science

Here's how to crack it: In spite of the fact that X rays and gamma rays were mentioned in the first sentence, we know that this was just an introductory thought to get to the real idea of the passage—the danger of microwaves. So eliminate choice (A). The federal guidelines in choice (B) were mentioned in the passage, but only at the very end. Could this be the main idea of the entire passage? No way. Choice (C) is the correct answer. While Cleary and Milham are discussed several times, they are never compared. Remember their purpose in the passage: to support the main idea that microwaves may be harmful. Eliminate (D). While the passage questions the methodologies of the two scientists, this is not the main idea. Eliminate choice (E) as well.

Specific Questions

- "The passage suggests which of the following about the "federal guidelines" on microwaves mentioned in lines 38–39?"

- According to the passage, which of the following best describes the weak point of Cleary's test-tube results?

Each of the questions above is a specific question. Specific questions have specific answers. Note the line numbers in the first question. All we have to do is go back to the cited lines and read quickly starting a little above the indicated place and finishing a little below.

The second question has no line number, but instead there is a very clear reference to a particular point in the passage—"Cleary's test-tube results." Even if you don't remember where this was in the passage, it is easy enough just to run your finger down the page until you find the place. Again read a little above and a little below the indicated line.

Inference Questions

- Which of the following can be inferred from the passage about the level of radiation from cellular telephones?

Although this question asks you to draw an inference, you'll find that ETS's idea of an inference will be much more timid than yours. GMAT inferences go at most a tiny bit further than the passage itself. If your thinking on this type of question becomes too subtle, you'll get it wrong. Here's an example:

> Which of the following can be inferred from the passage about the studies conducted by Cleary and Milham?
>
> (A) Cleary's results were better documented than Milham's
> (B) Neither study is scientifically valid.
> (C) Both studies indicated that microwaves were more harmful than X rays.
> (D) The final results were not in at the time the article was written.
> (E) The results were based on long-term observation

Here's how to crack it: The passage never said that one study was better than the other, so eliminate answer choice (A). While both studies were questioned in the third paragraph, it would be inferring far too far to say that neither was scientifically valid. Eliminate choice (B). The passage never said that microwaves were more harmful than X rays. It seems likely that they are less harmful. Eliminate choice (C). The results of both studies were called "preliminary" in paragraph two. Thus, choice (D) seems so obvious that you might almost hesitate to call it an inference. This is exactly the kind of inference ETS feels comfortable making. Choice (E) we know to be false. So far, there have been no long-term studies. The correct answer was (D).

Be Wary of Exact Quotations

You have already seen how ETS can set a trap for Joe Bloggs by putting the correct answer to a question after a trigger word. Here's one of the examples we showed you earlier:

> Small companies can be devastated by the loss of a major client, but they can usually survive a few smaller defections.
>
> Which of the following statements is true?
>
> (A) Small companies can be devastated by the loss of any client.
>
> (B) The loss of some types of clients will not necessarily endanger a small company.

Choice (A) was a trap for students who, like Joe Bloggs, didn't bother to read the entire sentence. Because Joe stopped paying attention before he got to the trigger word, he misunderstood the meaning of the sentence and got the question wrong.

Answer choice (A) was even more enticing for Joe Bloggs because it was almost an exact quotation from the sentence. When Joe reads answer choice (A), he says, "Yeah. I saw that in the passage." It looks familiar, so he picks it—and loses points.

To prevent Joe from getting the correct answer by mistake, ETS test-writers try not to let the correct answer choice be a direct quote from the passage. Instead, they change the wording slightly so that it will not look familiar to Joe.

In fact, ETS test-writers sometimes create incorrect answer choices that use catchy phrases from the passage to entice Joe to pick them. This is most obvious on questions that ask you to *infer* something from the passage. Since these questions are asking you to say something that was not said directly in the passage, an answer choice with wording taken directly from the passage is almost certainly wrong.

Attack Disputable Answer Choices

You've eliminated two answer choices on a Reading Comprehension question, but you can't decide which of the remaining three choices is best. All three seem to be saying the same thing. How do you choose between them? The test-writers at ETS want their correct answers to be indisputable so that no one will ever be able to complain.

Here are three statements. Which of them is indisputable?

(A) Shaw was the greatest dramatist of his time.
(B) Shaw's genius was never understood.
(C) Shaw was a great dramatist, although some critics disagree.

Shaw's status as a playwright will always be a matter of opinion. If ETS made statement (A) the correct answer to a Reading Comprehension question, people who got the question wrong might argue that not everyone considers Shaw to be the greatest dramatist of his time.

If ETS made statement (B) the correct answer to a Reading Comprehension question, people who got the question wrong could argue that someone, somewhere in the world, must have understood poor old Shaw.

Statement (C), by contrast, is indisputable. Most critics would agree that Shaw was a great dramatist. If there are any critics who do not, ETS covers itself with its little disclaimer: "although some critics disagree." Statement (C) is so vague that no one could possibly argue with it.

In general: An answer choice that is highly specific and unequivocal is *disputable* and is therefore usually not the correct answer.

An answer choice that is general and vague is *indisputable* and is therefore often the correct answer.

How to Pick an Indisputable Answer Choice

Certain words make a statement so vague that it is almost impossible to dispute. Here are some of these words:

> usually
> sometimes
> may
> can
> some
> most

If a statement says that Shaw is *sometimes* considered to be the greatest dramatist ever, who can dispute that?

How to Avoid a Disputable Answer Choice

Certain words make a statement so specific that it is easy to dispute. Here are some of these words:

> always
> must
> everybody
> all
> complete
> never

If a statement says that Shaw is *always* considered to be the greatest dramatist ever, who couldn't dispute that?

What Does Wally Want to Pick?

The GMAT was created in 1954. Very little thought has gone into it since then. Although some of the question types have changed, the philosophical outlook of the test has remained the same. Every year the same information is tested in pretty much the same way. The GMAT is frozen in time. It harks back to a more innocent era—a time when there were answers to every question, and America was always right, and all our problems were on the way to being solved. ETS reading passages are still written from that perspective.

It is a perspective you may not understand, since you probably weren't around in the '50s. But we've all experienced that era indirectly, in the form of 1950s television sitcoms. Think of the GMAT as the test Wally Cleaver would have had to take if he'd decided to go to business school.

Whenever you're in doubt about an answer, it always helps to ask yourself whether Wally would have felt comfortable selecting that answer.

Respect for Professionals

ETS has tremendous respect for all professionals—doctors, scientists, economists, writers, and artists. After all, Dr. Kildare never got sued for malpractice, and Wally would feel very uncomfortable selecting an answer choice that implied that any professional was a terrible person.

By the same token, it would be unusual to find a correct answer choice that took any but the lightest digs at America. Our country is pretty much beyond ETS's reproach.

Moderate Emotion

ETS avoids strong emotions on the GMAT. If Wally took the GMAT, he would never pick an answer choice that took too strong a position about anything. The author's tone might be "slightly critical," but it will not be "scornful and envious." The author's tone might be "admiring," but it will never be "wildly enthusiastic."

The Minority Passage

For many years minority groups have complained—justifiably—that ETS tests discriminate against them. ETS responded to this criticism by adding a minority passage to many of its tests. One of the reading passages on the GMAT you take will almost certainly be about some minority group—blacks, Chicanos, women (for some reason, they consider women to be a minority group), etc.

Designed to answer charges that ETS tests are biased, the minority passage is invariably positive in tone. This doesn't make the test any fairer to minorities, but it does sometimes make the test easier to beat. Any answer choice that expresses negative views of the minority in question is almost certainly wrong. Try the following example:

> The author considers women's literature to be
>
> (A) derivative
> (B) lacking in imagination
> (C) full of promise and hope
> (D) much better than the literature being written by
>   men today
> (E) uninteresting

Here's how to crack it: You don't need to see the passage to answer this question. The whole purpose of the minority passage is to illustrate to everyone how broad-minded and unbiased the GMAT really is. *Derivative, lacking in imagination,* and *uninteresting* all express negative opinions of literature written by (what ETS considers to be) a minority group. Wally would never have picked choices (A), (B), or (E).

Answer choice (D) goes too far in the other direction. As far as Wally and ETS are concerned, women's literature is just as good as, but no better than, anyone else's. The answer must be choice (C).

Putting All This to Work

Now that you know something about how to tackle GMAT passages, and what to look for, try the sample passage below. Find the main idea of each paragraph (and if you like, jot down a few key words about each in the margin); look for structural signposts (and circle them when you find them). Try not to spend much time "reading." Remember, you only get points for answering questions. Don't feel you have to do the questions in the order in which they are presented. As we've said, if you've understood the structure of the passage, it makes sense to do the general questions first. Leave for last any specific questions that don't seem to have an obvious reference place in the passage. (At the end of this chapter you will find the same passage repeated with all the handwritten markings one of our teachers made when she "read" the passage.)

Until recently, corporate ideology in the United
States has held firmly to the central belief that bigger
is better. This traditional view of the primacy of
huge, centralized companies is now being challenged
(05) as some of the giants of American business are being
outperformed by a new generation of smaller,
streamlined businesses. If it was the industrial
revolution that spawned the era of massive
industrialized companies, then it could be said that it
(10) is the information revolution of the 1990's that is
spawning the era of the small company.

For most of this century, big companies
dominated an American business scene that seemed
to thrive on its own grandness of scale. The
(15) expansion westward, the growth of the railroad and
steel industries, an almost limitless supply of cheap
raw materials, plus a population boom that provided
an ever-increasing demand for new products (if not
always a cheap source of labor) all coincided to
(20) encourage the growth of large companies.

But rapid developments in the marketplace have
begun to change the accepted rules of business
prosperity and have underscored the need for fast
reaction times. Small companies, without huge
(25) overhead and inventory, can respond quickly to a
technologically advanced age in which new products
and technologies can become outmoded within a year
of their being brought to market.

Despite sagging profit margins, and warnings
(30) from industry analysts, large companies initially have
been slow to recognize the threat posed to them by
the growth of new technologies, and the information
systems that have made them available so quickly.
This slow response by the industrial giants has not

(35) just been a problem in the United States: Large corporations in Japan and Germany have recently been learning the same hard lesson that no company can afford to be complacent in this business climate.

(40) Of course, successful emerging small companies face a potential dilemma in that their very success will tend to turn them into copies of the large corporate dinosaurs they are now supplanting. To avoid this trap, small companies may look to the example of several CEOs of large corporations who
(45) have learned the lessons of the information revolution and who are successfully breaking their sprawling organizations down into small, semi-independent divisions capable of making the leap into the next century.

1. The primary purpose of the passage is to

    (A) present evidence that resolves a contradiction in business theory
    (B) discuss reasons why an accepted business pattern is changing
    (C) describe a theoretical model and a method whereby that model can be tested
    (D) argue that a traditional ideology deserves new attention
    (E) resolve two conflicting explanations for a phenomenon

2. According to the passage, which of the following served as one warning of the changes in the marketplace that large companies initially failed to heed?

    (A) The emergence of small companies
    (B) The population boom
    (C) The coming of the industrial revolution
    (D) The hiring of industry analysts
    (E) The shrinking of profits

3. According to the passage, all of the following are examples of developments that helped promote the growth of large companies earlier in this century EXCEPT

    (A) the growth of the railroad industry
    (B) the expansion of the western frontier
    (C) an almost inexhaustible source of raw materials
    (D) the existence of an inexpensive source of labor
    (E) the development of an industry to produce steel

4. The author's attitude toward the "traditional view" (line 3) can best be described as

(A) scornful and denunciatory
(B) dispirited and morose
(C) critical but respectful
(D) admiring and deferential
(E) uncertain but interested

5. It can be inferred from the passage that which of the following actions would be most consistent with the traditional ideology described in the passage?

(A) Splitting a manufacturing company into several smaller divisions.
(B) Bringing a new product to market within a year.
(C) Creating a department to utilize new emerging technologies.
(D) Expanding an existing company in anticipation of growing demand.
(E) Cutting inventory and decreasing overhead.

6. According to the passage, to avoid the trap posed by the "potential dilemma" mentioned in line 40, emerging successful small companies will have to do which of the following?

(A) Turn for advice to the industry analysts who earlier predicted the problems of large companies.
(B) Avoid taking paths that will make them too successful.
(C) Learn to embrace the traditional ideology of large corporations.
(D) Create small interconnected divisions rather than expanding in traditional ways.
(E) Hire successful CEOs from other firms.

7. Which of the following best describes the organization of the first paragraph of the passage?

(A) A conventional model is dismissed and an alternative introduced.
(B) An assertion is made and a general supporting example is given.
(C) Two contradictory points of view are presented and evaluated.
(D) A historical overview is given to explain a phenomenon.
(E) A new theory is described and then qualified.

8. It can be inferred from the passage that small companies are better able to adapt to the new business climate due to which of the following factors?

    I. low overhead and inventory
    II. the ability to predict when new products will become outmoded
    III. the capacity to change quickly to meet new challenges

(A) I only
(B) II only
(C) III only
(D) I and III only
(E) I, II, and III

Attacking the Questions

1. The primary purpose of the passage is to

(A) present evidence that resolves a contradiction in business theory
(B) discuss reasons why an accepted business pattern is changing
(C) describe a theoretical model and a method whereby that model can be tested
(D) argue that a traditional ideology deserves new attention
(E) resolve two conflicting explanations for a phenomenon

Here's how to crack it: This is a general question, and general questions always reflect the structure of the passage. The first words of the passage were "until recently." We hope you recognized right away that this was "yin-yang" terminology, as was "this traditional view." Obviously this passage was about to present a *new* view.

The old view, according to the passage, was that in America large companies were always better off than small companies. Of course, the new view is that smaller companies are now doing better than big companies. This was probably enough for you to answer all the general questions in this section, but let's look quickly at the rest of the passage: paragraph two gave historical reasons why bigger used to be better; paragraph three explained why this was no longer true today; paragraph four examines the reactions of the large companies to the changes in the business climate; and paragraph five concludes by talking about how small companies can stay successful as they inevitably get bigger. Let's look at the answer choices.

(A) In yin-yang passages, new is virtually always better than old. There is really no contradiction here, and besides, how could a 500-word passage "resolve" anything definitively? Eliminate.

(B) This is the correct answer. It mirrors the yin-yang structure of the passage—the accepted pattern of almost a century is now changing.

(C) If you picked this one, you were thinking too hard. Perhaps you thought the primacy of the small company was the new theoretical model, about to be tested. However, the passage seems to imply that the decline of large companies and the ascendancy of small companies started before anyone even realized what was happening, let alone came up with some smart theory about it.

(D) Was the author arguing that in fact the traditional view that "bigger is better" is actually correct after all? Nope. Eliminate.

(E) As we said above, GMAT passages virtually never "resolve" anything. While there are two conflicting elements in this passage, they are not conflicting explanations for a single phenomenon.

2. According to the passage, which of the following served as one warning of the changes in the marketplace that large companies initially failed to heed?

   (A) The emergence of small companies
   (B) The population boom
   (C) The coming of the industrial revolution
   (D) The hiring of industry analysts
   (E) The shrinking of profits

Here's how to crack it: This is a specific question. There is no line reference, but can you tell where you are likely to find the correct answer? If you said paragraph four, you were absolutely correct. This was the paragraph that described the large companies' slow reaction to the changing business climate. The important line was "Despite sagging profit margins, and warnings from industry analysts . . ." Let's look at the answer choices:

(A) If the question says, "According to the passage," then there is one specific place in the passage that will tell us the answer to the question. While you could argue that the emergence of small companies could have served as a warning to the large companies, this was never explicitly said. The fourth paragraph gives us two more specific warnings. Eliminate choice (A).

(B) The population boom did come up in this passage, but in another paragraph. The population boom was one reason why big companies were able to expand. Eliminate.

(C) The industrial revolution also came up in the passage, but in paragraph one. Again, it was one of the factors in the expansion of big companies. So much for choice (C).

(D) Now we're getting warmer. Industry analysts gave warnings to big business that were ignored. But was it the *hiring* of these analysts that served as a warning? No.

(E) Bingo. Choice (E) is a nice paraphrase of "Despite sagging profit margins . . . "

3. According to the passage, all of the following are examples of developments that helped promote the growth of large companies earlier in this century EXCEPT

(A) the growth of the railroad industry
(B) the expansion of the western frontier
(C) an almost inexhaustible source of raw materials
(D) the existence of an inexpensive source of labor
(E) the development of an industry to produce steel

Here's how to crack it: This is a specific question without a line number, but you probably knew just where to look. Which paragraph gave historical background on the growth of large companies? If you said paragraph two, you are absolutely correct.

The first time you "read" this passage, you may have skipped over the specifics in this paragraph since they weren't necessary to understand the purpose of the paragraph. Now, of course, you are interested. But even if you had spent twenty minutes you didn't really have memorizing the entire passage, wouldn't you still have wanted to peek back at this paragraph just to make sure you remembered it correctly? Since you were going to have to look back anyway, it made sense to skip over the details the first time around. Remember, there was no guarantee that there would even be a question about this information. It is not unusual to find GMAT passages whose questions completely ignore whole paragraphs at a time.

This is an "except" question which means that every answer choice is correct but one. The answer to this question was buried inside the parentheses in lines 18–19: ("If not always a cheap source of labor.") The answer to this question is choice (D).

4. The author's attitude toward the "traditional view" (line 3) can best be described as

(A) scornful and denunciatory
(B) dispirited and morose
(C) critical but respectful
(D) admiring and deferential
(E) uncertain and uninterested

Here's how to crack it: You could eliminate two of these answer choices without even reading the passage. Wally would never have chosen an answer that described an attitude toward the ideology of companies like General Motors in terms like "scornful and denunciatory" or "dispirited and morose." As far as the passage is concerned, the traditional ideology no longer works, so we can pretty much rule out choice (D) admiring and deferential. Choice (E) is a little too vague. After all, the author was obviously interested enough to write this passage. Both choices (A) and (B) are so strong and out in left field that we can safely eliminate them. The only possible answer is choice (C).

5. It can be inferred from the passage that which of the following actions would be most consistent with the traditional ideology described in the passage?

   (A) Splitting a manufacturing company into several smaller divisions.
   (B) Bringing a new product to market within a year.
   (C) Creating a department to utilize new emerging technologies.
   (D) Expanding an existing company in anticipation of growing demand.
   (E) Cutting inventory and decreasing overhead.

Here's how to crack it: The trick in inference questions is to infer as little as possible. The traditional ideology is that bigger is better. Which of the answer choices shows a situation getting bigger? The correct answer is choice (D). Choices (A), and (E) both illustrate the process of down-sizing as described in the passage. Choices (B) and (C) illustrate the lean-and-mean tactics attributed in the passage to small companies.

6. According to the passage, to avoid the trap posed by the "potential dilemma" mentioned in line 40, emerging successful small companies will have to do which of the following?

   (A) Turn for advice to the industry analysts who earlier predicted the problems of large companies.
   (B) Avoid taking paths that will make them too successful.
   (C) Learn to embrace the traditional ideology of large corporations.
   (D) Create small interconnected divisions rather than expanding in traditional ways.
   (E) Hire successful CEOs from other firms.

Here's how to crack it: Whenever you see a specific question with line numbers, always remember to read a little above and a little below the cited line. In this case, we are not interested so much in the "dilemma" as how to avoid the trap posed by the dilemma. The answer to this question is in the last three lines of the passage. Let's look at the answer choices:

(A) is an interesting idea, but it is not said in the passage, so we can eliminate it.

(B) has the right idea, but takes it too far. It is practically un-American to think that a company would try not to become too successful.

(C) The traditional ideology is what got the big companies into trouble. Eliminate.

(D) This is the correct answer, and a nice paraphrase of what was said in the last three lines of the passage.

(E) The passage suggests that small companies could learn from these CEOs, but does not suggest that the small companies *hire* the CEOs.

7. Which of the following best describes the organization of the first paragraph of the passage?

   (A) A conventional model is dismissed and an alternative introduced.
   (B) An assertion is made and a general supporting example is given.
   (C) Two contradictory points of view are presented and evaluated.
   (D) A historical overview is given to explain a phenomenon.
   (E) A new theory is described and then qualified.

Here's how to crack it: This is a structure question pure and simple. Let's look at the answers:

Choice (A) correctly describes this yin-yang paragraph.

Choice (B) ignores the structure of the passage.

Choice (C) is close, but fails to show that one point of view is considered superior to the other.

Choice (D) describes paragraph two instead of paragraph one.

In choice (E), the word "qualified" means "limited." The author seems to like the idea of the small company, and certainly doesn't qualify it in the first paragraph.

8. It can be inferred from the passage that small companies are better able to adapt to the new business climate due to which of the following factors?

> I. low overhead and inventory
> II. the ability to predict when new products will become outmoded
> III. the capacity to change quickly to meet new challenges

(A) I only
(B) II only
(C) III only
(D) I and III only
(E) I, II, and III

Here's how to crack it: I,II,III questions are nasty because you have to answer three questions in order to get one right. It is often a good idea to leave these for last. Where in the passage were small companies actually described? If you said paragraph three, you were absolutely correct. Since this is an inference question, we need to make sure we don't infer too far. Let's look at statement I. Can we infer that small companies are better able to adapt because of low inventory? Sure. On line 24–25 the passage reads; "Small companies, without huge overhead and inventory . . . "

Since we know that statement I works, we can cross off choices (B) and (C). Let's look at statement II. While it seems likely that the ability to predict ahead of time which products are going to become outmoded would help small companies adapt faster, there is no indication in the passage that anyone has the ability to predict the future. If you aren't sure about statement II, you can skip it and go on to statement III. This statement is definitely true. It is a paraphrase of line 25–28. The correct answer is choice (D).

Here's What a Reading Passage Should Look Like After You've Finished Reading It

trad. view:
bigger better

(Until recently) corporate ideology in the United
States has held firmly to the central belief that bigger
is better. This traditional view of the primacy of
huge, centralized companies is now being challenged
(05) as some of the giants of American business are being
outperformed by a new generation of smaller,
streamlined businesses. If it was the industrial
revolution that spawned the era of massive
industrialized companies, then it could be said that it
(10) is information revolution of the 1990's that is
spawning the era of the small company.

new view:
small is better

For most of this century, big companies
dominated an American business scene that seemed
to thrive on its own grandness of scale. The
(15) expansion westward, the growth of the railroad and
steel industries, an almost limitless supply of cheap
raw materials, plus a population boom that provided
an ever-increasing demand for new products (if not
always a cheap source of labor) all coincided to
(20) encourage the growth of large companies.

hist. reasons for
big companies'
early success

(But) rapid developments in the marketplace have
begun to change the accepted rules of business
prosperity and have underscored the need for fast
reaction times. Small companies, without huge
(25) overhead and inventory, can respond quickly to a
technologically advanced age in which new products
and technologies can become outmoded within a year
of their being brought to market.

reasons for
small companies'
recent success

(Despite) sagging profit margins, and warnings
(30) from industry analysts, large companies initially have
been slow to recognize the threat posed to them by
the growth of new technologies, and the information
systems that have made them available so quickly.
This slow response by the industrial giants has not
(35) just been a problem in the United States: large
corporations in Japan and Germany have recently
been learning the same hard lesson that no company
can afford to be complacent in this business climate.

big companies'
slow response to
new conditions

Of course, successful emerging small companies
(40) face a potential dilemma in that their very success
will tend to turn them into copies of the large
corporate dinosaurs they are now supplanting. To
avoid this trap, small companies may look to the
example of several CEOs of large corporations who
(45) have learned the lessons of the information
revolution and who are successfully breaking their
sprawling organizations down into small, semi-
independent divisions capable of making the leap
into the next century.

danger for small
companies:
getting too big

Summary

1. A GMAT Reading Comprehension section contains three passages. Each passage is followed by 7 or 8 questions, for a total of 23 questions. The three types of passages that may appear on the test are social science, science, and humanities. However, on recent tests the Reading Comprehension section has consisted of

   2 social science passages

   and

   1 science passage

2. Reading Comprehension questions are not presented in order of difficulty, and while the _passages_ are usually arranged in order of difficulty, it is generally more effective strategy to decide on your _own_ order in which to do the passages.

3. If you insist on reading these passages the way you normally read, it might make sense to skip one entire passage and the questions based on that passage, in order to have enough time to read the other two thoroughly. However, if you can make the transition to GMAT reading, you may find that even if Reading Comprehension is not your strength, that you may have time to do all three passages well, perhaps skipping one or two difficult questions from each passage.

4. GMAT reading has nothing to do with reading, and even less to do with business reading. GMAT passages contain many more pieces of information than you'll be tested on. Trying to remember all this useless information is silly.

5. Read a passage for its structure. This will enable you to answer the general questions, and give you a good idea of where to look for the answers to specific questions.

6. Read each paragraph for the main idea, and to decide how it fits into the general structure of the entire passage. Specific facts are unimportant at this stage. Let your eyes skim over them. Write notes in the margin.

7. Structural signposts can help you see how a passage is organized.

8. Trigger words are important structural signposts. Circle all signposts.

9. Attack answer choices that repeat words from the passage. These are sometimes traps, particularly on inference questions.

10. Attack answer choices that are disputable. Specific, strong statements are often wrong. Vague, wimpy statements are often correct.

11. The tone of a minority passage is invariably positive. This can sometimes help you to answer questions even if you haven't had time to read the entire passage.

12. If the Beaver's older brother, Wally, wouldn't have liked a particular answer, there's a good chance it's wrong. Wally wouldn't have liked answers that

    A) are disrespectful to professionals
    B) are too strong
    C) are anti-American
    D) condone prejudicial attitudes

13. When line references are given, read a little above and a little below the cited lines.

14. I, II, III questions are best tackled by POE. If they're taking too much time, leave them for last.

CHAPTER EIGHT

Critical Reasoning

The Critical Reasoning section of the GMAT consists of very short reading passages (typically 20 to 100 words) arranged in order of difficulty. Each of these passages is followed by one or two questions, giving a total of 20 questions. These questions are supposed to test your ability to think clearly. ETS says that "no knowledge of the terminology and of the conventions of formal logic is presupposed." Nevertheless, you'll find that while it may not be presupposed, some knowledge of the rudiments of formal logic—as applied by The Princeton Review—can substantially increase your score.

The History of Critical Reasoning

Over the years ETS has tried several different formats in an attempt to test reasoning ability.

The original GMAT contained a section called Best Arguments. In 1961, ETS replaced this section ("in part because research indicated that [doing so] would increase the predictive effectiveness of the test") with something called Organization of Ideas. In 1966, this section was also phased out, and for six years reasoning ability went unmeasured by ETS. In 1972, ETS tried again, with a section called Analysis of Situations. Finally, on the October 1988 version of the GMAT, ETS unveiled Critical Reasoning for the first time.

Well, Not Exactly the *First* Time

In fact, Critical Reasoning looks a lot like Best Arguments. ETS has used this type of question for years on the LSAT and the GRE—respectively, the Law School Admission Test and the Graduate Record Exam.

Before we begin, take a moment to read a close approximation of the instructions at the beginning of each Critical Reasoning section:

> Directions: After reading each question, pick the
> best answer among the choices that follow.

Obviously you won't need to read these instructions again.

How to Increase Your Score on the Critical Reasoning Section

The terseness of ETS's instructions implies that all you need on this section is common sense. Common sense will certainly help, but you should also understand a bit about the formal logic on which Critical Reasoning is based.

Like the other types of questions found on the GMAT, Critical Reasoning questions tend to be predictable. There are only a few question types, and as you learn how the test-writers use their smattering of formal logic to write Critical Reasoning questions, you'll be able to anticipate the answers to certain of those questions.

In this chapter we'll teach you how to:

1. use clues in the questions to anticipate the kind of answer you're looking for in a passage
2. analyze and attack the passages in an organized fashion
3. understand the basic structure of the passages
4. use Process of Elimination to eliminate wrong choices

A Word About GMAT Logic

GMAT logic is different from the formal logic you may have studied in college. Our review of GMAT logic is not intended to be representative of logic as a whole. We don't intend to teach you logic. We're going to teach you *GMAT* logic.

The Passage

Most of the passages in the Critical Reasoning section are in the form of *arguments* in which the writer tries to convince the reader of something. Here's an example:

> In the past 10 years, advertising revenues for the magazine *True Investor* have fallen by 30%. The magazine has failed to attract new subscribers, and newsstand sales are down to an all-time low. Thus, sweeping editorial changes will be necessary if the magazine is to survive.

There are three main parts to an argument.

The Conclusion: This is what the author is trying to convince us of.

The Premises: These are the pieces of evidence the author gives to support the conclusion.

The Assumptions: These are unstated ideas or evidence without which the entire conclusion might be invalid.

In the passage above, the author's *conclusion* is found in the last line:

> *Thus, sweeping editorial changes will be neces-*
> *sary if the magazine is to survive.*

To support this, the author gives three pieces of evidence, or *premises*: Advertising revenue is down; there are no new subscribers; and very few people are buying the newspaper at the newsstand.

Are there any *assumptions* here? Well, not in the passage itself. Assumptions are never stated by the author. They are parts of the argument that have been left out. Even the best thought-out argument has assumptions. In this case one important assumption the author seems to be making is that it was the old editorial policy that caused the problems the magazine is now encountering. Another assumption is that editorial changes alone will be enough to restore the magazine's financial health.

A Critical Reasoning passage is not necessarily made up of only these three parts. The passage might contain other information as well—extraneous ideas, perhaps, or statements of an opposing point of view. It's also possible for some important part of an argument to be missing—its conclusion, for example. Sometimes ETS will ask *you* to supply the conclusion.

This Is Not Like Reading Comprehension

Reading Comprehension passages are long and filled with useless facts. By now you've gotten used to reading these passages for their structure, letting your eyes skip over factual data you probably won't be tested on anyway.

By contrast, Critical Reasoning passages are quite short, and every single word should be considered carefully. Shades of meaning are very important in this section.

The Question

Immediately after the passage, there will be a question. There is usually only one question per passage. In the chapter on Reading Comprehension, we told you that it was a waste of time to try to read Reading Comprehension questions *before* you read the passage; after all, each Reading Comprehension passage is followed by 7 or 8 questions. It is impossible to keep that many questions in your head.

In Critical Reasoning, however, since there is usually only one question per passage, it is essential that you

always read the question first.

The question contains important clues that will tell you what to look for as you read the passage.

There Are Seven Question Types

Here are examples of the seven question types you'll see (we'll go into much greater detail later in the chapter):

1. What is the conclusion in the passage above?

As you read the passage, you'll be looking to identify and separate the premises from the conclusion.

2. What conclusion is best supported by the passage above?

The passage connected to this type of question will simply be a list of premises. You will have to supply your own conclusion.

3. The passage above assumes that . . .

As you read the passage in question, you will be looking for an unstated premise on which the argument depends.

4. Which of the following, if true, would most strengthen the conclusion drawn above?

This type of question is like an assumption question in that it is asking you to find an unstated premise on which the argument depends, and then bolster it.

5. Which of the following, if true, would most seriously weaken the conclusion of the passage above?

This type of question, like an assumption question, is asking you to find an unstated premise of the argument and poke holes in it.

6. Which of the following can best be inferred from the passage above?

This question, like inference questions in the Reading Comprehension section, is at most asking you to go a tiny, tiny bit further than the passage does.

7. Which of the following most resembles the method used by the author to make the point above?

This type of question asks you to find an argument in the answer choices that mimics the original argument.

While the wording of the questions may vary, these are the question types you'll see—there are only seven. Each type of question has its own strategy.

The Answer Choices

As you read through this chapter you will notice that certain words keep coming up again and again in our discussions of how to eliminate wrong answers.

"This answer choice goes too far"
"That choice is out of the scope of the argument"

POE + Critical Reasoning = Scope

Scope is the single most valuable tool to eliminate answer choices in Critical Reasoning questions. It takes a little practice to figure out how scope works. We'll give you an introduction to the concept here, but you'll need to work through the entire chapter (and perhaps do some timed sections in the *Official Guide for GMAT Review*) to understand it completely. Here's an example:

In an effort to save money, a country's government is considering reducing its military spending. However, without military contracts, crucial industries in that country face bankruptcy, which could disrupt the economy. Thus, the same government that is reducing its military spending will eventually have to provide these industries with money for peacetime research and development.

Which of the following states the conclusion of the passage above?

(A) The necessity of providing money to keep crucial industries from going bankrupt will discourage the government from reducing its military budget.
(B) If the government decreases its military budget, it will eventually be forced to increase its military budget to its former level.
(C) The industries that receive research and development money will be successful in their efforts to convert to peacetime manufacturing.
(D) In the event of war, this country would be unprepared for military conflict.
(E) Reducing military spending to save money will result in some increases in other types of spending.

We will be discussing how to do this type of question (Find-the-conclusion) very shortly, but for now we're going to summarize the argument and skip right to the answer choices in order to illustrate how to use scope as an elimination technique. The argument states that a country wants to save money by decreasing its military budget; however, in order to keep the industries that depend on military contracts from collapsing, the country will have to *spend* some additional money as well.

ETS Rewards Narrow Minds

In critical reasoning it is easy to think too much. Answer choice (A) might look very tempting at first, because it seems to take the argument to its logical conclusion: "Heh, if cutting military spending is going to end up *costing* the country money, they may as well not do it." But the ETS test-writers consider answer choice (A) to be outside the scope of this argument. In fact, if you think about it, we have no idea whether the government will be discouraged or not, or even whether the costs of supplying R and D money will be greater than the savings in military spending. This answer goes much further than the argument itself.

Choice (B) goes too far as well. Perhaps cutting military spending will turn out to be a bad idea, but even if that is true, how do we know that the country will then eventually decide to increase military spending? What might happen in the future is well outside the scope of this argument.

We can eliminate choice (C) for the same reason, since it merely goes off on a tangent to speculate as to the ultimate fate of the industries mentioned in the passage. Whether these industries succeed in making the transition to peacetime manufacturing is not crucial to this argument.

If you are tempted by choice (D), you're still thinking too much. When a country reduces its military spending, you could argue that it might be less prepared for war—but that is way outside the scope of this passage. Be careful not to impose your own value judgments or thought processes on these questions.

Choice (E) may have seemed simplistic when you first read it. You might even have thought that it wasn't really a conclusion at all, that it was more like a summary. However, this is the answer the ETS test-writer would choose. And remember, *he's* the one who makes up the answer key. Choice (E) stayed within the scope of the argument.

Logical Reasoning

Before we get into specific strategies for dealing with Critical Reasoning questions, it's helpful to understand two major types of reasoning used in logic: **deduction** and **induction**.

Deduction is the process of finding a conclusion that *must* follow from the premises that are given. Here's an example:

> *All Marx Brothers movies are comedies.* Duck Soup *is a Marx Brothers movie. Therefore,* Duck Soup *is a comedy.*

In this example we are given two premises and a conclusion that must follow from these premises. There is no way to argue with this logic. As long as the premises are correct, the conclusion must be valid. This particular kind of deductive reasoning is called a *syllogism*. Make one up on your own—it's easy:

> *Warren Beatty always sleeps with his costars. This year he is costarring in a movie with Roseanne Arnold. Therefore Warren Beatty will sleep with Roseanne Arnold.*

The chances of seeing a syllogism on the GMAT are pretty slim, but it *is* likely that you'll see one type of question that uses deductive reasoning—a question that will give you a list of premises and then ask for a conclusion that *must* follow logically.

GMAT test-writers don't use deductive logic very often. For one thing, since deductive logic must be true, it's hard to come up with four enticing wrong answers. In addition, there's very little deductive logic to be found in real life. Most of the everyday logic we use is based on inductive reasoning. In a deductive argument, as long as the premises are true, the conclusion must be true.

In an *inductive* argument, even if the premises are true, the best we can say about the conclusion is that it *may* be true. In other words, the conclusion does not necessarily have to follow from the premises. In an inductive argument a conclusion is often predicted to be true based on the fact that a similar statement is true, or has been true in the past.

There are three types of inductive reasoning that appear on the GMAT: statistical arguments, arguments by analogy, and causal arguments.

Statistical Arguments

A statistical argument uses statistics to "prove" its point. Remember what Mark Twain said: "There are lies, damned lies, and statistics."

> *Four out of five doctors agree: The pain reliever in Sinutol is the most effective analgesic on the market today. You should try Sinutol.*

The conclusion (you should try Sinutol) is based on the premise that four out of five doctors found the pain reliever in Sinutol to be the most effective. However, a literal reading of the passage tells us that the statistic that the author uses in support of his conclusion is only based on the opinions of five doctors (all of whom are probably on the board of directors of Sinutol). The author's conclusion is based on the *assumption* that four out of *every* five doctors will find Sinutol to be wonderful. This may be correct, but we do not know for sure. Therefore, the most we can say about the conclusion is that it may be true.

Whenever you see statistics in an argument, always be sure to ask yourself the following question: Are the statistics representative?

Arguments by Analogy

An argument by analogy compares one situation to another, ignoring the question of whether the two situations are comparable.

> *Studies indicate that use of this product causes cancer in laboratory animals. Therefore, you should stop using this product.*

The author's conclusion (you should stop using the product) is based on the premise that the product causes cancer in laboratory animals. This argument is not really complete. It relies on the *assumption* that since this product causes cancer in laboratory animals, it will also cause cancer in humans.

Whenever you see a comparison in a Critical Reasoning passage, you should ask yourself: Are these two situations really comparable?

Causal Arguments

Causal arguments take an effect and suggest a cause for it:

> *Every time I wear my green suit, people like me. Therefore, it is my green suit that makes people like me.*

The author's conclusion (it is the green suit that makes people like him) is based on the premise that every time he wears it, he has observed that effect. But this argument relies on the *assumption* that there is no other possible cause for people liking him. Perhaps he always wears a red tie with his green suit, and it's really the tie that people like.

Whenever you spot a cause being suggested for an effect, ask yourself whether there might be an alternative cause.

You've now seen all the logic you'll need to attack Critical Reasoning. Let's apply your knowledge to the question types.

Find-the-Conclusion Questions

Here's a typical find-the-conclusion question. Remember, always read the question first.

1. When young students first look at modernist abstract painting, their eyes are assailed by a seemingly meaningless mass of squiggles. It is only after a study of the history of art and the forces which led up to abstraction that it is possible to appreciate the intellectual sophistication of modern art. Thus, a high-school study of modern art should always begin with a study of the history of art.

   Which of the following is the main point of the passage above?

   (A) To understand the history of art, it is necessary to study modern art.
   (B) Young students are unable to appreciate fully the complexities of modern art.
   (C) An understanding of the history of art is essential to an understanding of modern art.
   (D) To understand abstract art, students must first study the history of art.
   (E) A high-school study of modern art will have little relevance to students who lack a historical perspective.

Since you read the question first, you knew that as you began reading the passage you would need to separate the conclusion of the argument from its premises. Before you start analyzing the passage, here are a few pointers:

How to Find the Conclusion If It Is Stated in the Passage

• Look for conclusions at the beginning and end of a passage. Most arguments follow one of two common structures:

Premise, premise, premise, conclusion
or
conclusion, premise, premise, premise.

Therefore the conclusion can often be found in the first or last sentence of the passage.

• Look for the same kinds of structural signposts we showed you in the Reading Comprehension chapter. Words like

therefore
thus
so
hence
implies
indicates that

often signal that a conclusion is about to be made.

• Look for a statement that cannot stand alone; in other words, a statement that needs to be supported by premises.

• If you can't find the conclusion, look for the premises instead. These are the parts of the argument that support the conclusion. Premises are often preceded by another kind of signpost. Words like

> because
> since
> in view of
> given that

signal that evidence is about to be given to support a conclusion.

Now Let's Analyze the Passage

1. When young students first look at modernist abstract painting, their eyes are assailed by a seemingly meaningless mass of squiggles. It is only after a study of the history of art and the forces which led up to abstraction that it is possible to appreciate the intellectual sophistication of modern art. Thus, a high-school study of modern art should always begin with a study of the history of art.

   Which of the following is the main point of the passage above?

   (A) To understand the history of art, it is necessary to study modern art.
   (B) Young students are unable to appreciate fully the complexities of modern art.
   (C) An understanding of the history of art is essential to an understanding of modern art.
   (D) To understand abstract art, students must first study the history of art.
   (E) A high-school study of modern art will have little relevance to students who lack a historical perspective.

Here's how to crack it: Look at the first sentence of the passage. If this is the conclusion, it must be supported by other statements in the passage. Does the second sentence, for example, support the first? No, it goes on to make another point. The first sentence is probably not the conclusion. Look at the last sentence. This seems more like a conclusion. It follows the word "thus"—conclusion signpost—and makes a statement that cannot stand alone. Furthermore, the rest of the passage seems to be leading up to this sentence. We've found our conclusion. The passage can be broken down as follows:

1. Students don't understand modern art. (premise)
2. To understand modern art, it is necessary to study art history. (premise)
3. Therefore, students who study modern art should first study art history. (conclusion)

Let's look at the answer choices:

> (A) To understand the history of art, it is necessary to study modern art.

This statement actually reverses the second premise. Not only is it not the conclusion, it's not even a premise. Eliminate.

> (B) Young students are unable to appreciate fully the complexities of modern art.

This statement is the first premise, not the conclusion. Eliminate.

> (C) An understanding of the history of art is essential to an understanding of modern art.

This is a correct statement of the second premise, but, again, it is not the conclusion.

> (D) To understand abstract art, students must first study the history of art.

This looks pretty good. It's a restatement of the last sentence of the passage. Note that the Reading Comprehension strategy of avoiding words taken directly from the passage does not work in Critical Reasoning questions where you are being asked to identify a part of an argument that has already been stated in the passage. In these cases an answer choice that takes a quotation from the passage may well be correct.

> (E) A high-school study of modern art will have little relevance to students who lack a historical perspective.

Choice (E) may seem a little tempting at first. To be sure, it is *a* conclusion—and it begins with the same words found in the last sentence of the passage. The question you must ask yourself is whether this statement encapsulates the conclusion found in the passage. The conclusion in the passage states that a high-school study of art should begin with art history. Answer choice (E) does not restate the conclusion—it goes further to explain why students need art history. In other words, it is outside the scope of the argument.

Supply-Your-Own-Conclusion Questions

Supply-your-own-conclusion questions are much more common than find-the-conclusion questions. The passage gives you a list of premises. You will have to decide which of the answer choices is the best conclusion to the passage. There are two basic types: questions that require you to reason deductively and passages that test your ability to reason inductively.

A Deductive Supply-the-Conclusion Question

2. Fred is taller than Phil.
   Jane is taller than Phil.
   Susan is taller than Jane.
   Tom is taller than Fred.

   If the information above is true, which of the following statements must also be true?

   (A) Fred is taller than Jane.
   (B) Tom is taller than Phil.
   (C) Susan is shorter than Tom.
   (D) Fred is shorter than Jane.
   (E) Phil is taller than Jane.

Here's how to crack it: The question asks which of the statements *must* be true. You're being asked to make a conclusion based on the premises listed in the passage. You may have noticed that you're also being asked to reason deductively. The only type of reasoning that allows you to know that a conclusion *must* be true is deductive reasoning.

The best way to keep all the premises straight is to draw a diagram, or a series of diagrams:

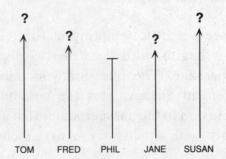

Be sure to distinguish what you *know* to be true from things that merely *could* be true. Now let's attack the answer choices:

(A) Fred is taller than Jane.

From the diagram you can see that while both Fred and Jane are taller than Phil, we do not know the exact relationship between the heights of Fred and Jane. Fred *could* be taller than Jane, but we do not know for certain. Eliminate.

(B) Tom is taller than Phil.

We know from the diagram that Tom is taller than Fred. Since we also know that Fred is taller than Phil, it follows that Tom is, in fact, taller than Phil. This must be the answer. All the same, you should always look at the other answer choices.

(C) Susan is shorter than Tom.

We know that Tom is taller than Fred, who is also taller than Phil. We know that Susan is taller than Jane, who is also taller than Phil. The only thing we know for certain is that both Susan and Tom are taller than Phil. The exact relationship between their heights is unknown. Eliminate.

(D) Fred is shorter than Jane.

Note that answer choice (D) is the exact opposite of answer choice (A). Since we could not tell who was taller in answer choice (A), we can eliminate choice (D) for the same reason.

(E) Phil is taller than Jane.

This one's easy. One of the premises directly contradicts this statement. Eliminate.

An Inductive Supply-the-Conclusion Question

3. Fewer elected officials are supporting
   environmental legislation this year than at any time
   in the last decade. In a study of thirty elected
   officials, only five were actively campaigning for
   new environmental legislation. This comes at a
   time when the public's concern for the environment
   is growing by leaps and bounds.

   Which of the following conclusions is best
   supported by the passage above?

   (A) More elected officials are needed to support
       environmental legislation.
   (B) Elected officials have lost touch with the
       concerns of the public.
   (C) The five elected officials who actively
       campaigned for new environmental
       legislation should be congratulated.
   (D) If the environment is to be saved, elected
       officials must support environmental
       legislation.
   (E) If elected officials are truly to represent their
       constituents, many of them must increase
       their support of environmental legislation.

Here's how to crack it: By reading the question, you can deduce two things: First, this is a supply-the-conclusion passage. Second, since the question does not ask you to supply a conclusion that *must* be true, the reasoning in this passage will be inductive. Here are some guidelines for spotting conclusions among the answer choices:

• Conclusions are supported by *all* the evidence in the passage. As you look at each answer choice, check to see whether the potential conclusion is supported not by some of the premises but by all of them. A statement that follows from only one of the premises will not be the conclusion.

• Because the conclusion in this type of question is not in the passage, the answer cannot be just a restatement of a sentence from the passage.

• Several answer choices will be obviously wrong. Eliminate these first, then decide which of the remaining answers follows most clearly from the premises.

• Be wary of answer choices that go further than the scope of the original argument. For example, if the passage has given you several noncontroversial facts about advertising, do not select an answer choice that says advertising is a waste of time.

Let's attack the answer choices:

   (A) More elected officials are needed to support
       environmental legislation.

This statement ignores the last premise of the passage—that the *public* is becoming more and more concerned about the environment. A conclusion must be supported by all its premises. Eliminate.

> (B) Elected officials have lost touch with the
> concerns of the public.

This is *a* conclusion, but it goes beyond the scope of the argument and ignores parts of the first two premises that relate to the environment.

> (C) The five elected officials who actively
> campaigned for new environmental
> legislation should be congratulated.

This statement, while consistent with the sentiments of the author, again does not deal with the last premise, relating to the concerns of the public.

> (D) If the environment is to be saved, elected
> officials must support environmental
> legislation.

This answer choice again ignores the last premise in the passage. The correct conclusion to this passage must support of all its premises. Eliminate.

> (E) If elected officials are truly to represent their
> constituents, many of them must increase
> their support of environmental legislation.

Bingo. This conclusion is supported by all the premises, and it does not go beyond the scope of the argument.

Assumption Questions

An assumption question asks you to identify an unstated premise of the passage from among the answer choices. Remember that if an argument depends on one or more unstated premises, it must be based on inductive reasoning. As you read the passage, watch for the three kinds of inductive reasoning we've classified.

You should also remember that in an inductive argument, the conclusion does not *have* to be true, although it *may* be true. Assumptions plug holes in the argument and help make a conclusion true. Here are some guidelines for spotting assumptions among the answer choices:

• Assumptions are never stated in the passage. If you see an answer choice that comes straight from the passage, it is not correct.

• Assumptions support the conclusion of the passage. Find the conclusion in the passage, then try out each answer choice to see whether it makes the conclusion stronger.

• Assumptions frequently trade on the gaps inherent in inductive reasoning. If the argument uses statistics, you should probably ask yourself whether the statistics involved are representative. If the argument offers an analogy, you should ask yourself whether the two situations are analogous. If the argument proposes a cause for an effect, you should ask yourself whether there might be some other cause.

Now Let's Try the Passage

4. Many people believe that gold and platinum are the most valuable commodities. To the true entrepreneur, however, gold and platinum are less valuable than opportunities that can enable him to further enrich himself. Therefore, in the world of high finance, information is the most valuable commodity.

    The author of the passage above makes which of the following assumptions?

    (A) Gold and platinum are not the most valuable commodities.
    (B) Entrepreneurs are not like most people.
    (C) The value of information is incalculably high.
    (D) Information about business opportunities is accurate and will lead to increased wealth.
    (E) Only entrepreneurs feel that information is the most valuable commodity.

Here's how to crack it: The question tells you that you are looking for an assumption, which means you can assume that the reasoning of the passage is inductive. You'll be looking for a hole in the argument.

Since an assumption supports the conclusion, it's a good idea to know what the conclusion is. Can you identify it? It was in the last sentence, preceded by "therefore": "In the world of high finance, information is the most valuable commodity."

As you read the passage, keep your eyes open for potential holes in the argument. For example, as you read it might occur to you that the author is assuming that there is no such thing as bad information.

Anyone who has ever taken a stock tip knows the error in that assumption.

Don't be upset if you can't find a hole in the argument as you read. The answer choices will give you a clue.

Let's attack the answer choices:

> (A) Gold and platinum are not the most valuable
>   commodities.

Does this support the conclusion? In a way, it does. If information is supposed to be the most valuable commodity, it might help to know that gold and platinum are *not* the most valuable commodities.

However, saying that gold and platinum are *not* the most valuable commodities does not necessarily mean that information *is* the most valuable commodity.

> (B) Entrepreneurs are not like most people.

If most people find gold and platinum to be the most valuable commodities, while entrepreneurs prefer information, then it *could* be inferred that entrepreneurs are not like most people. Does this support the conclusion, though? Not really. Remember, ETS rewards narrow thinking.

> (C) The value of information is incalculably high.

This answer seems to restate the conclusion. Remember, an assumption is an *unstated* premise. In addition, it goes beyond the scope of the argument. To say that information is valuable does not mean that its value is "incalculable."

> (D) Information about business opportunities is
>   accurate and will lead to increased wealth.

This is the correct answer. If the business information is not accurate, it could not possibly be valuable. Therefore this statement supports the conclusion by plugging a dangerous hole in the argument.

> (E) Only entrepreneurs feel that information is the
>   most valuable commodity.

Does this statement strengthen the conclusion? Actually, it might weaken it. The conclusion states that "in the world of high finance, information is the most valuable commodity." Presumably the world of high finance is not composed exclusively of entrepreneurs. If only entrepreneurs believe information to be the most valuable commodity, then not everyone in the world of high finance would feel the same way.

Strengthen-the-Argument Questions

If a question asks you to strengthen an argument, it is saying that the argument can be strengthened; in other words, again, you're going to be dealing with an inductive passage. The argument won't be complete by itself. The conclusion *may* be true, but it doesn't have to be.

Like assumption questions, strengthen-the-argument questions are really asking you to find a hole in the argument and to fix it with additional information. Here are some guidelines for spotting strengthen-the-argument statements among the answer choices:

• The correct answer will strengthen the argument with *new* information. If you see an answer choice that comes straight from the passage, it's wrong.

• The new information you're looking for will support the conclusion of the passage. Find the conclusion in the passage, then try out each answer choice to see whether it makes the conclusion stronger.

• Strengthen-the-argument questions frequently trade on the gaps inherent in inductive reasoning. If the argument uses statistics, you should probably ask yourself whether the statistics involved are representative. If the argument offers an analogy, you should ask yourself whether the two situations are analogous. If the argument proposes a cause for an effect, you should ask yourself whether there might be some other cause.

Now Let's Try the Passage

5. It has recently been proposed that we adopt an all-volunteer army. This policy was tried on a limited basis several years ago, and was a miserable failure. The level of education of the volunteers was unacceptably low, while levels of drug use and crime soared among army personnel. Can we trust our national defense to a volunteer army? The answer is clearly "No."

Which of the following statements, if true, most strengthens the author's claim that an all-volunteer army should not be implemented?

(A) The general level of education has risen since the first time an all-volunteer army was tried.
(B) The proposal was made by an organization called Citizens for Peace.
(C) The first attempt to create a volunteer army was carried out according to the same plan now under proposal and under the same conditions as those that exist today.
(D) A volunteer army would be less expensive than an army that relies on the draft.
(E) The size of the army needed today is smaller than that needed when a volunteer army was first tried.

Here's how to crack it: You know from reading the question that you're expected to fix a flaw in the argument. Even better, the question itself tells you the conclusion of the passage: "An all-volunteer army should not be implemented."

Since the reasoning in a strengthen-the-argument question has to be inductive, it pays to see whether the argument is statistical, causal, or analogous. You may have noticed that the argument *does*, in fact, use an analogy. The author is basing his conclusion on the results of one previous experience. In effect he is saying, "The idea didn't work then, so it won't work now." This is the potential flaw in the argument.

If you didn't spot the argument by analogy, don't worry. You would probably have seen it when you started attacking the answer choices:

(A) The general level of education has risen since the first time an all-volunteer army was tried.

Does this support the author's conclusion? Actually, it may weaken the conclusion. If the general level of education has risen, it could be argued that the level of education of army volunteers is also higher.

This would remove one of the author's objections to a volunteer army. Eliminate.

> (B) The proposal was made by an organization called Citizens for Peace.

This is irrelevant to the author's conclusion. You might have wondered whether a group called Citizens for Peace was the right organization to make suggestions about the army. Attacking the reputation of a person in order to cast doubt on that person's ideas is a very old pastime. There's even a name for it: an ad hominem fallacy. An ad hominem statement does not strengthen an argument. Eliminate.

> (C) The first attempt to create a volunteer army was carried out according to the same plan now under proposal and under the same conditions as those that exist today.

This is the correct answer. The passage as it stands is potentially flawed because we cannot know that a new attempt to institute an all-volunteer army would turn out the same way it did before. Answer choice (C) provides new information that suggests that the two situations *are* analogous.

> (D) A volunteer army would be less expensive than an army that relies on the draft.

Does this support the conclusion? No. In fact, it makes a case *for* a volunteer army. Eliminate.

> (E) The size of the army needed today is smaller than that needed when a volunteer army was first tried.

Like answer choice (D), this answer contradicts the conclusion of the passage. If we need a smaller army today, maybe we would be able to find enough smart and honest volunteers to make a volunteer army work. Eliminate.

Weaken-the-Argument Questions

If a question asks you to weaken an argument, it implies that the argument can be weakened; in other words, once again you're going to be dealing with an inductive argument. The argument won't be complete by itself. The conclusion *may* be true, but it doesn't have to be.

Like assumption questions and strengthen-the-argument questions, weaken-the-argument questions are really asking you to find a hole in the argument. This time, however, you don't need to fix the hole. All you have to do is expose it. Here are some guidelines for finding weaken-the-argument statements among the answer choices:

• The statement you'll be looking for should weaken the *conclusion* of the passage. Find the conclusion in the passage, then try out each answer choice to see whether it makes the conclusion less tenable.

• Weaken-the-argument questions frequently trade on the gaps inherent in inductive reasoning. If the argument uses statistics, ask yourself whether the statistics involved are representative. If the argument offers an analogy, ask yourself whether the two situations are analogous. If the argument proposes a cause for an effect, ask yourself whether there might be some other cause.

Now Let's Try the Passage

6. The recent turnaround of the LEX Corporation is a splendid example of how an astute chief executive officer can rechannel a company's assets toward profitability. With the new CEO at the helm, LEX has gone, in only three business quarters, from a 10 million dollar operating loss to a 22 million dollar operating gain.

   A major flaw in the reasoning of the passage above is that

   (A) the passage assumes that the new CEO was the only factor that affected the corporation's recent success
   (B) the recent success of the corporation may be only temporary
   (C) the chief executive officer may be drawing a salary and bonus that will set a damaging precedent for this and other corporations
   (D) the author does not define "profitability"
   (E) rechanneling assets is only a short-term solution

Here's how to crack it: You know from reading the question that you'll need to find a flaw in the reasoning of the argument. As you read the passage, look for the conclusion. The correct answer choice will weaken this conclusion. In this passage the conclusion is in the first sentence: "The recent turnaround of the LEX Corporation is a splendid example of how an astute chief executive officer can rechannel a company's assets toward profitability."

Because this is a weaken-the-argument question that uses inductive reasoning, you should look to see whether the argument is statistical, causal, or analogous. In this case the argument is causal. The passage implies that the sole cause of the LEX Corporation's turnaround is the new CEO. While this *may* be true, it is also possible that there are other causes. If you didn't spot the causal argument, don't worry. You would probably have seen it when you attacked the answer choices.

Let's do that now:

> (A) the passage assumes that the new CEO was the only factor that affected the corporation's recent success

This is the correct answer. The new chief executive officer may not have been the cause of the turnaround—there may have been some other cause we don't know about.

> (B) the recent success of the corporation may be only temporary

It may be hasty to crown LEX with laurels after only three economic quarters, but this statement doesn't point out a flaw in the *reasoning* of the passage. Eliminate.

> (C) the chief executive officer may be drawing a salary and bonus that will set a damaging precedent for this and other corporations

This answer choice may seem tempting because it's not in favor of the new CEO. But this alone doesn't represent a major flaw in the reasoning of the passage. Eliminate.

> (D) the author does not define "profitability"

An author can't define every word he uses. Profitability seems a common enough word, and a change in the balance sheet from minus 10 million to plus 22 million seems to qualify. Eliminate.

> (E) rechanneling assets is only a short-term solution

Like answer choice (B), this statement implies that all the votes aren't in yet. This does not affect the reasoning of the argument, however. Eliminate.

Inference Questions

Like inference questions in the Reading Comprehension section, Critical Reasoning inference questions do not really ask you to make an inference. In fact, you will often find that the answer to a Critical Reasoning inference question is so basic that you won't believe it could be correct the first time you read it. Inference questions often have little to do with the conclusion of the passage; instead they might ask you to make inferences about one or more of the premises.

7. In film and videotape, it is possible to induce viewers to project their feelings onto characters on the screen. In one study when a camera shot of a woman's face was preceded by a shot of a baby in a crib, the audience thought the woman's face was registering happiness. When the same shot of the woman's face was preceded by a shot of a lion running toward the camera, the audience thought the woman's face was registering fear. Television news teams must be careful to avoid such manipulation of their viewers.

Which of the following can be inferred from the passage?

(A) Television news teams have abused their position of trust in the past.
(B) The expression on the woman's face was, in actuality, blank.
(C) A camera shot of a baby in a crib provoked feelings of happiness in the audience.
(D) Audiences should strive to be less gullible.
(E) The technique described in the passage would work with film or videotape.

Here's how to crack it: This is an inference question. ETS is probably not interested in the conclusion of the passage. You'll be looking for a statement that seems so obvious that it almost doesn't need saying. Let's attack the questions:

(A) Television news teams have abused their position of trust in the past.

If you chose this answer, you inferred too much. The passage doesn't say that news teams have ever abused their position of trust. Eliminate.

(B) The expression on the woman's face was, in
actuality, blank.

The audience had no idea what the expression on the woman's face
was, and neither do we. It would make sense for the woman's face to
be blank, but we don't know whether this is so. This answer also goes
too far.

(C) A camera shot of a baby in a crib provoked
feelings of happiness in the audience.

This is the correct answer. The passage says that the audience
projects its own feelings onto characters on the screen. If the audience believes the woman's face reflects happiness, then that must
have been their own reaction.

(D) Audiences should strive to be less gullible.

This statement goes way beyond the intent of the passage. Eliminate.

(E) The technique for manipulating audiences
described in the passage would work with
film or videotape.

Again, this statement goes too far to be the correct answer to an
inference question. Eliminate.

Mimic-the-Reasoning Questions

Mimic-the-reasoning questions ask you to recognize the method of
reasoning used in a passage and then identify the same line of
reasoning in one of the answer choices. The best way to understand
the passage associated with a reasoning question is to simplify the
terms. Here's an example: "If it rains, I will stay home today." We
could simplify this by saying, "If A, then B."

8. World-class marathon runners do not run more than six miles a day when they are training. Therefore, if you run more than six miles a day, you are not world-class.

   Which of the following statements supports its conclusion in the same manner as the argument above?

   (A) Sprinters always run in the morning. If it is morning, and you see someone running, it will not be a sprinter.
   (B) Paint never dries in less than three hours. If it dries in less than three hours, it is not paint.
   (C) Little League games are more fun for the parents than for the children who actually play. Therefore, the parents should be made to play.
   (D) If a car starts in the morning, chances are it will start again that evening. Our car always starts in the morning, and it always starts in the evening as well.
   (E) If you sleep less than four hours a night, you may be doing yourself a disservice. Studies have shown that the most valuable sleep occurs in the fifth hour.

Here's how to crack it: First, simplify the argument in the passage. World-class marathon runners do not run more than six miles a day when they are training. (If A, then B.) Therefore, if you run more than six miles a day, you are not world-class. (If not B, then not A.)

Now let's attack the answer choices:

   (A) Sprinters always run in the morning. If it is morning, and you see someone running, it will not be a sprinter.

Just because this answer choice is also about running doesn't mean the reasoning will be the same. In fact, it is unlikely that ETS would use the same subject matter for the correct answer. If we simplify this argument, we get: If A, then B. If B, then not A. Is this the same reasoning used in the passage? No. Eliminate.

   (B) Paint never dries in less than three hours. If it dries in less than three hours, it is not paint.

If we simplify this argument, we get: If A, then B. If not B, then not A. This is the correct answer.

   (C) Little League games are more fun for the parents than for the children who actually play. Therefore, the parents should be made to play.

Simplifying this argument, we get . . . not much. The reasoning here is totally different. Also, note that the subject matter here is still about sports. Eliminate.

> (D) If a car starts in the morning, chances are it
>   will start again that evening. Our car always
>   starts in the morning, and it always starts in
>   the evening as well.

If we simplify this argument, we get: If A, then B. If always A, then always B. That doesn't sound right. Eliminate.

> (E) If you sleep less than four hours a night, you
>   may be doing yourself a disservice. Studies
>   have shown that the most valuable sleep
>   occurs in the fifth hour.

Simplifying this argument, we get . . . again, not much. The reasoning in this answer choice is very different from the reasoning in the passage. Eliminate.

Summary

1. Critical Reasoning is made up of short passages. Each of these passages is followed by one or two questions, giving 20 questions. The questions are roughly presented in order of difficulty.

2. ETS says that no formal logic is required to answer these questions, but in fact some knowledge of the rudiments of GMAT logic *will* increase your score.

3. Critical Reasoning is new to the GMAT, although this type of question has appeared on the LSAT and the GRE for years under the name Arguments.

4. There are three parts to an argument:

   A) the conclusion
   B) the premises
   C) assumptions

5. This section is not like Reading Comprehension in that

   A) you should never skim; each word is important
   B) you should always read the question first
   C) most of the Reading Comprehension techniques we
      have shown you are inappropriate in this section

6. Always read the question first because it will contain clues that
   will help you to find the answer as you read the passage.

7. In Critical Reasoning, the most important POE technique is
   eliminating answers that are outside the scope of the argument.

8. There are two main types of reasoning: *deductive* and *inductive*.
   In deductive logic the conclusion *must* follow from the premises.
   In inductive logic the conclusion may be true, but it does not have
   to be. Three popular kinds of inductive logic are

   A) statistical arguments—ask yourself whether the
      statistics are representative
   B) arguments by analogy—ask yourself whether the
      two situations are analogous
   C) causal arguments—ask yourself whether there
      might be an alternative cause

   These three kinds of inductive logic are very important in
   assumption questions, weaken-the-argument questions, and
   strengthen-the-argument questions.

9. There are seven question types. Each type has its own strategy.

   1) *Find-the-Conclusion Questions*
      Break the argument down into its parts and look
      for signposts. A conclusion must be supported by
      its premises.

   2) *Supply-the-Conclusion Questions*

      • If the question asks which conclusion *must* fol-
        low, the reasoning will be deductive. This type
        of question can usually be diagramed.

- All other supply-the-conclusion passages will be inductive. The correct answer will be supported by *all* the premises.

3) *Assumption Questions*

Assumptions are unstated premises that support the conclusion. Assumption questions always involve inductive logic. Look for a flaw in the argument that is fixed by the assumption.

4) *Strengthen-the-Argument Questions*

These are also based on inductive logic. Look for answer choices that support the conclusion with new information.

5) *Weaken-the-Argument Questions*

Also based on inductive logic, these questions ask you to find answers that point out flaws in the reasoning of passages.

6) *Inference Questions*

Like Reading Comprehension inference questions, these questions do not actually want you to infer. Unlike most Critical Reasoning questions, these questions will concern the *premises,* not the conclusion.

7) *Mimic-the-Reasoning Questions*

This type of question asks you to find an argument in one of the answer choices that mimics the method of reasoning used in the original argument. Most of these questions can be answered by simplifying (if A, then B).

PART THREE

HOW
TO CRACK
THE MATH
GMAT

CHAPTER NINE

GMAT Math: Basic Principles

What's Covered in the Math Sections

Of the six 30-minute sections that count on the GMAT, three will be math sections. One of these, called Data Sufficiency, has a peculiar format and will be covered in a later chapter. The other two math sections contain standard problem-solving questions. The two sections are identical in format. Each contains 20 problems that test your general knowledge of three subjects:

1. arithmetic
2. basic algebra
3. geometry

What Isn't Covered in the Math Sections

The good news is that you won't need to know calculus, trigonometry, or any of the complicated parts of geometry. The bad news is that the specialized, business-type math you're probably good at isn't tested, either. There will be no questions on computing the profit on three ticks of a particular bond sale, no questions about amortizing a loan, no need to calculate the bottom line of a small business.

Ancient History

For the most part what you'll find on the GMAT is a kind of math you haven't had to think about in years: high-school math. The GMAT is more difficult than your old nemesis, the SAT, but the problem-solving on the GMAT tests the same general body of knowledge tested by the SAT. Since most people who apply to business school have been out of college for several years, high-school math may seem a bit like ancient history. In the next few chapters, we'll give you a fast review of the important concepts, as well as show you some powerful techniques for cracking the system.

Order of Difficulty

The questions in each of the problem-solving sections are arranged in order of difficulty:

1. The first third of the section is relatively easy.
2. The middle third of the section is medium.
3. The final third of the section is difficult.

Of the 20 questions in this section:

$$1 - 7 \quad \text{relatively easy}$$
$$8 - 14 \quad \text{medium}$$
$$15 - 20 \quad \text{difficult}$$

The only exception is when ETS gives you two questions based on the same information. For example, problems 7 and 8 might refer to one chart. In this case, problem 7 is easier than a normal problem 7, but problem 8 is *much* tougher than a normal problem 8.

The Princeton Review Approach

When it comes to the GMAT, most people solve the easy questions, get some of the medium questions right, and miss most of the difficult questions. In order to get a very good score it isn't necessary to get every question right. As we told you in Chapter 3, you can do extremely well on this test by skipping a large number of questions.

Since each question is worth the same number of points, it makes sense to concentrate on the questions you know how to do. For the most part, that means you should do the easy questions first, then the medium questions, and, unless you're shooting for a very high score, skip most of the difficult questions. However, it may be that when you've finished this book some of the "difficult" questions won't seem difficult anymore.

Extra Help

Although we'll show you which mathematical principles are most important for the GMAT, this book cannot take the place of a basic foundation in math. We find that most people, even if they don't remember much of high-school math, pick it up again quickly. Our drills and examples will refresh your memory if you've gotten rusty, but if you have serious difficulties with the following chapters, you should consider a more thorough review. This book will enable you to see where you need the most work. Always keep in mind, though, that if your purpose is to raise your GMAT score, it's a waste of time to learn math that won't be tested.

Basic Information

Try the following problem:

2. How many even integers are there between 17 and 27?

(A) 9　(B) 7　(C) 5　(D) 4　(E) 3

This is a very easy question. You can tell by its number: It is question 2 out of 20 questions. Even so, if you don't know what an integer is, the question will be impossible to answer. Before moving on to arithmetic, you should be sure you're familiar with some basic terms and concepts. This material isn't difficult, but you must know it cold. (The answer, by the way, is C.)

Integers

Integers are the numbers we think of when we think of numbers. They can be negative or positive. They do not include fractions. The positive integers are:

1, 2, 3, 4, 5, etc.

The negative integers are:

−1, −2, −3, −4, −5, etc.

Zero (0) is also an integer. It is neither positive nor negative.

Positive integers get bigger as they move away from 0; negative integers get smaller. Look at this number line:

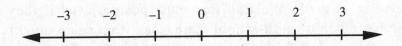

2 is bigger than 1, but −2 is smaller than −1.

Positive and Negative

Positive numbers are to the right of the zero on the number line above. Negative numbers are to the left of zero on the number line above.

There are three rules regarding the multiplication of positive and negative numbers:

1. pos. times pos. = pos.
   $2 \times 3 = 6$
2. pos. times neg. = neg.
   $3 \times -4 = -12$
3. neg times neg. = pos.
   $-2 \times -3 = 6$

If you add a positive number and a negative number, you're subtracting the number with the negative sign in front of it from the positive number.

$$4 + (-3) = 1$$

If you add two negative numbers, you add them as if they were positive, then put a negative sign in front of the sum.

$$-3 + -5 = -8$$

Digits

There are ten digits:

$$0, 1, 2, 3, 4, 5, 6, 7, 8, 9$$

All integers are made up of digits. In the integer 246, there are three digits—2, 4, and 6. Each of the digits has a different name:

6 is called the units digit
4 is called the tens digit
2 is called the hundreds digit

A number with decimal places is also composed of digits, although it is not an integer. In the decimal 27.63 there are four digits:

7 is the units digit
2 is the tens digit
6 is the tenths digit
3 is the hundredths digit

Odd or Even

Even numbers are integers that can be divided evenly by 2. Here are some examples:

−4, −2, 0, 2, 4, etc.   (note that 0 is even)

Any integer, no matter how large, is even if its last digit can be divided evenly by 2. Thus 777,772 is even.

Odd numbers are integers that cannot be divided evenly by 2. Here are some examples:

–5, –3, –1, 1, 3, 5, etc.   (note that 0 is not odd)

Any integer, no matter how large, is odd if its last digit cannot be divided evenly by 2. Thus 222,227 is odd.

There are several rules that always hold true with even and odd numbers:

even × even = even
odd × odd = odd
even × odd = even

even + even = even
odd + odd = even
even + odd = odd

It isn't necessary to memorize these, but you must know that the relationships always hold true. The individual rules can be derived in a second. If you need to know "even × even," just try 2 × 2. The answer in this case is even, as "even × even" always will be.

Remainders

If a number cannot be divided evenly by another number, the number that is left over at the end of division is called the remainder.

$$2\overline{)7}\;\;^{3\text{ r. }1}$$

Consecutive Integers

Consecutive integers are integers listed in order of increasing size without any integers missing in between. For example, –3, –2, –1, 0, 1, 2, 3 are consecutive integers. The formula for consecutive integers is $n, n + 1, n + 2, n + 3$, etc., where n is an integer.

Some consecutive even integers: –2, 0, 2, 4, 6, 8, etc.
Some consecutive odd integers: –3, –1, 1, 3, 5, etc.

Prime Numbers

A prime number is a number that can be divided evenly only by itself and by 1. Thus 2, 3, 5, 7, 11, 13 are all prime numbers. The number 2 is the only even prime number. Neither 0 nor 1 is a prime number.

Divisibility Rules

If a number can be divided evenly by another number, it is said to be divisible by that number.

Some useful shortcuts:

1. A number is divisible by 2 if its units digit can be divided evenly by 2. Thus 777,772 is divisible by 2.

2. A number is divisible by 3 if the sum of its digits can be divided evenly by 3. We can instantly tell that 216 is divisible by 3, because the sum of the digits $(2 + 1 + 6)$ is divisible by 3.

3. A number is divisible by 5 if its final digit is either 0 or 5. Thus 60, 85, and 15 are all divisible by 5.

Factors and Multiples

A number is a *factor* of another number if it can be divided evenly into that number. Thus the factors of 15, for example, are 1, 3, 5, and 15.

A number x is considered to be a *multiple* of another number y if y times another integer $= x$. For example, 15 is a multiple of 3 (3×5); 12 is also a multiple of 3 (3×4).

Absolute Value

The *absolute value* of a number is the distance between that number and 0 on the number line. The absolute value of 6 is expressed as $|6|$.

$|6| = 6$
$|-5| = 5$

Standard Symbols

The following standard symbols are frequently used on the GMAT:

SYMBOL	MEANING
$=$	is equal to
$\neq$	is not equal to
$<$	is less than
$>$	is greater than
$\leq$	is less than or equal to
$\geq$	is greater than or equal to

Now Let's Look at the Instructions

Both of the problem-solving sections on the GMAT have the same instructions. To avoid wasting time reading these during the test, read our version of the instructions now:

Directions: Solve the following problems, using the margins of your test booklet for space for your computations.

Numbers: This test uses only real numbers; no imaginary numbers are used or implied.

Diagrams: All diagrams in this section are drawn as accurately as possible UNLESS it is specifically noted that a diagram is "not drawn to scale." All diagrams are in a plane unless stated otherwise.

CHAPTER TEN

Joe Bloggs, POE, and GMAT Math

In Chapter 4 we introduced you to Joe Bloggs—the average test-taker. Understanding how Joe thinks can be as great an advantage to you on the math as it was on the verbal sections. It's important that you be able to identify the answer choices Joe Bloggs is attracted to on every math problem—easy or difficult.

Why?

On an easy problem, Joe's hunch is correct. This means that on easy problems you can trust choices that seem correct to you.

On a difficult problem, however, Joe's hunch is always wrong. By eliminating Joe's answers on the difficult problems, you can improve your odds tremendously.

Where Does Joe Go Wrong?

In Chapter 4 we introduced Joe Bloggs by showing you how he approached a difficult math question. In that example, we pointed out one answer choice that Joe Bloggs would have been irresistibly drawn to. In fact, there were two other answer choices in that problem that might have appealed to Joe as well.

To understand how ETS comes up with traps for Joe Bloggs, let's look at that same problem again from a slightly different perspective:

18. The output of a factory was increased by 10% to keep up with rising demand. To handle the Christmas rush, this new output was increased by 20%. By approximately what percent would the output now have to be decreased in order to restore the original output?

(A)　　　(B) 24%　(C)　　　(D)　　　(E)

Zen and the Art of Test Writing

Let's put ourselves in the place of the ETS test-writer who has just written this difficult math problem. He's finished with his question, and he has his correct answer (24%), but he isn't done yet. He still has four empty slots to fill in. He needs to come up with incorrect numbers for answer choices A, C, D, and E.

He *could* simply choose numbers at random, or numbers that are closely clustered around the correct answer. If the test-writer did that, however, Joe Bloggs wouldn't see an obvious answer and might therefore guess at random. The test-writer does *not* want Joe to guess at random. If Joe guesses at random, he might actually pick the right answer. So our test-writer comes up with incorrect answer choices that whisper seductively, "Pick *me*, Joe." If Joe's going to guess, our test-writer wants to make sure he guesses wrong.

Psst! Hey, Joe, Looking for a Good Time?

To come up with answers that will appeal to Joe Bloggs, the ETS test-writer has to know how Joe thinks. Fortunately for the test-writer, he can draw on over thirty years of statistical information ETS has compiled. From this, he knows that

1. **On difficult math problems, Joe Bloggs is always attracted to easy solutions that he can find in one or two steps.**

For example, Joe might just add together the numbers mentioned in the problem.

2. On difficult math problems, Joe Bloggs is attracted to numbers that he has already seen in the problem.

It's pretty silly, but frequently Joe picks a number simply because he remembers it from the problem itself.

Now let's look at the same problem complete with answer choices:

18. The output of a factory was increased by 10% to keep up with rising demand. To handle the Christmas rush, this new output was increased by 20%. By approximately what percent would the output now have to be decreased in order to restore the original output?

(A) 20%   (B) 24%   (C) 30%   (D) 32%   (E) 70%

If the test-writer has done his job properly, Joe Bloggs will never even consider the correct answer (24%). He's too smitten by the other answer choices.

Here's how to crack it: As we said in Chapter 4, Joe's favorite answer to this question is undoubtedly choice (C). Joe notices that the output seems to have increased by 30% and figures that to get rid of that increase, you would have to decrease it by 30%. What Joe has just done is add the two numbers he saw in the problem. This was a one-step operation.

Another answer Joe might find enticing is choice (E). The word *percent* means "out of a hundred." If Joe adds the two numbers contained in the problem to get 30 and then subtracts the sum from 100, he gets 70. This is a two-step operation.

On difficult math problems, Joe Bloggs is attracted to easy solutions that he can find in one or two steps.

Another answer Joe might be attracted to is choice (A). Twenty (20%) is simply one of the numbers from the problem. There is no logical reason to think this is the correct answer, but Joe isn't always logical.

On difficult math problems, Joe Bloggs is attracted to answer choices that simply repeat numbers from the problem.

Joe wants to select choice (A), (C), or (E). On a difficult question, Joe's answers are always wrong. This means that you can eliminate these three choices. At this point, if you aren't sure of how to solve the problem mathematically, guess choice (B) or (D) and move on. You'll have a fifty-fifty shot at being correct.

Even if you do think you know how to solve the problem mathematically, you might still want to guess instead of taking the time to work it out.

Why?

Suppose there's only one minute left for this math section. You're pretty sure you can solve this problem, but looking ahead to the next problem, you realize you can solve that one, too. One minute isn't enough time for two problems, though. Wouldn't it make sense to take the fifty-fifty odds on this problem in order to get to the next one?

Does Every Difficult Math Problem Have Joe Bloggs Answers?

No. Some types of problems (in particular, problems with variables in the answer choice) have no obvious solutions that can be used to trap Joe. But even when there are no obvious traps, ETS test-writers are very careful in creating incorrect answer choices. They try to figure out all the mistakes a careless test-taker might make, then they include those answers among the choices.

Partial Answers

People often go wrong on GMAT math problems by thinking that they are finished before they really are. Here's an example:

8. 22% of the cars produced in America are manufactured in Michigan. If the total number of cars produced in America is 40 million, how many cars are produced outside of Michigan?

(A) 4.4 million (B) 8.8 million (C) 15 million
(D) 27 million (E) 31.2 million

Here's how to crack it: The first step in this problem is to find out how many actual cars are produced in Michigan; in other words, we need to know what 22% of 40 million equals. If you aren't sure how to do this, don't worry; we'll show you how to do percent problems in the arithmetic chapter. For the moment, take our word for it that 22% of 40 million equals 8.8 million.

If you were feeling smug about having figured this out, you might just look at the answer choices, notice that answer choice (B) says 8.8 million, and figure that you're done. Unfortunately, the problem didn't ask how many cars were produced in Michigan; it asked how many cars were *not* produced in Michigan.

ETS provided answer choice (B) just in case you got halfway through the problem and decided you'd done enough work. It was a *partial* answer. To find the correct answer you have to subtract 8.8 from 40 million. The correct answer is choice (E) 31.2 million.

You can prevent yourself from selecting partial answers by doing two things:

1. When you finish a problem, always take two seconds to reread the last line of the problem to make sure you've actually answered the question.

2. Always look at the number of the problem you're working on to decide whether you've done enough work for ETS to think you "deserve" to get the problem right. For example, that last problem was a number 8. It was a medium problem. There's no way a medium problem can be solved in just one step.

Common Sense

ETS is so caught up in trying to provide answer choices that anticipate all the mistakes a test-taker might make on a problem that they often forget to make certain that all of these answer choices make sense.

Look at the following difficult problem:

14. A student took 6 courses last year and received an average grade of 100. The year before, the student took 5 courses and received an average grade of 90. To the nearest tenth of a point, what was the student's average grade for the entire two-year period?

(A) 79 (B) 89 (C) 95 (D) 95.5 (E) 97.2

Here's how to crack it: Because this is a difficult problem, the first thing to do is see whether there are any Joe Bloggs answers. There's one big one—Joe likes answer choice (C) a lot. He figures that to find the average of the entire two-year period, all he has to do is find that the average of 90 and 100 is 95.

If this problem were that easy, it wouldn't be number 14. Eliminate choice (C).

There are no other obvious Joe Bloggs answers, but it *is* possible to eliminate a couple of other choices by using common sense. The student's average for the first year was 90. The student's average for the second year was 100. Obviously the student's second-year grades are going to bring his average *up*. We may not be sure by exactly how much, but the average for the entire two-year period has to be higher than it was for the first year. Both choices (A) and (B) are less than the first year's average. We can therefore eliminate both of them.

Now we're down to a fifty-fifty shot. The answer has to be either choice (D) or (E). We can either guess and move on or start solving the problem in earnest. (By the way, the answer to this problem is choice (D), but don't worry about how to solve it just yet. We'll cover average problems in the next chapter.)

Eliminating Crazy Answers

Many of the problems on the GMAT are both time-consuming and difficult. You can make things easier for yourself by eliminating choices that don't make sense before you actually solve the problem. Some answer choices seem pretty crazy when you look at them in the cold light of day.

Here's an example:

15. Three typists are hired to type a 180-page report. Typist A can type 4 pages an hour, typist B can type 5 pages an hour, and typist C can type 6 pages an hour. If all three work continuously at their respective rates until the report is finished, what fraction of the report will be typed by typist A?

(A) $\frac{2}{9}$ (B) $\frac{4}{15}$ (C) $\frac{1}{3}$ (D) $\frac{4}{9}$ (E) $\frac{2}{3}$

Here's how to crack it: Is there a Joe Bloggs answer here? Joe is strongly attracted to choice (C). After all, there are three typists, so Joe (conveniently forgetting that they're working at different rates) reasons that each of them does one third of the work. Eliminate choice (C).

Now let's try some common sense. If the three typists were working at the *same* rate, each would do one third of the work. In this case, however, the problem tells us that typist A is *slower* than the other two. Since they all plan to work continuously until the report is done, is it possible that typist A will be able to do a third of the report? No. Typist A will do *less* than a third. This means that any choice *greater* than a third is crazy. Eliminate choices (D) and (E).

(By the way, the correct answer to this problem is choice (B), but don't worry about how to solve it yet. We'll cover work problems in the algebra chapter.)

You can use common sense to eliminate crazy choices even on easy and medium problems. Sometimes eliminating crazy choices will lead you directly to the correct answer.

Summary

1. Joe Bloggs tends to get the easy math problems right, but he always gets the difficult math problems wrong because of the traps ETS has set for him.

2. On difficult problems, Joe Bloggs is attracted to easy solutions that he can arrive at in one or two steps. Therefore eliminate all obvious answers on difficult questions.

3. On difficult problems, Joe Bloggs is attracted to answer choices that simply repeat numbers from the problem. Therefore eliminate those choices.

4. On all problems, always take a moment to see whether the answer choices make sense. Eliminate crazy answer choices.

CHAPTER ELEVEN

Arithmetic

Although arithmetic is only one of the three types of math tested on the GMAT, arithmetic problems comprise about half of the total number of questions. In each 20-question math section, about ten problems will involve arithmetic.

It is also interesting to note that most of these ten problems will be found in the easy and medium parts of the section. Therefore it is crucial that you know the information in this chapter cold.

Here are the specific arithmetic topics tested on the GMAT:

1. Axioms and Fundamentals (properties of integers, positive and negative numbers, even and odd). These were covered in Chapter 9.
2. Arithmetic Operations
3. Fractions
4. Decimals
5. Ratios
6. Percentages
7. Averages
8. Exponents and Radicals

In this chapter we will first discuss the fundamentals of each topic and then show how ETS constructs questions based on that topic.

Arithmetic Operations

There are six arithmetic operations you will need for the GMAT:

1. addition $(2 + 2)$ the result of addition is a sum or total

2. subtraction $(6 - 2)$ the result of subtraction is a difference

3. multiplication (2×2) the result of multiplication is a product

4. division $(8 \div 2)$ the result of division is a quotient

5. raising to a power (x^2) in the expression x^2 the little 2 is called an exponent

6. finding a square root $(\sqrt{4}) = \sqrt{2 \cdot 2} = 2$

Which One Do I Do First?

In a problem that involves several different operations, the operations must be performed in a particular order, and occasionally ETS likes to see whether you know what that order is. Here's an easy way to remember the order of operations:

Please Excuse My Dear Aunt Sally

This stands for Parentheses, Exponents, Multiplication, Division, Addition, Subtraction. Do operations enclosed in parentheses first; then take care of exponents; then multiply, divide, add, and subtract.

Drill 1
Just to get you started, solve each of the following problems by performing the indicated operation in the proper order. The answers can be found on page 260.

1. $74 + (27 - 24) =$
2. $(8 \times 9) + 7 =$
3. $2[9 - (8 \div 2)] =$
4. $2(7 - 3) + (-4)(5 - 7) =$

It is not uncommon to see a problem like this on the GMAT:

5. $4[-3(3 - 5) + 10 - 17] =$

(A) –27   (B) –4   (C) –1   (D) 32   (E) 84

There are two operations that can be done in any order, provided they are the only operations involved: **When you are adding or multiplying a series of numbers, you can group or regroup the numbers any way you like.**

$2 + 3 + 4$ is the same as $4 + 2 + 3$

and

$4 \times 5 \times 6$ is the same as $6 \times 5 \times 4$

This is called the *associative law*, but the name will not be tested on the GMAT.

The *distributive law* states that $a(b + c) = ab + ac$

and

$$a(b - c) = ab - ac$$

ETS likes to see whether you remember this. Sometimes the distributive law can provide you with a shortcut to the solution of a problem. If a problem gives you information in "factored form"—$a(b + c)$—you should distribute it immediately. If the information is given in distributed form—$ab + ac$—you should factor it.

Drill 2

If the following problems are in distributed form, factor them; if they are in factored form, distribute them. Then do the indicated operation. Answers are on page 260.

1. $9(27 + 3)$
2. $(55 \times 12) + (55 \times 88)$
3. $a(b + c - d)$
4. $abc + xyc$

A GMAT problem might look like this:

5. If $x = 6$ what is the value of $\dfrac{2xy - xy}{y}$?

(A) –30   (B) 6   (C) 8   (D) 30
(E) it cannot be determined

Fractions

Fractions can be thought of in two ways:

• A fraction is just another way of expressing division. The expression $\frac{1}{2}$ is exactly the same thing as 1 divided by 2. $\frac{x}{y}$ is nothing more than x divided by y. In the fraction $\frac{x}{y}$, x is known as the numerator, and y is known as the denominator.

• The other important way to think of a fraction is as

$$\frac{\text{part}}{\text{whole}}$$

The fraction $\frac{7}{10}$ can be thought of as 7 parts out of a total of 10 parts.

Adding and Subtracting Fractions with the Same Denominator

To add two or more fractions that have the same denominator, simply add up the numerators and put the sum over the common denominator. For example:

$$\frac{1}{7} + \frac{5}{7} = \frac{(1+5)}{7} = \frac{6}{7}$$

Subtraction works exactly the same way:

$$\frac{6}{7} - \frac{2}{7} = \frac{(6-2)}{7} = \frac{4}{7}$$

Adding and Subtracting Fractions with Different Denominators

Before you can add or subtract two or more fractions with different denominators, you must give all of them the same denominator. To do this, multiply each fraction by a number that will give it a denominator in common with the others. If you multiplied each fraction by any old number, the fractions wouldn't have their original values, so the number you multiply by has to be some value of 1. For example, if you wanted to change $\frac{1}{2}$ into sixths, you could do the following:

$$\frac{1}{2} \times \frac{3}{3} = \frac{3}{6}$$

We haven't actually changed the value of the fraction, because we multiplied it by 1. $\frac{3}{6}$ reduces to $\frac{1}{2}$. If we wanted to add

$$\frac{1}{2} + \frac{2}{3} \qquad =$$

$$\frac{1}{2} \times \frac{3}{3} + \frac{2}{3} \times \frac{2}{2} =$$

$$\frac{3}{6} + \frac{4}{6} \qquad = \frac{7}{6}$$

Multiplying Fractions

To multiply fractions, just multiply the numerators and put the product over the product of the denominators. For example:

$$\frac{2}{3} \times \frac{6}{5} = \frac{12}{15}$$

Reducing Fractions

When you add or multiply fractions, you often end up with a big fraction that is hard to work with. You can usually reduce such a fraction. To reduce a fraction, find a factor of the numerator that is also a factor of the denominator. It saves time to find the biggest factor they have in common, but this isn't critical. You may just have to repeat the process a few times. When you find a common factor, cancel it. For example, let's take the product we just found when we multiplied the fractions above:

$$\frac{12}{15} = \frac{4 \times 3}{5 \times 3} = \frac{4}{5}$$

Get used to reducing all fractions (if they can be reduced) *before* you do any work with them. It saves a lot of time and prevents errors in computation.

Dividing Fractions

To divide one fraction by another, just invert the second fraction and multiply:

$$\frac{2}{3} \div \frac{3}{4}$$

is the same thing as

$$\frac{2}{3} \times \frac{4}{3} = \frac{8}{9}$$

You may see this same operation written like this:

$$\frac{\frac{2}{3}}{\frac{3}{4}}$$

Again, just invert and multiply. This next example is handled the same way:

$$\frac{6}{\frac{2}{3}} = \frac{6}{1} \times \frac{3}{2} = \frac{18}{2} = 9$$

Converting to Fractions

An integer can always be expressed as a fraction by making the integer the numerator and 1 the denominator. $16 = \frac{16}{1}$.

The GMAT sometimes gives you numbers that are mixtures of integers and fractions, for example, $3\frac{1}{2}$. It's easier to work with these numbers if you convert them into ordinary fractions. $3\frac{1}{2}$ would be converted like this:

Since the fractional part of this number was expressed in halves, let's convert the integer part of the number into halves as well. $3 = \frac{6}{2}$. Now just add the $\frac{1}{2}$ to the $\frac{6}{2}$. $3\frac{1}{2} = \frac{7}{2}$.

Comparing Fractions

In the course of a problem you may have to compare two or more fractions and determine which is larger. This is easy to do as long as you remember that you can compare fractions directly only if they have the same denominator. Suppose you had to decide which of these three fractions is largest:

$$\frac{1}{2} \qquad \frac{5}{9} \qquad \frac{7}{15}$$

To compare these fractions directly you need a common denominator, but finding a common denominator that works for all three fractions would be complicated and time-consuming. It makes more sense to compare these fractions two at a time. We showed you the classical way to find common denominators when we talked about adding fractions earlier.

Let's start with $\frac{1}{2}$ and $\frac{5}{9}$. An easy common denominator for these two fractions is 18 (9×2).

$$\frac{1}{2} \qquad\qquad \frac{5}{9}$$

$$\frac{1}{2} \times \frac{9}{9} \qquad\qquad \frac{5}{9} \times \frac{2}{2}$$

$$= \frac{9}{18} \qquad\qquad = \frac{10}{18}$$

Since $\frac{5}{9}$ is bigger, let's compare it with $\frac{7}{15}$. Here the easiest common denominator is 45.

$$\frac{5}{9} \qquad\qquad \frac{7}{15}$$

$$\frac{5}{9} \times \frac{5}{5} \qquad\qquad \frac{7}{15} \times \frac{3}{3}$$

$$= \frac{25}{45} \qquad\qquad = \frac{21}{45}$$

So $\frac{5}{9}$ is bigger than $\frac{7}{15}$, which means it's also the biggest of the three.

Two Shortcuts

One good shortcut is to compare fractions by cross-multiplying. The idea is that if all you need to know is which fraction is bigger, you just have to compare the new numerators.

$$9 \quad \frac{1}{2} \qquad \frac{5}{9} \quad 10$$

$$10 > 9, \text{ therefore, } \frac{5}{9} > \frac{1}{2}$$

You could also have saved yourself some time on the last problem by a little fast estimation. Again, which is larger?

$$\frac{1}{2} \qquad \frac{5}{9} \qquad \frac{7}{15}$$

Let's think about $\frac{5}{9}$ in terms of $\frac{1}{2}$. How many ninths equal a half? To put it another way, what is half of 9? 4.5. So $\frac{4.5}{9} = \frac{1}{2}$. That means $\frac{5}{9}$ is *bigger* than $\frac{1}{2}$.

Now let's think about $\frac{7}{15}$. Half of 15 is 7.5. $\frac{7.5}{15} = \frac{1}{2}$, which means that $\frac{7}{15}$ is *less* than $\frac{1}{2}$.

Proportions

A fraction can be expressed in many ways. $\frac{1}{2}$ also equals $\frac{2}{4}$ or $\frac{4}{8}$, etc. A proportion is just a different way of expressing a fraction. Here's an example:

> If 2 boxes hold a total of 14 shirts, how many shirts are contained in 3 boxes?

Here's how to crack it: The number of shirts per box can be expressed as a fraction. What you're being asked to do is express the fraction $\frac{2}{14}$ in a different way.

$$\frac{2 \text{ (boxes)}}{14 \text{ (shirts)}} = \frac{3 \text{ (boxes)}}{x \text{ (shirts)}}$$

To find the answer, all you need to do is find a value for x so that $3/x = 2/14$. The easiest way to do this is to cross-multiply.

$$\frac{2}{14} = \frac{3}{x}$$

$2x = 42$, which means $x = 21$. There are 21 shirts in 3 boxes.

Drill 3
The answers to these questions can be found on page 260.

1. $5\frac{2}{3} + \frac{3}{8} =$

2. Reduce $\frac{12}{60}$

3. Convert $9\frac{2}{3}$ to a fraction

4. $\frac{9}{2} = \frac{x}{4}$

A relatively easy GMAT fraction problem might look like this:

5. $$\frac{\left(\dfrac{\frac{4}{5}}{\frac{3}{5}}\right)\left(\dfrac{\frac{1}{8}}{\frac{2}{3}}\right)}{\dfrac{3}{4}} = ?$$

(A) $\frac{3}{100}$ (B) $\frac{3}{16}$ (C) $\frac{1}{3}$ (D) 1   (E) $\frac{7}{6}$

Fractions: Advanced Principles

Now that you've been reacquainted with the basics of fractions, let's go a little further. More complicated fraction problems usually involve all of the rules we've just mentioned, with the addition of two concepts: part/whole, and the rest. Here's a typical medium fraction problem:

9. A cement mixture is composed of 3 elements: by weight, $\frac{1}{3}$ of the mixture is sand, $\frac{3}{5}$ of the mixture is water and the remaining 12 pounds of the mixture is gravel. What is the weight of the entire mixture in pounds?

(A) 11.2   (B) 12.8   (C) 36   (D) 60   (E) 180

> **Easy Eliminations:** The weight of the gravel alone is 12 pounds. Since we know that sand and water make up the bulk of the mixture—sand $\frac{1}{3}$, water $\frac{3}{5}$ (which is a bit more than half)—the entire mixture must weigh a great deal more than 12 pounds. Answer choices (A), (B), and (C) are out of the question.

Here's how to crack it: The difficulty in solving this problem is that the ingredients of cement are expressed in two different units of measurement. Sand and water are expressed as fractions, while gravel is expressed in pounds. At first there seems to be no way of knowing what fractional part of the mixture the 12 pounds of gravel represents; nor do we know how many pounds of sand and water there are.

The first step is to add up the fractional parts that we do have:

$$\frac{1}{3} + \frac{3}{5} = \frac{1}{3}\left(\frac{5}{5}\right) + \frac{3}{5}\left(\frac{3}{3}\right) = \frac{14}{15}$$

Sand and water make up 14 parts out of the whole of 15. This means that gravel makes up what is left over—the rest: 1 part out of the whole of 15. Now the problem is simple. Set up a proportion: gravel as part over whole equals another part over whole:

$$\frac{\text{part}}{\text{whole}} \quad \frac{1}{15} = \frac{12}{x} \quad \begin{array}{l}\text{pounds (of gravel)}\\ \text{pounds (total pounds)}\end{array}$$

Cross-multiply: $x = 180$. The answer is choice (E).

Decimals Are a Lot Like Fractions

A decimal can be expressed as a fraction, and a fraction can be expressed as a decimal.

$$.6 = \frac{6}{10} \text{ which is reduced to } \frac{3}{5}$$

$$\frac{3}{5} \text{ is the same thing as } 3 \div 5$$

$$5\overline{\smash{\big)}3.0}^{\,.6}$$
$$= .6$$

But Fractions Are Easier

Which would you rather figure out—the square of $\frac{1}{4}$ or the square of 0.25? There may be a few of you out there who've had so much practice with decimals in your work that you prefer decimals to fractions, but for the rest of us, fractions are infinitely easier to deal with.

Whenever possible, convert decimals to fractions. It will save time and eliminate careless mistakes. Occasionally, however, you will have to work with decimals.

Adding and Subtracting Decimals

To add or subtract decimals, just line up the decimal points and proceed as usual. Adding 6, 2.5, and 0.3 looks like this:

$$\begin{array}{r} 6.0 \\ 2.5 \\ +0.3 \\ \hline 8.8 \end{array}$$

Multiplying Decimals

To multiply decimals, simply ignore the decimal points and multiply the two numbers. When you've finished, count all the digits that were to the right of the decimal points in the original numbers you multiplied. Now place the decimal point in your answer so that there are the same number of digits to the right of it. Here are two examples:

0.3

× .7

.21   (3 times 7 = 21. There were a total of two digits to the right of the decimal point in the original numbers, so we place the decimal so that there are two digits to the right in the answer.)

2.32

× .03

.0696   (3 times 232 = 696. There were a total of four digits to the right of the decimal point in the original numbers, so we place the decimal so that there are four digits to the right in the answer.)

Dividing Decimals

The best way to divide one decimal by another is to convert the number you are dividing by (in mathematical terminology, the divisor) into a whole number. You do this simply by moving the decimal point as many places as necessary. This works as long as you remember to move the decimal point in the number that you are *dividing* (in mathematical terminology, the dividend) the same number of spaces.

For example, to divide 12 by .6, set it up the way you would an ordinary division problem:

$$.6\overline{)12}$$

To make .6 (the divisor) a whole number, you simply move the decimal point over one place to the right. You must also move the decimal one place to the right in the dividend. Now the operation looks like this:

$$6\overline{)120} \qquad \overset{20}{6\overline{)120}}$$

Rounding off Decimals

9.4 rounded to the nearest whole number is 9.
9.5 rounded to the nearest whole number is 10.

When ETS asks you to give an approximate answer on an easy question, it is safe to round off numbers. But you should be leery about rounding off numbers on a difficult question.

Drill 4
The answers to these questions can be found on page 260.

1. $\begin{array}{r} 34.26 \\ -\ 9.6 \\ \hline \end{array}$

2. $\begin{array}{r} 27.3 \\ \times\ 9.75 \\ \hline \end{array}$

3. $\dfrac{19.6}{3.22}$

4. $\dfrac{\frac{4}{.25}}{\frac{1}{.50}}$

On the GMAT, there might be questions that mix decimals and fractions:

5. $\dfrac{\frac{3}{10} \times 4 \times .8}{.32}$

(A) .96 (B) .333 (C) 3 (D) 30 (E) 96

Ratios

Ratios are close relatives of fractions. A ratio can be expressed as a fraction and visa versa. The ratio 3 to 4 can be written as $\frac{3}{4}$ as well as in standard ratio format: 3:4.

There Is Only One Difference Between a Ratio and a Fraction

One way of defining the *fraction* $\frac{3}{4}$ is to say that there are 3 equal *parts* out of a *whole* of 4.

    Let's take the ratio of 3 women to 4 men in a room, which could also be expressed as $\frac{3}{4}$. Is 4 the whole in this ratio? Of course not. There are 3 women and 4 men, giving a total of 7 people in the room. The *whole* in a ratio is the sum of all the parts. If the ratio is expressed as a fraction, the *whole* is the sum of the numerator and the denominator.

Fraction:	*ratio:*
part 3	3 women
whole 7	4 men (The *whole* is 7)

Aside from That, All the Rules of Fractions Apply to Ratios

A ratio can be converted to a percentage or a decimal. It can be cross-multiplied, reduced, or expanded—just like a fraction. The ratio of 1 to 3 can be expressed as:

$$\frac{1}{3}$$
$$1:3$$
$$0.333\ldots$$
$$33\frac{1}{3}\%$$
$$\frac{2}{6}$$
$$\frac{3}{9}$$

An Easy Ratio Problem

The ratio of men to women in a room is 3 to 4.
What is the number of men in the room if there are
20 women?

Here's how to crack it: No matter how many people are actually in the room, the ratio of men to women will always stay the same: 3 to 4. What you're being asked to do is find the numerator of a fraction whose denominator is 20, and which can be reduced to $\frac{3}{4}$. Just set one fraction equal to another and cross-multiply:

$$\frac{3}{4} = \frac{x}{20} \qquad 60 = 4x, \quad x = 15$$

The answer to the question is 15 men. Note that $\frac{15}{20}$ reduces to $\frac{3}{4}$. The two fractions are equal, which is just another way of saying they are still in the same ratio.

A More Difficult Ratio Problem

The ratio of women to men in a room is 3 to 4. If there are a total of 28 people in the room, how many women are there?

This problem is more difficult because, while we are given the ratio of women to men, we do not have a specific value for either women or men. If we tried to set this problem up the way we did the previous one, it would look like this:

$$\frac{3}{4} = \frac{x}{y}$$

You can't solve an equation if it has two variables.

Here's how to crack it: The trick here is to remember how a ratio differs from a fraction. If the ratio is 3 parts to 4 parts, then there are a total of 7 parts. This means that the 28 people in that room are made up of groups of 7 people (3 women and 4 men in each group). How many groups of 7 people make up 28 people? 4 groups ($4 \times 7 = 28$).

If there are 4 groups—each made up of 3 women and 4 men—the total number of women would be 4×3, or 12. The number of men would be 4×4, or 16. To check this, make sure $\frac{12}{16}$ equals $\frac{3}{4}$ (it does) and that $12 + 16$ adds up to 28 (it does).

Percentages

A percentage is just a fraction in which the denominator is always equal to 100. Fifty percent means 50 parts out of a whole of 100. Like any fraction, a percentage can be reduced, expanded, cross-multiplied, converted to a decimal, or converted to another fraction.

$$50\% = \frac{1}{2} = .50$$

An Easy Percent Problem

The number 5 is what percent of the number 20?

Here's how to crack it: Whenever you see a percent problem, you should be thinking part/whole. In this case, the question is asking you to expand $\frac{5}{20}$ into another fraction in which the denominator is 100.

$$\frac{\text{part}}{\text{whole}} \quad \frac{5}{20} = \frac{x}{100} \qquad 500 = 20x \quad x = 25\%$$

Percent Shortcuts

In the last problem, reducing $\frac{5}{20}$ to $\frac{1}{4}$ would have saved time if you knew that $\frac{1}{4} = 25\%$. Here are some fractions and decimals whose percent equivalents you should know:

$$\frac{1}{4} = .25 = 25\%$$
$$\frac{1}{2} = .50 = 50\%$$
$$\frac{1}{3} = 0.333 \text{ etc. (a repeating decimal)} = 33\frac{1}{3}\%$$
$$\frac{1}{5} = .20 = 20\%$$

• Some percentages simply involve moving a decimal point: To get 10 percent of any number, you simply move the decimal point of that number over one place to the left:

$$10\% \text{ of } 6 = 0.6$$
$$10\% \text{ of } 60 = 6$$
$$10\% \text{ of } 600 = 60$$

To get 1 percent of any number, you just move the decimal point of that number over two places to the left:

$$1\% \text{ of } 600 = 6$$
$$1\% \text{ of } 60 = 0.6$$
$$1\% \text{ of } 6 = .06$$

• To find a more complicated percentage, it's easy to break the percentage down into easy-to-find chunks:

20% of 60:   10% of 60 = 6. 20% of 60 is double 10%, so the answer is 2×6, or 12.

30% of 60:   10% of 60 = 6. 30% of 60 is three times 10%, so the answer is 3×6, or 18.

3% of 200:   1% of 200 = 2. 3% of 200 is just three times 1%, so the answer is 3×2, or 6.

23% of 400:   10% of 400 = 40. Therefore 20% equals 2×40, or 80.
1% of 400 = 4. Therefore 3% equals 3×4, or 12.
Putting it all together, 23% of 400 equals $80 + 12$, or 92.

A More Difficult Percent Problem

Like advanced fraction problems, more difficult percent problems often involve remembering the principles of part/whole and the rest.

14.   A motor pool has 300 vehicles of which 30% are trucks. 20% of all the vehicles in the motor pool are diesel, including 15 trucks. What percent of the motor pool is composed of vehicles that are neither truck nor diesel?

(A) 165% (B) 90% (C) 65% (D) 55% (E) 10%

Here's how to crack it: Do this problem one sentence at a time.

1. A motor pool has 300 vehicles, of which 30% are trucks. 30% of 300 = 90 trucks, which means that 210 (the rest) are *not* trucks.

2. 20% of all the vehicles are diesel, including 15 trucks. 20% of 300 = 60 diesel vehicles, 15 of which are trucks, which means there are 45 diesel vehicles which are *not* trucks.

3. What percent of the motor pool is composed of vehicles that are neither truck nor diesel? We know from sentence number 1 that there are 210 nontrucks. We know from sentence number 2 that of these 210 nontrucks, 45 are diesel. Therefore 210 – 45, or 165, are neither diesel nor truck.

The question asks what percent of the entire motor pool these 165 nondiesel nontrucks are.

$$\frac{165}{300} = \frac{x}{100} \qquad 300x = 16,500$$

$$x = 55 \text{ and the answer is choice (D).}$$

Easy Eliminations:

1. Since the problem asks us to find a portion of the entire motor pool, it's impossible for that portion to be larger than the motor pool itself. Therefore answer choice (A) 165% is crazy.

2. If the problem simply asked what percent of the motor pool was not made up of trucks, the answer would be 70%. But since there is a further condition (the vehicles must be both nontruck and nondiesel), the answer must be even less than 70%. This makes answer choice (B) impossible, too.

3. Answer choice (C) is probably a Joe Bloggs answer. You can get it simply by adding 30 + 20 + 15.

4. Answer choice (A) was a trap for people who successfully got all the way to the end of the problem and then forgot that the answer was supposed to be expressed as a percent, not as a specific number.

Percent Increase

Another type of percent problem you'll probably see on the GMAT has to do with *percentage increase* or *percentage decrease*. In these problems the trick is always to put the increase or decrease in terms of the *original* amount. Here's an example:

9. The cost of a one-family home was $120,000 in 1980. In 1988, the price had increased to $180,000. What was the percent increase in the cost of the home?

   (A) 60% (B) 50% (C) 55% (D) 40% (E) 33.3%

Here's how to crack it: The actual increase was $60,000. To find the percent increase, set up the following equation:

$$\frac{\text{amount of increase}}{\text{original amount}} = \frac{x}{100}$$

In this case, $\dfrac{\$60,000}{\$120,000} = \dfrac{x}{100}$ $x = 50$ and the answer is choice (B).

Compound Interest

Another type of percentage problem involves *compound interest*. If you kept $1,000 in the bank for a year at 6% simple interest, you would get $60 in interest at the end of the year. Compound interest would pay you slightly more. Let's look at a compound-interest problem:

8. Ms. Lopez deposits $100 in an account that pays 20% interest, compounded semiannually. How much money will there be in the account at the end of one year?

   (A) $118.00 (B) $120.00 (C) $121.00 (D) $122.00
   (E) $140.00

Here's how to crack it: To find compound interest, divide the interest into as many parts as are being compounded. For example, if you're compounding interest semiannually, you divide the interest into two equal parts. If you're compounding quarterly, you divide the interest into four equal parts.

When Ms. Lopez deposited $100 into her account at a rate of 20% compound semiannually, the bank divided the interest into two equal parts. Halfway through the year, the bank put the first half of the interest into her account. In this case, since the full rate was 20% compounded semiannually, the bank deposited 10% of $100 (10% of $100 = $10). Halfway through the year, Ms. Lopez had $110.

For the second half of the year, the bank paid 10% interest on the $110 (10% of $110 = $11). At the end of the year, Ms. Lopez had $121.00 in her account. She earned $1 more than she would have earned if the account had paid only simple interest. The answer is choice (C).

Averages

To find the *average* of a set of *n* numbers, you simply add the numbers and divide by *n*. For example:

$$\text{The average of 10, 3, and 5 is } \frac{10+3+5}{3}=6$$

A good way to handle average problems is to set them up the same way every time. Whenever you see the word *average*, you should think:

$$\frac{\text{total sum of the items}}{\text{total number of the items}} = \text{average}$$

An Easy Average Problem

In a simple problem ETS will give you two parts of this equation, and it will be up to you to figure out the third. For example, ETS might ask:

What is the average of the numbers 3, 4, 5, and 8?

Here's how to crack it: In this case ETS has given us the actual numbers, which means we know the total sum (3 + 4 + 5 + 8 = 20) and the total number of items (there are four numbers). What we're missing is the average.

$$\frac{\text{total sum of the items}}{\text{total number of the items}} = \text{average} \qquad \frac{20}{4} = x \quad (x = 5)$$

Or ETS might ask:

If the average of 7 numbers is 5, what is the sum of the numbers?

Here's how to crack it: In this case we know the total number of items and the average, but not the total sum of the numbers.

$$\frac{\text{total sum of the items}}{\text{total number of the items}} = \text{average} \qquad \frac{x}{7} = 5 \quad (x = 35)$$

A More Difficult Average Problem

This is the same problem you just did, made a little more difficult:

The average of 7 numbers is 5. If two of the numbers are 11 and 14, what is the average of the remaining numbers?

Here's how to crack it: Always set up an average problem the way we showed you above—and with more complicated average problems, take things one sentence at a time. Set up correctly, the first sentence says

$$\frac{\text{total sum of the averages}}{\text{total number of the items}} = \text{average} \quad \frac{x}{7} = 5 \quad (x = 35)$$

The sum of *all* the numbers is 35. If two of those numbers are 11 and 14, then the sum of the remaining numbers is 35 − (11 + 14), or 10. The question asks "what is the average of the remaining numbers?" Again, let's set this up properly:

$$\frac{\text{total sum of the remaining numbers}}{\text{total number of the remaining numbers}} = \text{average} \quad \frac{10}{5} = x \quad (x = 2)$$

Why did we divide the total sum of the remaining numbers by 5? There were only 5 remaining numbers!

Means

When ETS talks about an average, the words "arithmetic mean" will often follow in parentheses. This is not just to make the problem sound scarier. Arithmetic mean is the precise term for the process of finding an average that we've illustrated in the problems above.

Exponents

An **exponent** is a short way of writing the value of a number multiplied several times by itself. $4 \times 4 \times 4 \times 4 \times 4$ can also be written as 4^5. This is expressed as "4 to the fifth power." The large number (4) is called the base, and the little number (5) is called the exponent.

There are several rules to remember about exponents:

• *Multiplying numbers with the same base:* When you multiply numbers that have the same base, you simply add the exponents.

$$6^2 \times 6^3 = 6^{(2+3)} = 6^5 \qquad (y^4)(y^6) = y^{(4+6)} = y^{10}$$

• *Dividing numbers with the same base:* When you divide numbers that have the same base, you can simply subtract the exponents.

$$\frac{3^6}{3^2} = 3^{(6-2)} = 3^4 \qquad \frac{x^7}{x^4} = x^{(7-4)} = x^3$$

• *Raising a power to a power:* When you raise a power to a power, you can simply multiply the exponents.

$$(4^3)^2 = 4^{(3 \times 2)} = 4^6 \qquad (z^2)^4 = z^{(2 \times 4)} = z^8$$

• *Distributing exponents:* When several numbers are inside parentheses, the exponent outside the parentheses must be distributed to all of the numbers within.

$$(4 \times y)^2 = 4^2 \times y^2$$

There are several operations which *seem* like they ought to work with exponents but don't.

• Does $x^2 + x^3 = x^5$? NO!
• Does $x^6 - x^2 = x^4$? NO!

• Does $\dfrac{\left(x^2 + y^2 + z^2\right)}{\left(x^2 + y^2\right)} = z^2$? NO!

The Strange Powers of Powers

If you raise a positive integer to a power, the number gets larger. For example, $6^2 = 36$. However, raising a number to a power can sometimes have unexpected results:

• If you raise a positive fraction that is less than 1 to a power, the fraction gets *smaller*.

$$\left(\frac{1}{3}\right)^2 = \frac{1}{3} \times \frac{1}{3} = \frac{1}{9}$$

• If you raise a negative number to an odd power, the number gets *smaller*.

$$(-3)^3 = (-3)(-3)(-3) = -27$$
(remember, −27 is smaller than −3)

- If you raise a negative number to an even power, the number becomes positive.

$$(-3)^2 = (-3)(-3) = 9$$
(remember, negative times negative = positive)

- Any number to the first power = itself.
- Any number to the 0 power = 1.
- Any number to the negative power y = the reciprocal of the same number to the positive power y. For example, $3^{-2} = \frac{1}{9}$.

Radicals

The square root of a positive number x is the number that, when squared, equals x. For example, the square root of 9 is 3 or –3, because 3 times 3 = 9, or –3 times –3 = 9. However, ETS is interested only in the *positive* square root. So for our purposes the square root of 9 is 3 only. The symbol for a positive square root is $\sqrt{\ }$. A number inside the $\sqrt{\ }$ is also called a *radical*.

$$\sqrt{4} = 2$$
$$\sqrt{9} = 3$$

There are several rules to remember about radicals:

1. $\sqrt{x}\sqrt{y} = \sqrt{xy}$. For example, $\sqrt{12}\sqrt{3} = \sqrt{36} = 6$

2. $\sqrt{\dfrac{x}{y}} = \dfrac{\sqrt{x}}{\sqrt{y}}$. For example, $\sqrt{\dfrac{3}{16}} = \dfrac{\sqrt{3}}{\sqrt{16}} = \dfrac{\sqrt{3}}{4}$

3. To simplify a radical, try factoring. For example,
   $\sqrt{32} = \sqrt{16}\sqrt{2} = 4\sqrt{2}$

4. The square root of a positive fraction less than 1 is actually larger than the original fraction. For example, $\sqrt{\frac{1}{4}} = \frac{1}{2}$.

Summary

1. The six arithmetic operations are addition, subtraction, multiplication, division, raising to a power, and finding a square root.

2. These operations must be performed in the proper order (**Please Excuse My Dear Aunt Sally**).

3. If you are adding or multiplying a group of numbers, you can regroup them in any order. This is called the associative law.

4. If you are adding or subtracting numbers with common factors, you can regroup them in the following way:

$$ab + ac = a(b + c)$$
$$ab - ac = a(b - c)$$

This is called the distributive law.

5. A fraction can be thought of in two ways:

- another way of expressing division
- as a part/whole

6. You must know how to add, subtract, multiply, and divide fractions. You must also know how to raise them to a power and find their roots.

7. Always reduce fractions (when you can) before doing a complicated operation. This will reduce your chances of making a careless error.

8. In tough fraction problems always think *part/whole* and *the rest*.

9. A decimal is just another way of expressing a fraction.

10. You must know how to add, subtract, multiply, and divide decimals.

11. In general it is easier to work with fractions than with decimals, so convert decimals to fractions.

12. A ratio is a fraction in all ways but one:

a fraction is a $\dfrac{\text{part}}{\text{whole}}$ a ratio is a $\dfrac{\text{part}}{\text{part}}$

In a ratio, the whole is the sum of all its parts.

13. A percentage is just a fraction whose denominator is always 100.

14. You must know the percentage shortcuts outlined in this chapter.

15. In tough percent problems, like tough fraction problems, think *part/whole* and *the rest.*

16. In a percentage increase or decrease problem, you must put the amount of the increase or decrease over the *original* amount.

17. In compound-interest problems, the answer will always be *a little bit more* than simple interest.

18. To find the average of several values, add the values and divide the total by the number of values.

19. Always set up average problems in the same way:

$$\frac{\text{total sum of the averages}}{\text{total number of the items}} = \text{average}$$

20. An exponent is a shorter way of expressing the result of multiplying a number several times by itself.

21. When you multiply numbers with the same base, you simply add the exponents.

22. When you divide numbers with the same base, you simply subtract the exponents.

23. When you raise a power to a power, you multiply the exponents.

24. You *cannot* add or subtract numbers with the same or different bases by adding their exponents.

25. On the GMAT, the square root of a number x is the positive number that when multiplied by itself $= x$.

26. The two radical rules you need to know:

$$\sqrt{x}\,\sqrt{y} = \sqrt{xy} \qquad \sqrt{\frac{x}{y}} = \frac{\sqrt{x}}{\sqrt{y}}$$

27. There are some unusual features of exponents and radicals:

    1. The square root of a positive fraction is larger than the original fraction.
    2. When you raise a positive fraction to an exponent, the resulting fraction is smaller.
    3. When you raise a negative number to an even exponent, the resulting number is positive.
    4. When you raise a negative number to an odd exponent, the resulting number is still a negative number.

CHAPTER TWELVE

Algebra

About a quarter of the problems in a regular 20-question problem-solving section will involve traditional algebra. These problems can often be found in the difficult third of the section, because ETS thinks algebra is difficult.

We don't. In this chapter we'll show you some powerful techniques that will enable you to solve these problems without using traditional algebra. The first half of this chapter will discuss these new techniques. The second half will show you how to do the few algebra problems that must be tackled algebraically.

Not Exactly Algebra: Basic Principles

There are certain problems in math that aren't meant to have just one specific number as an answer. Here's an example:

What is two more than 3 times a certain number x?

To find *one* specific number that answers this question, we would need to know the value of that "certain number *x*." Here's the way ETS would ask the same question:

1. What is two more than 3 times a certain number *x*?

    (A) $3x - 2$ (B) $3x$ (C) $2x - 3$ (D) $2x + 3$ (E) $3x + 2$

Cosmic Problems

In other words, this is kind of a cosmic problem. ETS is asking you to write an equation that will answer this question no matter what the "certain number" is. *X* could be *any* number, and that equation would still give you the correct answer.

ETS expects you to use algebra to answer this question, but there is a better way. Since the correct answer will work for *every* value of *x*, why not just pick *one* value for *x*?

We call this **plugging in.** Plugging in is easy. There are three steps involved:

1. Pick numbers for the letters in the problem.
2. Using your numbers, find an answer to the problem.
3. Plug your numbers into the answer choices to see which choice equals the answer you found in Step 2.

Let's look at that same problem again:

1. What is two more than 3 times a certain number *x*?
    (A) $3x - 2$ (B) $3x$ (C) $2x - 3$ (D) $2x + 3$ (E) $3x + 2$

Here's how to crack it: Let's pick a number for *x*. How about 4? In your test booklet, write in "*x* = 4" above the *x* in the problem. By substituting 4 for the *x*, we now have a specific rather than a cosmic problem. The question now reads,

"What is two more than 3 times 4?"

$3 \times 4 = 12$.
What is 2 more than 12?
14.

Using the number we chose for x, the answer to this question is 14. Write 14 in the margin next to the question and circle it. All you need to do now is figure out which of the answer choices equals 14 when you substitute 4 for x.

When you're plugging in, always start with answer choice (A). If that doesn't work, try choice (E), then (B), then (D), then (C). In other words, start from the outside and work toward the center.

Let's start with choice (A) $3x - 2$. Plugging in 4 for x, do we get 14? No, we get 10. Eliminate.

Go to choice (E) $3x + 2$. Plugging in 4 for x, we get $12 + 2$, or 14. This is the answer we wanted. Choice (E) is the correct answer to this question.

You might be thinking, "Wait a minute. It was just as easy to solve this problem algebraically. Why should I plug in?" There are two answers:

1. This was an easy problem. Plugging in makes even difficult problems easy.
2. ETS has spent hours coming up with all the possible ways you might screw this problem up using algebra. If you make one of these mistakes, your answer will be among the answer choices, and you will pick it and get it wrong.

There Are Three Kinds of Cosmic Problems—and You Can Plug In on All of Them

A cosmic problem is any problem in which the answer choices are not specific numbers. You can plug in if you see:
1. variables in the answer choices
2. percents in the answer choices (when they are percents of some unspecified amount)
3. fractions or ratios in the answer choices (when they are fractional parts or ratios of unspecified amounts)

Variables in the Answers

ETS wants you to use algebra on problems that have variables in the answers, but plugging in is easier, faster, and less likely to produce errors. Here's an example:

10. At a photocopy center, the first 10 copies cost x cents each. Each of the next 50 copies cost 5 cents less per copy. From the 61st copy on, the cost is 2 cents per copy. In terms of x, how much does it cost in cents to have 200 copies made?

(A) $60x + 30$ (B) $50x - 10$ (C) $50(x - 5)$ (D) $60x - 110$
(E) $10x + 490$

Here's how to crack it: Pick a number for x. How about 8?

The first 10 copies = 10×8 = <u>80 cents</u>
The next 50 copies each cost 5 cents less than the first 10, so each of these copies cost $8 - 5$ or 3 cents each.
The next 50 copies = 50×3 = <u>150 cents</u>

From now on, the cost is 2 cents for any additional copies. We need a total of 200 copies. So far we've done 60 copies. We need an additional 140 copies.

The final 140 copies = 140×2 = <u>280 cents</u>

Let's add it all up.

$$
\begin{array}{r}
80 \text{ cents} \\
150 \text{ cents} \\
+\,280 \text{ cents} \\
\hline
510 \text{ cents}
\end{array}
$$

This is the answer to the question. All we have to do is find out which answer choice equals 510. Start with choice (A) $60x + 30$, and remember that we plugged in 8 for x. Does $60(8) + 30 = 510$? Yes, it does. The answer to this question is choice (A). (Try the other choices if you're not convinced.)

What Number Should I Plug In?

A cosmic problem is designed to work with any number, but you'll find that certain numbers work better than others. Plugging in a number that's simple to use is obviously a good idea. In general you should stick to small numbers. But if the problem concerns hours and days, it might make sense to pick 24. If the problem concerns minutes and hours, a good number would probably be 60.

Avoid 0 and 1, and numbers that are already in the problem or the answer choices. Why? If you plug in one of these numbers, you may find that more than one answer choice appears to be correct.

Sometimes the best way to select a number is to use a little common sense. Here's an example:

14. If Jim can drive the distance k miles in 50 minutes, how many minutes, in terms of k, will it take him to drive 10 miles at the same speed?

(A) $\dfrac{500}{k}$ (B) $\dfrac{k}{50}$ (C) $60k$ (D) $10k$ (E) $\dfrac{50}{k}$

Here's how to crack it: ETS wants you to write a complicated equation based on the formula rate × time = distance, or perhaps set up a proportion. But this isn't necessary. Because there are variables in the answer choices, you can simply plug in.

Any number you choose to plug in for k will eventually give you the answer to this problem, but there are some numbers that will make your task even easier.

If it takes Jim 50 minutes to drive k *miles*, how long will it take him to drive *10 miles* at the same rate?

We need a number for k. What if we made k = half of 10? See how the question reads now:

If it takes Jim 50 minutes to drive 5 miles, how long will it take him to drive 10 miles at the same rate?

Suddenly the problem is simple. It will take him twice as long: 100 minutes. Now all we need to know is which of the answer choices equals 100, given that $k = 5$. Start with answer choice (A). Divide 500 by 5 and you have 100.

The answer to this question is choice (A).

Percents in the Answers

ETS wants you to use algebra on certain problems where there are percents in the answers, but plugging in is easier, and less likely to produce errors. Here's an example:

15. A merchant was selling an item at a certain price, then marked it down 20% for a spring sale. During the summer, he marked the item down another 20% from its spring price. If the item sold at the summer price, what percent of the original price did it sell for?

(A) 40% (B) 60% (C) 64% (D) 67% (E) 80%

> **Easy Eliminations:** This is a difficult question. The first thing to do here is eliminate any answers that are too good to be true. There are two 20s in the problem. Adding them together gives you answer choice (A). Eliminate choice (A). Joe's favorite answer is probably choice (B). Joe reasons that if an item is discounted 20% and then another 20%, there must be 60% left. Eliminate choice (B). Choice (E) seems too large. The answer is probably choice (C) or (D).

Here's how to crack it: You may have noticed that while this problem gave us lots of information, it never told us how much the item sold for originally. This is another cosmic problem. ETS wants you to write an equation that will work regardless of the original price of the item. But since this problem is supposed to work for *any* original amount, we may as well pick *one* amount.

Let's plug in 100. *When you are dealing with a percent problem, 100 is usually a convenient number.* The merchant was selling the item for $100. He discounted it by 20% for the spring sale. 20% of $100 is $20, so the spring price was $80. For the summer, he discounted it again, by 20% of the spring price. 20% of $80 is $16. Therefore he took $20 and then $16 off the original price. The summer price is $64.

The question asks what percent of the original price the item sold for. It sold for $64. What percent of 100 is 64? 64%. The answer is choice (C).

Fractions or Ratios in the Answers

ETS wants you to use traditional math on certain problems with fractions or ratios in the answer choices, but plugging in is easier, faster, and less likely to produce errors. Here's an example:

10. Half the graduating class of a college was accepted by a business school. One third of the class was accepted by a law school. If one fifth of the class was accepted to both types of school, what fraction of the class was accepted only by a law school?

(A) 1/60 (B) 2/15 (C) 1/3 (D) 1/2 (E) 4/5

Here's how to crack it: You may have noticed that while this problem gave us lots of fractions to work with, it never told us how many people were in the graduating class. This is yet another cosmic problem. ETS wants you to find a fractional *part* without knowing what the specific *whole* is. Since this problem is supposed to work with *any* number of people in the graduating class, we may as well pick *one* number.

This problem will work with any number, but some numbers are easier to work with than others. For example, if we chose 47 for the number of people in the graduating class, that would mean that $23\frac{1}{2}$ people were accepted by a business school; while this might make a good plot for a Stephen King novel, wouldn't it be easier to pick a number that can be divided evenly by all the fractions in the problem? One number that is evenly divisible by 2, 3, and 5 is 30. So let's plug in 30 for the number of people in the graduating class.

One half of the class got into business school ($\frac{1}{2}$ of 30 = 15).

One third of the class got into law school ($\frac{1}{3}$ of 30 = 10).

One fifth of the class got into both ($\frac{1}{5}$ of 30 = 6).

ETS wants to know what fraction of the class was accepted only by a law school. Ten people were accepted by a law school, but 6 of those 10 were also accepted by a business school. Therefore 4 people out of 30 were accepted only by a law school. Reduced, $\frac{4}{30}$ is $\frac{2}{15}$, so the answer is choice (B).

Working Backward

Any cosmic algebra problem can be solved, as we have seen, by plugging in numbers. But not all algebra problems are cosmic. What about a problem that asks for a specific numeric answer?

A company's profits have doubled for each of the 4 years it has been in existence. If the total profits for those 4 years were $30 million, what were the profits in the first year of operation?

There is only one number in the whole world that will answer this question. If you tried plugging in amounts for the first year of operation in hopes of happening upon the correct answer, you would be busy for a very, very long time.

ETS expects you to use algebra to answer this question. They want you to assign a variable for the first year's profits, say x, in which case the second year's profits would be $2x$, the third year's profits would be $4x$, and the fourth year's profits would be $8x$. Altogether, we get $15x = 30$, and $x = 2$.

Unfortunately, it is extremely easy to make a mistake when you set up an equation. You could add up the number of x's incorrectly, or think that the profits of the third year were equal to $3x$. While this is not a difficult problem, it does represent the potential difficulties of using algebra.

ETS expects you to use algebra to answer this question, but *there is a better way.* Each time ETS asks you to find a specific numeric answer, they are forced to give you five clues. Here is how ETS would ask this question:

7. A company's profits have doubled for each of the 4 years it has been in existence. If the total profits for the last 4 years were $30 million, what were the profits in the first year of operation?

    (A) $1 million (B) $2 million (C) $4 million
    (D) $4.5 million (E) $6 million

Here's how to crack it: Without answer choices this problem is difficult, and the only way to solve it is to use algebra. Now, however, there are only five possible answers. One of them has to be correct. Why not **work backward** from the answer choices?

Working backward is easy. There are three steps involved:

1. Always start with answer choice (C). Plug that number into the problem and see whether it makes the problem work.
2. If choice (C) is too small, choose the next larger number.
3. If choice (C) is too big, choose the next smaller number.

Numeric answers on the GMAT are always given in order of size (with one or two rare exceptions that we'll discuss in the geometry chapter). Therefore when you're working backward, always start with answer choice (C). Plug that number into the problem and see whether it works. If it does, you've already found the answer. If it's too big, you can try a lower number. If it's too small, try a larger number.

Let's try answer choice (C).

If the first year's profits were	$4 million
the second year's profits would be	$8 million
the third year's profits would be	$16 million
and the fourth year's profits would be	$32 million
the total profits =	$60 million

This is too big. The total profits were only $30 million. We don't even have to look at choice (D) or (E), which are even bigger. We can eliminate choices (C), (D), and (E).

Let's try answer choice (B).

If the first year's profits were	$2 million
the second year's profits would be	$4 million
the third year's profits would be	$8 million
and the fourth year's profits would be	$16 million
the total profits =	$30 million

Bingo! The correct answer is choice (B). Note that if choice (B) had been too big, the only possible answer would have been choice (A).

When to Work Backward

You can work backward as long as:

A) The answer choices are numbers.
B) The question is relatively straightforward. For example, it's easy to work backward on a question that asks, "What is x?" It's difficult and not worth the bother to work backward on a problem that asks, "What is $(x + y)$?"

5. If x is a positive number such that $x^2 + 5x - 14 = 0$, what is the value of x?

(A) –7 (B) –5 (C) 0 (D) 2 (E) 5

Here's how to crack it: There is only one number in the world that will make this problem work, and fortunately it has to be one of the five answer choices. Let's work backward. Start with choice (C). (Zero squared) plus (zero times 5) minus 14 does *not* equal 0. Eliminate. We don't have to try choice (A) or (B) because the problem asks for a positive number. Let's try choice (D). (Two squared) plus (5 times 2)—we're up to 14 so far—minus 14 *does* equal 0. The answer is choice (D).

> **Easy Eliminations:** Obviously, if *x* is a positive number, choices (A), (B), and (C) are out of the question.

Working Backward: Advanced Principles

Sometimes when you're working backward you'll be able to eliminate choice (C), but you may not be sure whether you need a larger number or a smaller one. Rather than waste time trying to decide, just try all the answer choices until you hit the right one. You'll never have to try more than four of them.

14. Today Jim is twice as old as Fred, and Sam is 2 years younger than Fred. Four years ago Jim was 4 times as old as Sam. How old is Jim now?

    (A) 8 (B) 12 (C) 16 (D) 20 (E) 24

Here's how to crack it: One of these five answer choices is the right answer.

Let's work backward.

Start with choice (C). Jim is 16 years old today. He is twice as old as Fred, so Fred is 8. Sam is 2 years younger than Fred, so Sam is 6. Therefore, 4 years ago Jim was 12 and Sam was 2. If these numbers agree with the rest of the problem, then choice (C) is the answer to this question. The problem says that four years ago Jim was 4 times as old as Sam. Does 12 times 4 equal 2? No. Choice (C) is the wrong answer. Does anybody want to guess which direction to go in now? Rather than hem and haw, just try the other answers until you get the right one.

Let's try choice (D). Jim is 20 years old today. He is twice as old as Fred, so Fred is 10. Sam is 2 years younger than Fred, so Sam is 8. Therefore, four years ago Jim was 16 and Sam was 4. If these numbers agree with the rest of the problem choice (D) is the right answer. The problem says that four years ago Jim was 4 times as old as Sam. Does 4 times 4 equal 16? Yes. The answer is choice (D).

Must Be/Could Be

From time to time ETS will write a question that contains the words "must be," "could be," or "cannot be." This type of problem can almost always be solved by plugging in, *but you may need to plug in more than one number*. Here's an example:

> 5. If x and y are consecutive integers, which of the following must be an even integer?
>
> (A) x (B) y (C) $\dfrac{xy}{2}$ (D) $\dfrac{y}{x}$ (E) xy

Here's how to crack it: Plug in numbers for x and y. How about 2 for x and 3 for y? Now go through each of the answer choices. Using these numbers, choice (A) is even, but because of the words "*must be*," we cannot assume that it will *always* be even, or that this is necessarily the right answer. Keep going. Using the numbers we plugged in, choices (B), (C), and (D) turn out to be odd. Since the question asks us for an answer that is *always* even, we can eliminate all of these. However, choice (E) is also even. We're down to either choice (A) or (E). Which is correct?

Try plugging in a different set of numbers. The problem concerns even and odd numbers, so this time let's try an odd number first. How about 3 and 4? This time choice (A) is odd. Eliminate. Choice (E) is still even; this must be our answer.

Basic Algebra

Plugging in and working backward will take care of most of your algebraic needs, but there are a few other types of problems that require some knowledge of basic algebra. After reading the rest of this chapter and working out the problems contained in it, if you still feel rusty, you might want to dig out your old high-school algebra book.

Solving Equalities

Even the simplest equalities can be solved by working backward, but it's probably easier to solve a *simple* equation algebraically. If there is one variable in an equation, isolate the variable on one side of the equation and solve it. Here's an example:

6. If $x - 5 = 3x + 2$, then $x =$

(A) -8 (B) $-\dfrac{7}{2}$ (C) -7 (D) $\dfrac{10}{3}$ (E) $\dfrac{7}{5}$

Here's how to crack it: Get all of the x's on one side of the equation. If we subtract x from both sides we have:

$$\begin{aligned} x - 5 &= 3x + 2 \\ -x \qquad &\quad -x \\ \hline -5 &= 2x + 2 \end{aligned}$$

Now subtract 2 from both sides:

$$\begin{aligned} -5 &= 2x + 2 \\ -2 \quad &\quad -2 \\ \hline -7 &= 2x \end{aligned}$$

Finally, divide both sides by 2:

$$\frac{-7}{2} = \frac{2x}{2}$$

$x = -\dfrac{7}{2}$. The answer is choice (B).

Solving Inequalities

To solve inequalities, you must be able to recognize the following symbols:

> is greater than
< is less than
≥ is greater than or equal to
≤ is less than or equal to

As with an equation, you can add or subtract a number to both sides of an inequality without changing it; you can collect similar terms and simplify them.

In fact, an inequality behaves just like a regular equation except in one way: *If you multiply or divide both sides of an equality by a negative number, the direction of the inequality symbol changes*. For example,

$$-2x > 5$$

To solve for x, you would divide both sides by -2, just as you would in an equality. But when you do, the sign flips:

$$\frac{-2x}{-2} < \frac{5}{-2} \qquad x < -\frac{5}{2}$$

Solving Simultaneous Equations

It's impossible to solve one equation with two variables. But if there are two equations, both of which have the same two variables, then it is possible to solve for both variables. An easy problem might look like this:

If $3x + 2y = 6$ and $5x - 2y = 10$ then $x = ?$

To solve simultaneous equations, add or subtract the equations so that one of the variables disappears.

$$\begin{aligned} 3x + 2y &= 6 \\ 5x - 2y &= 10 \\ \hline 8x &= 16 \qquad x = 2 \end{aligned}$$

In more difficult simultaneous equations, you'll find that neither of the variables will disappear when you try to add or subtract the two equations. In such cases you must multiply both sides of one of the equations by some number in order to get the coefficient in front of the variable you want to disappear to be the same in both equations. This sounds more complicated than it is. A difficult problem might look like this:

If $3x + 2y = 6$ and $5x - y = 10$, then $x = ?$

Let's set it up the same way:

$$\begin{aligned} 3x + 2y &= 6 \\ 5x - y &= 10 \end{aligned}$$

Unfortunately, in this example neither adding nor subtracting the two equations gets rid of either variable. But look what happens when we multiply the bottom equation by 2:

$$3x + 2y = 6 \qquad \text{or} \qquad 3x + 2y = 6$$
$$(2)5x - (2)y = (2)10 \qquad \qquad \underline{+\ 10x - 2y = 20}$$
$$13x \qquad = 26 \quad x = 2$$

Quadratic Equations

On the GMAT, quadratic equations always come in one of two forms: factored or unfactored. Here's an example:

$$\textit{factored} \qquad \textit{unfactored}$$
$$(x + 2)(x + 5) = x^2 + 7x + 10$$

The trick to solving a problem that involves a quadratic equation is to see which form the equation is in. If the quadratic equation is in an unfactored form, factor it immediately. If the quadratic equation is in a factored form, unfactor it. ETS likes to see whether you know how to do these things.

To unfactor a factored expression, just multiply it out:

$$(x + 2)(x + 5) = (x + 2)(x + 5)$$
$$= (x \text{ times } x) + (x \text{ times } 5) + (2 \text{ times } x) + (2 \text{ times } 5)$$
$$= x^2 + 5x + 2x + 10$$
$$= x^2 + 7x + 10$$

To factor an unfactored expression, put it into the following format and start by looking for the factors of the first and last terms.

$$x^2 + 2x - 15$$
$$= (\quad)(\quad)$$
$$= (x \quad)(x \quad)$$
$$= (x \quad 5)(x \quad 3)$$
$$= (x + 5)(x - 3)$$

Quadratic equations are usually set equal to 0. Here's an example:

4. What are all the values of x that satisfy the equation $x^2 + 4x + 3 = 0$?

(A) -3 (B) -1 (C) -3 and -1 (D) 3 and 4 (E) 4

Here's how to crack it: This problem contains an unfactored equation, so let's factor it.

$$
\begin{aligned}
x^2 + 4x + 3 &= 0 \\
(x \quad)(x \quad) &= 0 \\
(x \quad 3)(x \quad 1) &= 0 \\
(x + 3)(x + 1) &= 0
\end{aligned}
$$

In order for this equation to be correct, x must be either -3 or -1. The correct answer is choice (C).

Note: This problem would also have been easy to solve by working backward. It asked a specific question, and there were five specific answer choices. One of them was correct. All you had to do was try the choices until you found the right one. Bear in mind, however, that in a quadratic equation there are usually two values that will make the equation work.

Fetishes of GMAT Test-Writers

There are two types of quadratic equations the test-writers at ETS find endlessly fascinating. These equations appear on the GMAT with great regularity, both in the regular math sections and the Data Sufficiency section.

$$
\begin{aligned}
(x + y)^2 &= x^2 + 2xy + y^2 \\
(x + y)(x - y) &= x^2 - y^2
\end{aligned}
$$

Memorize both of these. As with all quadratic equations, if ETS presents the equation in factored form, you should immediately unfactor it; if it's unfactored, factor it immediately.

5. If $\dfrac{x^2 - 4}{x + 2} = 5$, then $x = ?$

(A) 3 (B) 5 (C) 6 (D) 7 (E) 9

Here's how to crack it: This problem contains one of ETS's fetishes. It is unfactored, so let's factor it:

$$\frac{(x + 2)(x - 2)}{(x + 2)} = 5$$

The $(x + 2)$s cancel out, leaving us with $(x - 2) = 5$. $X = 7$ and the answer is choice (D).

Rate × Time = Distance

Any problem that mentions planes, trains, cars, bicycles, distance, miles per hour, or any other travel-related terminology is asking you to write an equation based on the formula *rate × time = distance*. This formula is easy to reconstruct if you forget it; just think of a real-life situation. If you drove at 50 miles per hour for 2 hours, how far did you go? That's right, 100 miles. We just derived the formula. The rate is 50 miles per hour. The time is 2 hours. The distance is 100 miles.

8. Pam and Sue drove to a business meeting 120 miles away in the same car. Pam drove to the meeting and Sue drove back along the same route. If Pam drove at 60 miles per hour and Sue drove at 50 miles per hour, how much longer, in minutes, did it take Sue to travel the distance than it did Pam?

(A) 4 (B) 10 (C) 20 (D) 24 (E) 30

Here's how to crack it: As soon as you see the words "drove" and "travel," make a little chart for yourself:

R × T = D

Pam _____

Sue _____

The problem says the meeting was 120 miles away from wherever they started. This tells us not only how far Pam drove but how far Sue drove as well, since she returned along the same route. We are also given the rates of both women.

Let's fill in the chart with the information we have:

R × T = D

Pam   60 × ? = 120

Sue   50 × ? = 120

60 times what equals 120? It took Pam 2 hours to drive to the meeting. 50 times what equals 120? It took Sue 2.4 hours to drive back from the meeting. Sue took .4 hours longer, but the problem asks for the answer in minutes. .4 equals $\frac{4}{10}$ or $\frac{2}{5}$. There are 60 minutes in an hour, so just find $\frac{2}{5}$ of 60. The answer is choice (D), 24 minutes.

Work Problems

Another type of GMAT problem that requires an equation is the work problem. These are easy to spot because they always involve two people (or factories or machines) working at different rates. In these problems the trick is not to think about how long it takes to do an entire job, but rather how much of the job can be done in *one hour*.

9. If Sam can finish a job in 3 hours and Mark can finish a job in 12 hours, in how many hours could they finish the job if they worked on it together at their respective rates?

(A) 1 (B) $2\frac{2}{5}$ (C) $2\frac{5}{8}$ (D) $3\frac{1}{4}$ (E) 4

Here's how to crack it: If Sam can finish a job in 3 hours, then in one hour he can finish $\frac{1}{3}$ of the job. If Mark can finish a job in 12 hours, then in one hour, he can finish $\frac{1}{12}$ of the job. Working together, how much of the job can they do in one hour?

$$\frac{1}{3} + \frac{1}{12} = \frac{1}{x}$$

Now we only need to solve for x. First find a common denominator for $\frac{1}{3}$ and $\frac{1}{12}$.

$$\frac{1}{3} + \frac{1}{12} = \frac{1}{x}$$

$$\frac{4}{12} + \frac{1}{12} = \frac{1}{x}$$

$$= \frac{5}{12} = \frac{1}{x}$$

Cross-multiply and divide. $X = 2\frac{2}{5}$. The answer is choice (B).

> **Easy Eliminations:** It stands to reason that two men working together would take less time to finish a job than they would if each of them worked alone. Since Sam, working alone, could finish the job in 3 hours, it must be true that the two of them, working together, could do it in less time. The answer to this question has to be less than 3. Therefore we can eliminate answer choices (D) and (E).

Functions

You'll know you've hit a function problem by the sensation of panic and fear you get when you see some strange symbol ($ or # or* or Δ) and say, "I studied for two months for this test and somehow managed to miss the part where they told me about $ or # or* or Δ." Relax. Any strange-looking symbol on the GMAT is just a function, and on this test functions are easy.

A function is basically a set of directions. Let's look at an example:

$$\text{If } x * y = 3x - y, \text{ then what is } 4 * 2?$$

What the first half of this problem says is that for any two numbers with a * in between, you must multiply the number on the left by 3 and then subtract the number on the right. These are the directions. The second half of the problem asks you to use these directions with two specific numbers: 4 * 2.

To solve this problem, all we need to do is plug the specific numbers into the set of directions:

$$x * y = 3x - y$$
$$4 * 2 = 3(4) - (2)$$
$$= 12 - 2$$
$$= 10$$

Functions don't always involve two numbers. Sometimes they look like this:

13. If $\Delta x = x$ if x is positive, or $2x$ if x is negative, what is $\dfrac{\Delta 30}{\Delta -5}$?

(A) –12 (B) –6 (C) –3 (D) 6 (E) 30

Let's take this one step at a time. In this case the directions say that the function of any number x is simply that same number x, if x is positive. However, if the number x is negative, then the function of that number is $2x$. Thus:

$$\frac{\Delta 30}{\Delta -5} = \frac{30}{2(-5)} = \frac{30}{-10} \text{ or } -3. \text{ The answer is choice (C).}$$

Easy Eliminations: Joe has no idea what to do with Δ, so he just ignores it. Because $30/{-5} = -6$, Joe picks answer choice (B). On the other hand, Joe might also think he can reduce functions. In other words, he might think he could do this:

$$\frac{\Delta 30}{\Delta -5} = \Delta -6$$

The function of $-6 = -12$, so Joe might also select answer choice (A).

Summary

1. Most of the algebra problems on the GMAT are simpler to solve *without* algebra, using two Princeton Review techniques: *plugging in* and *working backward*.

2. Plugging in will work on any cosmic problem; that is, any problem that does not include specific numbers in the answer choices. You can always plug in if you see

   - variables in the answer choices
   - fractional parts in the answer choices
   - ratios in the answer choices

You can usually plug in when you see

- percentages in the answer choices

3. Plugging in is easy. There are three steps:

    1. Pick numbers for the variables in the problem.
    2. Using your numbers, find an answer to the problem.
    3. Plug your numbers into the answer choices to see which choice equals the answer you found in Step 2.

4. When you plug in, try to choose convenient numbers—those that are simple to work with and make the problem easier to manipulate.

5. When you plug in, avoid choosing 0 or 1, or a number that already appears in the problem or in the answer choices.

6. On problems with variables in the answers that contain the words "must be" or "could be," you may have to plug in more than once to find the correct answer.

7. Working backward will solve algebra problems that are *not* cosmic—in other words, problems that are highly specific. You can always work backward on an algebra problem if the answer choices contain specific numbers, and if the question being asked is relatively straightforward.

8. Working backward is easy. There are three steps:

    1. Always start with answer choice (C). Plug that number into the problem and see whether it makes the problem work.
    2. If choice (C) is too small, choose the next larger number.
    3. If choice (C) is too big, choose the next smaller number.

9. If you see a problem with a quadratic equation in factored form, the easiest way to get the answer is to unfactor it immediately. If it is unfactored, factor it immediately.

10. Memorize the factored and unfactored forms of the two most common quadratic equations on the GMAT:

$$(x + y)^2 = x^2 + 2xy + y^2$$
$$(x + y)(x - y) = x^2 - y^2$$

11. On problems containing inequalities, remember that when you multiply or divide both sides of an inequality by a negative number, the sign flips.

12. In solving simultaneous equations, add or subtract one equation to or from another so that one of the two variables disappears.

13. Any travel-related problem is probably concerned with the formula **rate × time = distance**.

14. The key to work problems is to think about how much of the job can be done in one hour.

15. Function problems have strange symbols like °, Δ, or *, but they are really just a set of directions.

CHAPTER THIRTEEN

Geometry

About a quarter of the problems in a regular 20-question problem-solving section will involve geometry. While this tends to be the math subject most people remember least from high school, the good news is that the GMAT tests only a small portion of the geometry you used to know. It will be relatively easy to refresh your memory.

The bad news is that unlike the SAT, the GMAT does not provide you with the formulas and terms you'll need to solve the problems. You'll have to memorize them.

The first half of this chapter will show you how to eliminate answer choices on certain geometry problems without using traditional geometry. The second half will review all the geometry you need to know in order to answer the problems that must be solved using more traditional methods.

Crazy Answers

Eliminating choices that don't make sense has already proven to be a valuable technique on arithmetic and algebra questions. On geometry questions you can develop this technique into a science. The reason for this is that many geometry problems come complete with a diagram *drawn to scale*.

Most people get so caught up in solving a geometry problem geometrically that they forget to look at the diagram to see whether their answer is reasonable.

Crazy Answers on Easy Questions

How big is angle *x*?

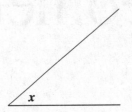

Obviously you don't know exactly how big this angle is, but it would be easy to compare it with an angle whose measure you *do* know exactly. Let's compare it with a 90-degree angle:

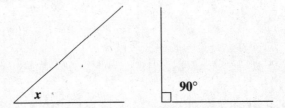

Angle *x* is less than 90 degrees. How much less? It looks as though it's about half of a 90-degree angle, or 45 degrees. Now look at the following problem, which asks about the same angle *x*:

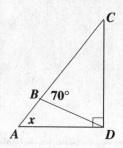

3. In this figure, if $BC = CD$, and angle $ADC = 90$
degrees, then what is the value of x?

(A) 45   (B) 50   (C) 70   (D) 75   (E) 100

Here's how to crack it: This is an easy problem, but before you
launch into solving it, it's still a good idea to take a moment to decide
whether any of the answer choices are clearly out of the question.
We've already decided that angle x is less than 90 degrees, which
means that answer choice (E) can be eliminated. How much less is it?
Well, we estimated before that it was about half, which rules out
answer choices (C) and (D) as well.

There is another way to eliminate choices (C) and (D). We can
compare angle x with the other marked angle in the problem—angle
DBC. If the answer to this problem is choice (C), then angle x should
look exactly the same as angle DBC. Does it? No. Angle x looks a
little bit smaller than angle DBC, which means that both choices (C)
and (D) can be eliminated.

Eliminating crazy answers will prevent you from making careless mistakes on easy problems. (By the way, we'll show you how to
solve this problem using geometry later in the chapter.)

Crazy Answers on Difficult Questions

If it's important to cross off crazy answer choices on easy questions,
it's even more important to eliminate crazy answer choices when
you're tackling a *difficult* geometry problem. On a difficult problem,
you may not know how to find the answer geometrically, and even
if you do, you could still fall victim to one of the traps ETS has placed
in your path. Take a look at the following difficult geometry problem:

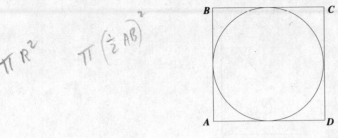

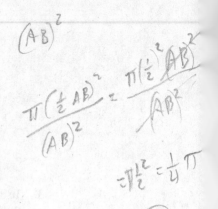

16. In the figure above, circle *C* is inscribed inside square *ABCD* as shown. What is the ratio of the area of circle *C* to the area of square *ABCD*?

(A) $\dfrac{\pi}{2}$ (B) $\dfrac{4}{\pi}$ (C) $\dfrac{\pi}{3}$ (D) $\dfrac{\pi}{4}$ (E) $\dfrac{2}{\pi}$

Here's how to crack it: This is a difficult problem, and it's worth noting that you didn't need to do this one at all. You can get a good score on the GMAT by skipping difficult questions entirely. But before you decide not to do this problem, let's see whether you can eliminate any of the answer choices just by looking at the diagram and using some common sense.

The problem asks you for the ratio of the area of the circle to the area of the square. Just by looking at the diagram, you can tell that the circle is smaller than the square. The correct answer to this question has to be the ratio of a smaller number to a bigger number. Let's look at the answer choices.

In choice (A), the ratio is π over 2. An approximate value of π is 3.14, so this really reads

$$\frac{3.14}{2}$$

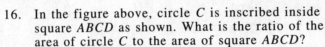

Is this the ratio of a smaller number to a bigger number? Just the opposite. Therefore choice (A) is a crazy answer. Eliminate.

In choice (B), the ratio is 4 over π. This really reads

$$\frac{4}{3.14}$$

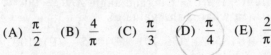

Is this the ratio of a smaller number to a bigger number? No. Choice (B) is a crazy answer. Eliminate.

In choice (C), the ratio is π over 3. This really reads

$$\frac{3.14}{3}$$

Is this the ratio of a smaller number to a bigger number? No. Choice (C) is a crazy answer. Eliminate.

Answer choices (D) and (E) both contain ratios of smaller numbers to bigger numbers, so they're both still possibilities. However, we've eliminated three of the answer choices without doing any math. If you know how to solve the problem geometrically, then proceed. If not, guess and move on. (By the way, we will show you how to solve this problem using geometry later in the chapter.)

The Basic Tools

In eliminating crazy answers, it helps to have the following approximations memorized.

$$\pi \approx 3$$
$$\sqrt{1} \approx 1$$
$$\sqrt{2} \approx 1.4$$
$$\sqrt{3} \approx 1.7$$
$$\sqrt{4} \approx 2$$

It's also useful to have a feel for the way certain common angles look:

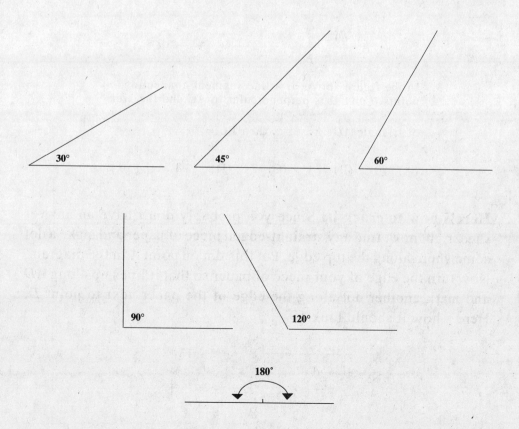

Getting More Precise

When a geometry problem has a diagram drawing drawn to scale, you can get even more precise in eliminating wrong answer choices.

How?

By measuring the diagram.

The instructions at the beginning of each problem-solving section say that unless a diagram is marked "not drawn to scale," it is drawn "as accurately as possible." ETS finds it possible to draw diagrams very accurately indeed. All you need now is something with which to measure the diagram. Fortunately the folks at ETS provide you with a ruler—your answer sheet. The computer that scores your answer sheet will be very interested in the left and right edges (the markings there tell the computer what page it's scanning) and in the bulk of the page where you mark down your answer choices, but it doesn't scan the top or bottom edges of the answer sheet. You can use one of these edges to construct a ruler. Look at the problem below:

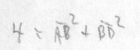

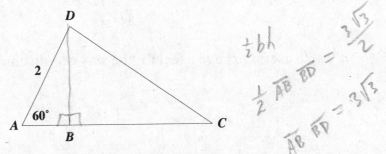

13. In the figure above, if a line segment connecting points B and D is perpendicular to AC and the area of triangle ADC is $\dfrac{3\sqrt{3}}{2}$, then $BC = ?$

(A) $\sqrt{2}$　(B) $\sqrt{3}$　(C) 2　(D) $3\sqrt{3}$　(E) 6

Here's how to crack it: Since you probably don't have an answer sheet right now, find any straight-edged piece of paper and make a dot somewhere along the top edge. Put this dot on point A in the diagram. Now turn the edge of your piece of paper so that it lines up along AD and mark another dot along the edge of the paper next to point D. Here's how it should look:

You now have a ruler. The distance between the dots at the top of your answer sheet is exactly the same as the distance between points *A* and *D* on the diagram. Use the ruler to measure the distance between point *B* and *C*.

If you measure carefully, you'll notice that the distance between *A* and *D* is the same as the distance between *B* and *C*—exactly 2. Let's look at the answer choices. Because you memorized the values we told you to memorize earlier, you know that answer choice (A) is equal to 1.4. Eliminate. Answer choice (B) is equal to 1.7. This is close enough for us to hold on to it while we look at the other choices. Choice (C) is exactly what we're looking for—2. Choice (D) is 3 times 1.7, which equals 5.1. This is much too large. Choice (E) is even larger. Eliminate (D) and (E). We're down to choices (B) and (C). The correct answer is choice (C).

Three Important Notes

1. While all diagrams in the regular problem-solving sections of the GMAT are drawn to scale (unless otherwise indicated), they are not *all* drawn to the *same* scale. A ruler that measures 2 on one diagram won't measure 2 on another. For every new problem with a diagram, you will have to make a new ruler.

2. Diagrams marked "not drawn to scale" cannot be measured. In fact, the drawings in these problems are often purposely misleading to the eye.

3. Drawings in the Data Sufficiency section of the GMAT are *not* drawn to scale. They *cannot* be estimated with your eye or with a ruler.

What Should I Do If There Is No Diagram?

Draw one. It's always difficult to imagine a geometry problem in your head. The first thing you should do with any geometry problem that doesn't have a diagram is sketch it out in the margin of the test booklet. And when you draw the diagram, try to draw it to scale. That way, you'll be in a position to estimate.

What Should I Do If the Diagram Is Not Drawn to Scale?

The same thing you would do if there were no diagram at all—draw it yourself. Draw it as accurately as possible so you'll be able to see what a realistic answer should be.

Basic Principles: Fundamentals of GMAT Geometry

The techniques outlined above will enable you to eliminate many incorrect choices on geometry problems. In some cases, you'll be able to eliminate every choice but one. However, there will be some geometry problems on which you will need geometry. Fortunately, ETS chooses to test only a small number of concepts.

For the sake of simplicity, we've divided GMAT geometry into five basic topics:

1. degrees and angles
2. triangles
3. circles
4. rectangles, squares, and other four-sided objects
5. solids and volume

Degrees and Angles

There are a total of 360 degrees in a circle. It doesn't matter how large or small a circle is, it still has precisely 360 degrees. If you drew a circle on the ground and then walked a quarter of the distance around it, you would have traveled 90 degrees of that circle. If you walked halfway around the circle, you would have traveled 180 degrees of it.

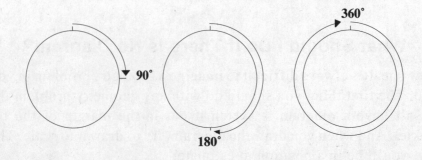

An angle is formed when two line segments extend from a common point. If you think of that point as the center of a circle, the measure of the angle is the number of degrees enclosed by the lines when they pass through the edge of the circle.

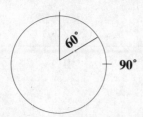

A line is just a 180-degree angle.

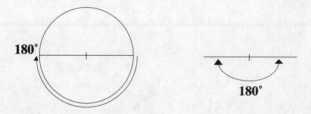

l is the symbol for a line. A line can be referred to as *l* or by naming two points on that line. For example, in the diagram below both points *A* and *B* are on the line *l*. This line could also be called line *AB*. The part of the line that is between points *A* and *B* is called a line segment. *A* and *B* are the end points of the line segment.

If a line is cut by another line, as in the diagram below, angle *x* and angle *y* add up to one straight line, or 180 degrees. If you knew that angle *x* equaled 120 degrees, you could find the measure of angle *y* by subtracting 120 degrees from 180 degrees. Thus angle *y* would equal 60 degrees.

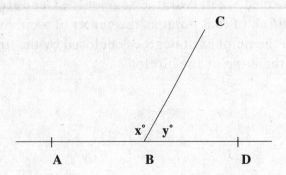

Note that in the diagram above angle *x* could also be called angle *ABC*, with *B* being the point in the middle.

When two lines intersect—as in the diagram below—four angles are formed. The four angles are indicated by letters.

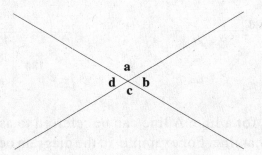

The four angles add up to 360 degrees (remember the circle).

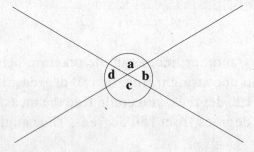

$a + b + c + d = 360$. Angle *a* + angle *b*, since they add up to a straight line, are equal to 180 degrees. Angle *b* + angle *c* also add up to a straight line, as do $c + d$ and $d + a$. Angles that are opposite each other are called *vertical angles* and have the same number of degrees. For example, in the diagram above, angle *a* is equal to angle *c*. Angle *d* is also equal to angle *b*.

Therefore when two lines intersect, there appear to be four different angles, but there are really only two:

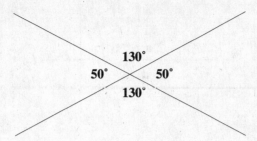

Two lines in the same plane are said to be parallel if they could extend infinitely in both directions without touching. The symbol for parallel is ∥. If two parallel lines are cut by a third line, eight separate angles are formed. Look at the diagram below:

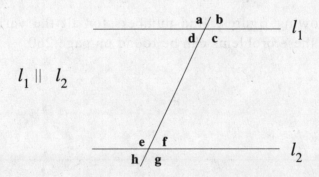

When two parallel lines are cut by a third line, there appear to be eight separate angles, but there are really only two. There is a big one (greater than 90°) and a little one (less than 90°). Angle *a* (a big one) is also equal to angles *c, e,* and *g.* Angle *b* (a little one) is also equal to angles *d, f,* and *h.*

If two lines intersect in such a way that one line is perpendicular to the other, all the angles formed will be 90-degree angles. These are also known as right angles:

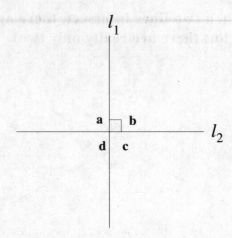

Angles *a, b, c,* and *d* each equal 90 degrees. The little box at the intersection of the two lines is the symbol for a right angle.

Angles and Lengths Drill

In the following figures, find numbers for all the variables. The answers to these problems can be found on page 260.

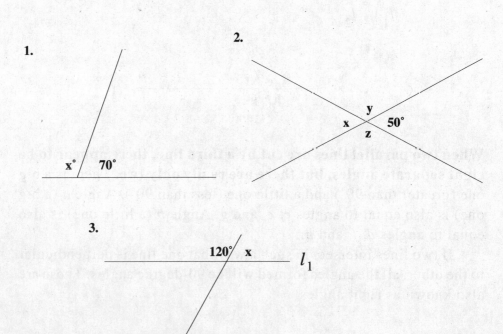

4. If a driver has traveled 270 degrees around a circular race track, what fractional part of the track has he driven?

A real GMAT angle problem might look like this:

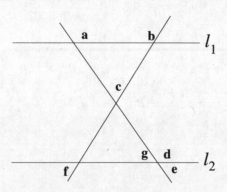

Note: Figure not drawn to scale.

5. In the figure above, if $l_1 \parallel l_2$, then which of the following angles must be equivalent?

   (A) *a* and *b*   (B) *g* and *f*   (C) *d* and *e*
   (D) *a* and *d*   (E) *f* and *d*

Triangles

A triangle is a three-sided figure that contains three interior angles. The interior angles of a triangle always add up to 180 degrees. Several kinds of triangles appear on the GMAT:

An *equilateral* triangle has three sides that are equal in length. Because the angles opposite equal sides are also equal, all three angles in an equilateral triangle are also equal.

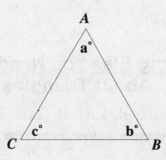

$AB = BC = CA$
$a = b = c = 60$

An *isosceles* triangle has two sides that are equal in length. The angles opposite those equal sides are also equal.

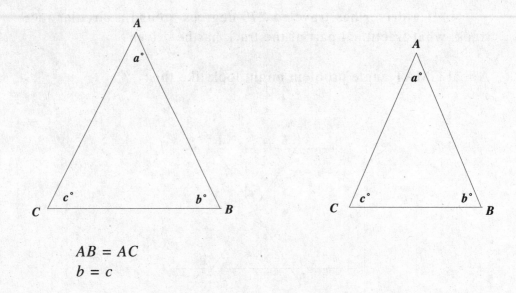

$AB = AC$
$b = c$

A *right* triangle has one interior angle that is equal to 90 degrees. The longest side of a right triangle (the one opposite the 90 degree angle) is called the *hypotenuse*.

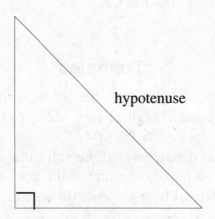

hypotenuse

Everything Else You Need to Know About Triangles

1. The sides of a triangle are in the same proportion as its angles. For example, in the triangle below, which is the longest side?

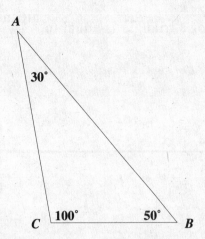

The longest side is opposite the longest angle. The longest side in the triangle above is *AB*. The next longest side would be *AC*.

2. *One side of a triangle can never be longer than the sum of the lengths of the other two sides of the triangle, or less than their difference.* Why? Look at the diagram below:

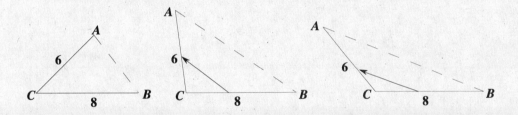

At the point where angle *ACB* = 180 degrees, this figure ceases to be a triangle. Angle *ACB* becomes 180 degrees when side *AB* equals the sum of the other two sides, in this case 6 + 8. Side *AB* can never quite reach 14.

By the same token, if we make angle *ACB* get smaller and smaller, at some point, when angle *ACB* = 0 degrees, the figure also ceases to be a triangle. Angle *ACB* becomes 0 degrees when side *AB* equals the difference of the other two sides, in this case 8 − 6. So *AB* can never quite reach 2.

3. The *perimeter* of a triangle is the sum of the lengths of the three sides.

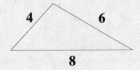

perimeter = 18

4. The *area* of a triangle is equal to $\dfrac{\text{altitude} \times \text{base}}{2}$

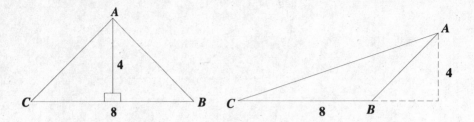

In both of the above triangles, the area $= \dfrac{8 \times 4}{2} = 16$

In a right triangle, the altitude also happens to be one of the sides of the triangle:

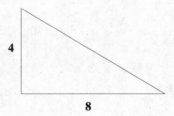

5. Don't expect triangles to be right side up:

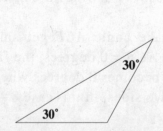

This is an *isosceles* triangle.

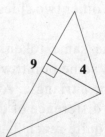

The area of this triangle is

$\dfrac{9 \times 4}{2}$, or 18.

6. In a right triangle, the square of the hypotenuse equals the sum of the squares of the other two sides. In the triangle below:

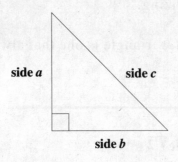

$$a^2 + b^2 = c^2$$

This is called the *Pythagorean* theorem. ETS loves to test this theorem, but usually you won't actually have to make use of it if you've memorized a few of the most common right-triangle proportions. The Pythagorean triangle that comes up most frequently on the GMAT is one that has sides of lengths 3, 4 and 5, or multiples of those numbers. Look at the following examples:

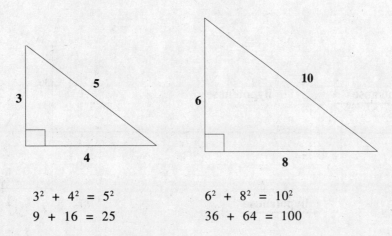

$$3^2 + 4^2 = 5^2$$
$$9 + 16 = 25$$

$$6^2 + 8^2 = 10^2$$
$$36 + 64 = 100$$

Some other Pythagorean triples:

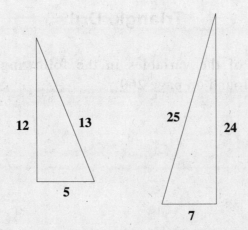

There are two other kinds of right triangles ETS loves to test. These are a little complicated to remember, but they come up so often that they're worth memorizing.

7. A *right isosceles* triangle is one that always has the following proportions:

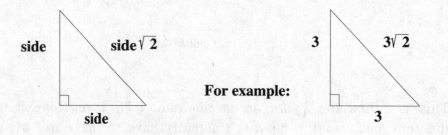

For example:

8. A *30-60-90* triangle is one that always has the following proportions:

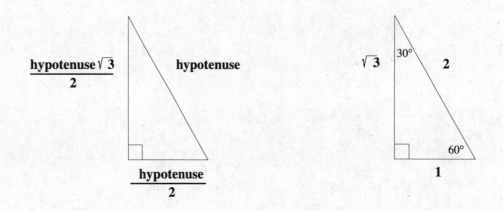

Triangle Drill

Find the value of the variables in the following problems. The answers can be found on page 260.

1.

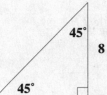

2.

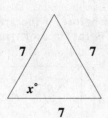

3.

4. What value must x be less than in the triangle below? What value must x be greater than?

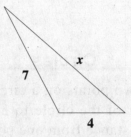

5. In the square $ABCD$ below, what is the value of line segment AC?

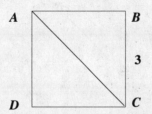

6. In the triangle below, what is the value of the line segment BC?

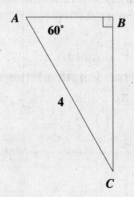

A real GMAT triangle problem might look like this:

7. In the diagram below, if the area of triangle *LNP* is 32, then what is the area of triangle *LMN*?

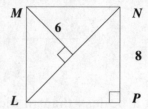

Note: Figure not drawn to scale.

(A) 24 (B) $24\sqrt{2}$ (C) $24\sqrt{3}$ (D) 32 (E) 48

Circles

A line connecting any two points on a circle is called a *chord*. The distance from the center of the circle to any point on the circle is called the *radius*. The distance from one point on the circle through the center of the circle to another point on the circle is called the *diameter*. The diameter is equal to twice the radius.

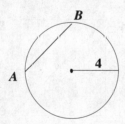

radius = 4
diameter = 8
AB is a chord
The rounded portion of the circle between points *A* and *B* is called an *arc*.

The *area* of a circle is equal to πr^2.
The *circumference* (the length of the entire outer edge of the circle) is equal to $2\pi r$ or πd.

Circle Drill

Answer the following questions. The answers can be found on page 260.

    1. In the diagram below, what is the area of the circle? What is the circumference?

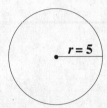

    2. If the area of a circle is 36π, what is the circumference?

    3. In the circle below, if the arc RT is equal to $\frac{1}{6}$ of the circumference, what is the value of angle x?

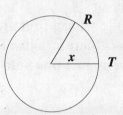

A real GMAT circle problem might look like this:

    4.   In the figure above, P is the center of the larger circle, and N is the center of the smaller, shaded circle. If the radius of the smaller circle is 5, what is the area of the unshaded region?

       (A) 100π (B) 75π (C) 25π (D) 20π (E) 10π

Rectangles, Squares, and Other Four-Sided Objects

A four-sided figure is called a **quadrilateral.** The perimeter of any four-sided object is the sum of the length of its sides. A rectangle is a quadrilateral whose four interior angles are each equal to 90 degrees.

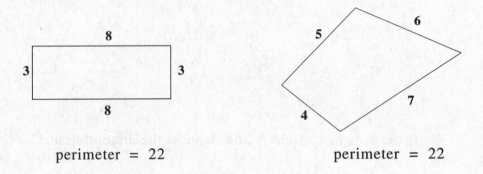

perimeter = 22   perimeter = 22

The area of a rectangle is *length × width*. The area of the rectangle above is therefore 3 × 8, or 24.

A *square* is a rectangle whose four sides are all equal in length. The perimeter of a square is therefore just four times the length of one side. The area of a square is just one side squared.

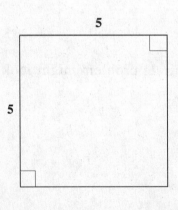

perimeter = 4 × 5 = 20
area = 5 × 5 = 25

A *parallelogram* is a quadrilateral in which the two pairs of opposite sides are parallel to each other and equal to each other, and in which opposite angles are equal to each other. A rectangle is obviously a parallelogram, but so is a figure like this:

228

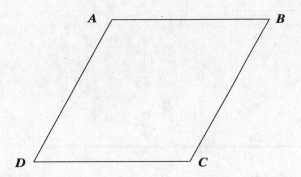

$$AB = DC. \quad AD = BC$$

Angle *ADC* = angle *ABC* and angle *DAB* = angle *DCB*.

The area of a parallelogram equals *base* × *height*.

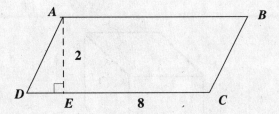

The area of parallelogram *ABCD* = 8 × 2 = 16. (If you are having trouble picturing this, imagine cutting off triangular region *ADE* and sticking it onto the other end of the figure. What you get is a rectangle with the dimensions 8 by 2.)

Solids, Volume, and Surface Area

The GMAT will occasionally ask you to find the volume or surface area of a three-dimensional object.

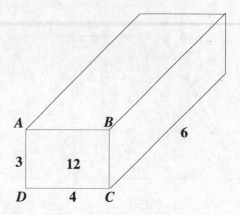

The volume of the *rectangular solid* above is equal to the area of
the rectangle *ABCD* times depth—in this case 12 × 6, or 72. Another
way to think of it is *length × width × depth* = 3 × 4 × 6, or 72.

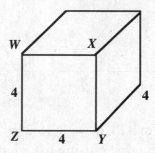

The volume of a *cube* is equal to the area of the square *WXYZ*
times depth, or again, *length × width × depth*. In the case of a square,
the length, width, and depth are all the same, so the volume of a cube
is always side cubed. The volume of this cube is 4 × 4 × 4, or 64.

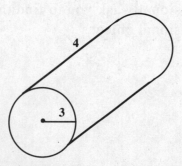

The volume of a *cylinder* is equal to the area of the circular base
times the depth. The area of this circle is 9π. Thus the volume of the
cylinder is 36π.

You may need to find the surface area of a solid. Surface area is just the sum of the areas of all the two-dimensional outer surfaces of the object. The surface area of a rectangular solid is just the sum of the two-dimensional areas of each of the six faces of the solid. For example, in the rectangular solid below, the surface area would be

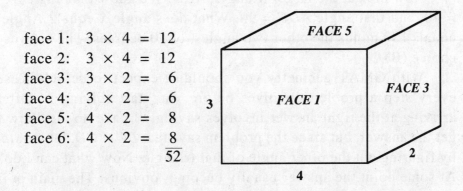

face 1: $3 \times 4 = 12$
face 2: $3 \times 4 = 12$
face 3: $3 \times 2 = 6$
face 4: $3 \times 2 = 6$
face 5: $4 \times 2 = 8$
face 6: $4 \times 2 = \underline{8}$
52

GMAT Geometry: Advanced Principles

All geometry problems (even easy ones) involve more than one step. Remember the first problem we looked at in this chapter?

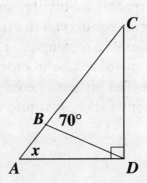

3. In the figure above, if $BC = CD$, and angle ADC = 90 degrees, then what is the value of x?

    (A) 45 (B) 50 (C) 70 (D) 75 (E) 100

Here's how to crack it: Just by looking at the figure, we were able to eliminate answer choices (C), (D), and (E). Now let's solve the problem using geometry. The figure includes two—actually three— different triangles: *ABD, BCD,* and *ACD.* ETS wants even this easy problem to be a little challenging; there must be more than one step involved. To find angle *x,* which is part of triangles *ABD* and *ACD,* we must first work on triangle *BCD.*

What do we know about triangle *BCD*? The problem itself tell us that *BC* = *CD*. This is an isosceles triangle. Since angle *DBC* equals 70, so does angle *BDC*. Angle *BCD* must therefore equal 180 minus the other two angles. Angle *BCD* = 40. In the diagram, write in the measure of angle *BCD*.

Now look at the larger triangle, *ACD*. We know that angle *ACD* = 40, and that angle *ADC* = 90. What does angle *x* equal? Angle *x* equals 180 minus the other two angles, or 50 degrees. The answer is choice (B).

With GMAT geometry you shouldn't expect to be able to see every step a problem involves before you start solving it. Often, arriving at the right answer involves saying, "I have no idea how to get the answer, but since the problem says that *BC* = *CD*, let me *start* by figuring out the other angle of that triangle. Now what can I do?" At some point the answer usually becomes obvious. The main point is not to stare at a geometry problem looking for a complete solution. Just wade in there and *start*.

Walking and Chewing Gum at the Same Time

Most GMAT geometry problems involve more than one geometric concept. A problem might require you to use both the properties of a triangle and the properties of a rectangle; or you might need to know the formula for the volume of a cube in order to find the dimensions of a cube's surface area. The difficult geometry problems do not test more complicated concepts—they just pile up easier concepts.

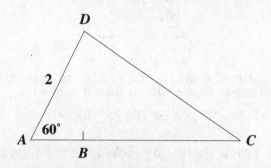

13. In the figure above, if a line segment connecting points *B* and *D* is perpendicular to *AC*, and the area of triangle *ADC* is $\frac{3\sqrt{3}}{2}$, then *BC* = ?

(A) $\sqrt{2}$ (B) $\sqrt{3}$ (C) 2   (D) $3\sqrt{3}$ (E) 5

Here's how to crack it: We already got the correct answer to this question by measuring; now let's solve it using geometry. If we draw in the line DB (which is perpendicular to AC), we form a 30-60-90 triangle on the left side of the diagram (triangle ADB). The hypotenuse of this triangle is 2. Using the rules we've learned, the measurements of triangle ADB are as follows:

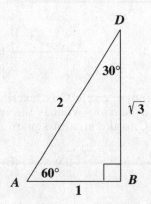

Thus $DB = \sqrt{3}$. At first you might think we're no closer to the solution, but don't despair. Just look for something else to *start*. The problem tells us that the area of triangle ADC is $\frac{3\sqrt{3}}{2}$. The area of a triangle is $\frac{\text{base} \times \text{altitude}}{2}$. DB is the altitude. Let's find out what the base is. In other words, $\frac{\text{base} \times \sqrt{3}}{2} = \frac{3\sqrt{3}}{2}$, so the base equals 3. We know from the 30-60-90 triangle that $AB = 1$. What is BC? 2. The answer is choice (C).

Plugging In on Geometry?

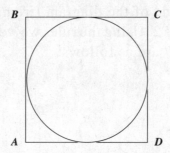

16. In the figure above, circle C is inscribed inside square *ABCD* as shown. What is the ratio of the area of circle C to the area of square *ABCD*?

(A) $\dfrac{\pi}{2}$ (B) $\dfrac{4}{\pi}$ (C) $\dfrac{\pi}{3}$ (D) $\dfrac{\pi}{4}$ (E) $\dfrac{2}{\pi}$

Here's how to crack it: We already saw this problem in the first half of the chapter when we discussed eliminating crazy answers. As you recall, we were able to eliminate answer choices (A), (B), and (C) because we determined that the correct answer had to be the ratio of a smaller number to a bigger number.

Now let's solve this problem completely. You may have noticed that the answer choices do not contain *specific numbers* for the areas of the two figures—all we have here are *ratios* in the answer choices. Sound familiar? That's right! This is just another cosmic problem, and the best way to solve it is to plug in.

To find the area of the circle, we need a radius. Let's just pick one—3. If the radius is 3, the area of the circle is 9π. Now let's tackle the square. The circle is inscribed inside the square, which means that the diameter of the circle is also the length of the side of the square. Since the radius of the circle is 3, the diameter is 6. Therefore the side of the square is 6, and the area is 36.

The problem asks for the ratio of the area of the circle to the area of the square:

$$\frac{9\pi}{36} = \frac{\pi}{4}$$ The answer is choice (D).

Summary

1. While the geometry found on the GMAT is rudimentary, you will have to memorize all formulas because they are not provided on the test.

2. Always estimate any problem drawn to scale in order to eliminate crazy answer choices.

3. You must know the following values:

$$\pi \approx 3 \quad \sqrt{2} \approx 1.4 \quad \sqrt{3} \approx 1.7$$

4. You must be familiar with the size of certain common angles:

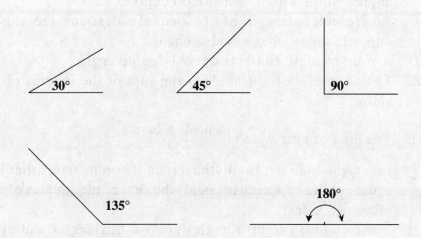

5. To estimate very precisely, you can use the top or bottom edge of your answer sheet as a ruler.

6. You can *never* estimate drawings on the Data Sufficiency section.

7. When no diagram is provided, make your own.

8. When the diagram is not drawn to scale, redraw it.

9. Degrees and angles:

    A. A circle contains 360 degrees.

    B. When you think about angles, remember circles.

    C. A line is a 180-degree angle.

    D. When two lines intersect, four angles are formed, but in reality there are only two.

    E. When two parallel lines are cut by a third line, eight angles are formed, but in reality there are only two: a big one and a little one.

10. Triangles:

    A. Every triangle contains 180 degrees.

    B. An equilateral triangle has three equal sides and three equal angles, all of which measure 60 degrees.

    C. An isosceles triangle has two equal sides, and the angles opposite those sides are also equal.

    D. A right triangle contains one 90-degree angle.

    E. The perimeter of a triangle is the sum of the lengths of its sides.

    F. The area of a triangle is $\dfrac{\text{altitude} \times \text{base}}{2}$.

    G. In a right triangle, the Pythagorean theorem states that the square of the hypotenuse equals the sum of the squares of the other two sides.

    H. Some common right triangles are 3-4-5 triangles and multiples of 3-4-5 triangles.

    I. Two other triangles that often appear on the GMAT are the right isosceles triangle and the 30-60-90 triangle. Memorize the formulas for these two triangles.

    J. The longest side of a triangle is opposite the largest angle; the shortest side is opposite the smallest angle.

    K. One side of a triangle can never be as large as the sum of the two remaining sides; nor can it ever be as small as the difference of the two remaining sides.

11. Circles:

    A. The circumference of a circle is $2\pi r$ or πd, where r is the radius of the circle and d is the diameter.

    B. The area of a circle is πr^2, where r is the radius of the circle.

GEOMETRY

12. Rectangles, squares, and other four-sided objects:

   A. Any four-sided object is called a quadrilateral.
   B. The perimeter of a quadrilateral is the sum of the lengths of the four sides.
   C. The area of a rectangle, or of a square, is equal to length times width.
   D. The area of a parallelogram is equal to altitude times base.

13. Solids and volume:

   A. The volume of most objects is equal to their two-dimensional area times depth.
   B. The volume of a rectangular solid is equal to length times width times depth.
   C. The volume of a cylinder is equal to the area of the circular base times depth.

14. GMAT geometry problems always involve more than one step. Difficult GMAT geometry problems layer several concepts on top of one another. Don't be intimidated if you don't see the entire process necessary to solve the problem. Start somewhere. You'll be amazed at how often you arrive at the answer.

CHAPTER FOURTEEN

Data Sufficiency

In the Data Sufficiency section there are 25 questions to be completed within thirty minutes. Like the regular math sections, the Data Sufficiency section gets more difficult as it goes along. It helps to think of Data Sufficiency problems as being in three separate groups:

Problems 1–8   relatively easy
Problems 9–17   medium
Problems 18–25   very difficult

For each group there is a different strategy. Joe Bloggs comes in very handy on Data Sufficiency questions.

What Is Data Sufficiency?

This question type requires some getting used to. When you take the exam, you'll notice that some of the people sitting around you in the examination room will spend at least the first ten minutes of the Data Sufficiency section just reading the directions. To avoid being among those unfortunate people, look at our version of the directions now:

Directions: In each of the Data Sufficiency problems below, you will find a question followed by two statements. You are not required to find the answer to the question; instead you must decide WHETHER the information given in the two statements is sufficient to answer the question, based on a knowledge of common facts (for example, the fact that an hour contains 60 minutes) and your understanding of the principles of math.

The answer to a data sufficiency question is

(A) if statement (1) BY ITSELF is sufficient to answer the question but statement (2) is not sufficient by itself;
(B) if statement (2) BY ITSELF is sufficient to answer the question but statement (1) is not sufficient by itself;
(C) if neither statement is sufficient by itself, but if the two statements IN COMBINATION are sufficient to answer the question.
(D) if EACH statement by itself is sufficient to answer the question;
(E) if NEITHER statement (1) nor statement (2) is sufficient to answer the question separately or in combination.

Numbers: This test uses only real numbers; no imaginary numbers are used or implied.

Diagrams: Diagrams in Data Sufficiency are drawn to scale according to the data contained in the QUESTION, but may not be drawn to scale in light of the new information contained in the two STATEMENTS:

All diagrams lie in a plane unless stated otherwise.
Angles shown cannot have a measure of 0 degrees.
A line shown as straight cannot bend.
Relative positions of objects, points, and angles cannot change.

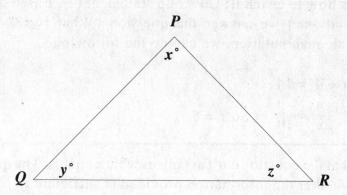

Example:

In triangle QPR above, what is the value of y?

(1) $x = 50$
(2) $z = 40$

Explanation: A triangle has a total of 180 degrees.

Statement (1) gives us one of the three angles, but without angle z we cannot know the measure of angle y. By itself, statement (1) does not answer the question.

Statement (2) gives us another of the three angles, but without angle x, we cannot know the measure of angle y. By itself, statement (2) does not answer the question.

In combination, however, statement (1) and statement (2) give us two out of three of the angles of the triangle. By subtracting the sum of the two angles from the measure of the entire triangle, we can determine the value of y. Thus, the answer is (C).

Basic Principles

You can see why it is absolutely necessary to learn these directions NOW. You shouldn't even have to glance at them when you take the test. Let's start with a simple example:

EXAMPLE 1

What is x?

(1) $2x + 4 = 14$
(2) $x + y = 7$

Here's how to crack it: Cover up statement (2). Based on statement (1) *alone,* can we answer the question "What is x?" Yes. Using algebraic manipulation, we can do the following:

$$2x + 4 = 14$$
$$\frac{-4}{2x} = \frac{-4}{10} \quad \text{So } x = 5$$

Note that the question isn't asking us what x equals. The question asks only whether the information provided is sufficient to *find out* what x equals.

In this case it is. Statement (1) gives us enough information to answer the question "What is x?"

If statement (1) is sufficient, you have narrowed your answer choice down to two possibilities:

    A) Statement (1) alone is sufficient, but statement (2) alone is not sufficient.

or

    D) EACH statement alone is sufficient

Now forget you ever saw statement (1). Cover it up with your finger and look only at statement (2). Based on statement (2) *alone,* can we find a single value for x?

No. The statement tells us that $x + y = 7$, in which case there are many possible values of x: If y equaled 2, then x could equal 5. On the other hand, if y equaled 3, then x could equal 4. Statement (2) is *not* sufficient to give us a single value for x.

Since (1) is sufficient and (2) is not, the answer to this question is choice (A).

Let's look at the same problem with the two statements reversed:

EXAMPLE 2
    What is x?

        (1) $x + y = 7$
        (2) $2x + 4 = 14$

Here's how to crack it: Cover up statement (2) and look at statement (1). Well, we know from the previous example that $x + y = 7$ does not give us a single value for x. So this time statement (1) is *not* sufficient.

In the first example, by deciding that statement (1) was sufficient, we narrowed our answer down to choice (A) or (D).

In this example, however, because (1) is *not* sufficient, we can eliminate answer choices (A) and (D).

Now cover up statement (1) and look at statement (2). Well, we already know from the first example that $2x + 4 = 14$ gives us a single value for x.

Since we know that (2) is sufficient, but (1) is not, the answer is choice (B).

EXAMPLE 3
What is x?

(1) $x + y = 7$
(2) $y = 2$

Here's how to crack it: Cover up statement (2) and look only at statement (1). By itself, (1) is not sufficient to answer the question. Eliminate answer choices (A) and (D).

Cover up statement (1) and look at statement (2). By itself, this statement tells us what y equals, but we need a value for x. Eliminate answer choice (B).

We're down to answer choice (C) or (E).

Now let's look at the two statements at the same time. Since we know from the second statement that $y = 2$, we can substitute for y in the first statement. Now it reads $x + 2 = 7$.

Do we have a single value for x? You bet!

Since neither statement by itself is sufficient, but both statements together are sufficient, the answer is choice (C).

EXAMPLE 4
What is x?

(1) $2x + 4 = 14$
(2) $3x = 15$

Here's how to crack it: Cover up statement (2). Based on statement (1) *alone,* can we get a single value for x? Yes. Using algebraic manipulation, we know that $x = 5$.

Since statement (1) is sufficient, we are already down to two possible answer choices: (A) or (D).

Now cover up statement (1). Based on statement (2) *alone,* can we get a single value for x? Yes. Using algebraic manipulation, we find that, again, $x = 5$.

Since each statement alone is sufficient, the answer is choice (D).

EXAMPLE 5

What is x?

(1) $x + y = 7$
(2) $y + z = 3$

Here's how to crack it: Cover up statement (2). Based on statement (1) alone, can we get a single value for x? No. Eliminate answer choices (A) and (D).

Cover up statement (1). Based on statement (2) alone, we still can't arrive at a single value for x. Eliminate answer choice (B).

We're down to answer choice (C) or (E).

Looking at both statements together, can we find a single value for x?

No. Because there are three different variables in the two equations, x could have many different values.

Since statements (1) and (2) are not sufficient by themselves OR together, the answer is choice (E).

Danish Data Sufficiency

In the examples above you may have noticed that we were already using the Process of Elimination. In Data Sufficiency a little knowledge goes a long way. Suppose you saw the following Data Sufficiency problem:

12. How tall is Frank?

(1) Frank is 6'2".
(2) Frank er en stor mand.

When we don't know something about a problem, our impulse is to skip the entire problem. Since you probably don't speak Danish, you have no idea whether the second statement is sufficient to answer the question.

However, it would be a mistake to skip this question.

Heads You Win a Dollar; Tails You Lose a Quarter

Let's focus on what you DO know. Cover up statement (2). Based on statement (1) *alone*, do you know how tall Frank is? Of course. He is 6'2". Since statement (1) is sufficient, the answer to this question is either

A) Statement (1) alone is sufficient

or

D) EACH statement ALONE is sufficient

By using POE, you've narrowed your choice down to two possibilities. You now have a fifty-fifty chance of getting this question correct, even though you know absolutely nothing about statement (2).

Tails You Lose a Quarter; Heads You Win a Dollar

As long as you know *something* about a Data Sufficiency problem, you can do some shrewd guessing. Look at the following problem:

12. How tall is Frank?

   (1) Frank er en stor mand.
   (2) Frank is pretty tall.

Since we have no idea what statement (1) says, let's cover it up and look at statement (2). Based on statement (2) *alone,* can you tell exactly how tall Frank is? Of course not. Since (2) is not sufficient, you can rule out choices (B) and (D).

By using POE in this case, you've narrowed your choice down to three possibilities—a one-in-three shot—even though the only thing you knew for certain about this problem was that one of the statements *did not* work.

Can't Make Head or Tail of the First Statement?

If you're having trouble understanding the first statement, skip it for a minute and look at the second statement. If it is sufficient, you can eliminate answer choices (A), (C), and (E) and be down to a fifty-fifty guess—choice (B) or (D). If it is not sufficient, you can eliminate answer choices (B) and (D), and have a one-in-three shot at getting the problem right.

How Does Joe Do on Data Sufficiency?

Joe Bloggs does well on the easy Data Sufficiency problems (1–8). He gets a few of the medium problems (9–17), and then he gets *all* of the difficult problems wrong.

This is bad news for Joe, but good news for you. On the early problems, if you pay close attention to the method we've outlined in the preceding five examples, you'll get the correct answer most of the time. There are no tricks in those first eight problems. ETS has designed them so that Joe will get most of them right.

On the medium problems, however, it isn't enough to merely understand the directions; you must begin using POE to eliminate answers. Some of these medium problems will contain traps that ETS hopes will trip you up. We'll show you some of ETS's favorite traps in just a minute.

On the difficult problems, virtually every question contains a trap. Joe Bloggs invariably picks the wrong answer on the last seven problems of Data Sufficiency. By learning to recognize the traps ETS has set for Joe, you can eliminate even more wrong answers. Sometimes all that remains is the correct answer.

Data Sufficiency Math Versus Problem-Solving Math

In terms of mathematical content, the Data Sufficiency section tests the same kinds of topics tested by the regular math sections. You'll find problems involving integers, percents, averages, ratios, algebra, and geometry. Only the format is different.

Let's do an easy "regular" math problem and then turn it into a Data Sufficiency problem.

3. A certain factory has filled 92 orders. If the total number of orders on file is 230, what percent of the orders have been filled?

    (A) 20% (B) 30% (C) 40% (D) 50% (E) 60%

If you've already done the math review in the preceding chapters, this problem should be very easy. It's a percent problem, and as soon as you see the word "percent," you should immediately be thinking

$$\frac{\text{part}}{\text{whole}} = \frac{92}{230} = \frac{x}{100}$$

(the answer, by the way, is (C) 40%)

Now let's turn this same problem into a Data Sufficiency problem.

3. If a certain factory has filled 92 orders, what percent of the total number of orders has been filled?

   (1) The total number of orders on file is 230.
   (2) The number of orders the factory has already filled represents two-fifths of the total number of orders.

Here's how to crack it: Although the problem is now in a different format, the math involved is exactly the same. Again, as soon as you see the word "percent," you should be thinking

$$\frac{\text{part}}{\text{whole}}$$

Without looking at the two statements, let's look at the information contained in the question itself and set that up as a part-over-whole equation:

$$\frac{\text{part}}{\text{whole}} \quad \frac{92}{?} = \frac{x}{100}$$

As this equation stands, there is no way to find a value for x. We have the **part** (the number of orders that have already been filled), but we do not have the **whole** (total number of orders).

Cover up statement (2). Does statement (1) alone give us the missing whole? Yes, it does. Therefore, the answer to this question is either choice (A) or (D).

Now cover up statement (1). Statement (2) expresses the number of orders already filled as a fraction of the total number of orders. Remember, a fraction is *also* a part over whole. Let's see what we have:

$$\frac{\text{part}}{\text{whole}} \quad \frac{2}{5} = \frac{x}{100}$$

Can we find a value for x in this equation? Of course. Therefore statement (2) is also sufficient, and the answer to this question is choice (D).

Math Is Math Is Math

All Data Sufficiency problems are just standard math problems in a new format. Look for the clue that tells you what to do, then see whether the two statements provide you with enough information to answer the question.

Except on Yes or No Questions

Leave it to ETS to come up with a way to give you five different answer choices on a "yes or no" question. Let's look at an example:

> 7. Did candidate x receive more than 40% of the 30,000 votes cast in the general election?
>
> (1) Candidate y received 45% of the votes.
> (2) Candidate x received exactly 11,000 votes.

Here's how to crack it: When all is said and done, the answer to this question is either yes or no.

Cover up statement (2). Does statement (1) alone answer the question? If you were in a hurry, you might think so. Many people just assume that statement (1) is talking about candidate x—in which case they get the problem wrong. Other people notice that statement (1) is talking about candidate y but assume that these are the only two candidates running in the election (in which case, since candidate y received 45%, candidate x must have received 55%). Since the problem doesn't *say* that there were only two candidates, statement (1) doesn't answer the question.

Now cover up statement (1) and let's look at statement (2). This seems more promising. Like the problem we saw earlier involving factory orders, this problem is also about percents, so again we think:

$$\frac{\text{part}}{\text{whole}} \quad \frac{11,000}{30,000} = \frac{x}{100}$$

Using algebraic manipulation, we learn that $x = 36.6\%$. At which point many people say, "The guy got less than 40%—this statement doesn't answer the question, either."

But they're wrong.

Just Say No

Broken down to its basics, the question we were asked was, "Did he get more than 40% of the vote—yes or no?"

Statement (2) *does* answer the question. The answer is, "No, he didn't."

On a yes or no Data Sufficiency problem, if a statement answers the question in the affirmative *or* in the negative, it is sufficient. The answer to question number 7 above is choice (B).

How to Keep It All Straight

Since there can be as many as nine yes or no problems in a Data Sufficiency section, it's a good idea to have a strategy. When yes or no questions involve variables, there's a good way to keep everything straight. Here's an example:

10. Is x an integer?

    (1) $5x$ is a positive integer
    (2) $5x = 1$

Here's how to crack it: As always, cover up statement (2). Look only at statement (1). Let's plug in a value for x, a number that anyone, even Joe Bloggs, might pick. How about 2? We know that $5 \times 2 = 10$, which is a positive integer. Is 2 an integer? Yes.

What we've just found is *one case* in which the answer to question 10 is yes. If x is *always* an integer, then the answer is always yes, and statement (1) is sufficient. If x is *never* an integer, the answer would always be no, and statement (1) would *still* be sufficient (remember, the answer to a yes or no question can be no).

But if statement (1) gives us an answer that is sometimes yes and sometimes no, then the statement is no good.

By plugging in, we found *one case* in which the answer to the question is yes. Now all we need to do is see whether we can find *one case* in which the answer to the question is no. The statement says,

(1) $5x$ is a positive integer

Most numbers we could plug in for x to make the statement true are integers. Is there ANY value of x that makes the statement true, but isn't itself an integer? What if x were $\frac{1}{5}$?

We know that $5 \times \frac{1}{5} = 1$, which *is* a positive integer; but now x is *not* an integer. By plugging in $\frac{1}{5}$, we have found one case in which the answer is no. Since statement (1) gives us an answer that is sometimes yes and sometimes no, the statement is not sufficient.

Cover up statement (1) and look at statement (2):

$$(2)\ 5x = 1$$

To make this statement true, x *must* equal $\frac{1}{5}$. Is x an integer? No. We have now found *one case* in which the answer is no. Is there any other number we could plug in for x that would make the statement true? No.

Since statement (2) gives us an answer that is *always* no, the statement is sufficient, and the answer to this question is choice (B).

Dr. Livingston, I Presume?

Stanley would not have done well on the GMAT with that kind of careless presumption. The test-makers at ETS like to see whether they can get you to make careless assumptions. Here's an example:

10. Two people went into an executive trainee program at the same time. How much more money per week does trainee A now earn than trainee B?

   (1) Trainee A earns $300 per week more than she did when she began the program.
   (2) Trainee B earns $100 more per week than she did when she began the program.

Here's how to crack it: In this problem everyone's first impression is that the answer is choice (C) (both statements together are sufficient). Most people make the perfectly natural assumption that both trainees started at the same salary. But do we *know* this?

Never Assume

On medium or difficult questions, you can never assume *anything*. The answer to this question is choice (E) because the two trainees may have had different starting salaries.

14. At a business dinner, people were offered coffee or tea. If all the diners had either coffee or tea, how many of the diners had tea?

(1) Of 60 people at the dinner, 10% had tea.
(2) Fifty-four people had coffee.

Here's how to crack it: Statement (1) is sufficient because 10% of 60 = 6. Now look at statement (2). At first glance this seems sufficient as well. We just found out from statement (1) that there were a total of 60 people at the dinner. If 54 of them had coffee, then the other 6 had tea, which agrees with the number we got in statement (1). There is only one hitch: Statement (2) by itself does not tell us the total number of people at the dinner. We are subconsciously relying on information in statement (1).

Just Because One Statement Seems to Agree with the Other Doesn't Mean They Are Necessarily Saying the Same Thing

If statement (2) had said "two people had coffee," you would have eliminated it right away. But because it seemed to agree with statement (1), it became much more tempting. Just remember: When you look at statement (2), *always cover up statement* (1) *and forget you ever saw it.* The answer to this question is choice (A).

Cracking Data Sufficiency: Advanced Principles

When our students take their first practice GMAT with us, they generally get less than 10 percent of the difficult Data Sufficiency problems correct. When you consider that random guessing would have gotten them 20 percent correct, you begin to see that the axiom we gave you for the regular math sections is true here as well:

On difficult problems, answers that seem correct at first glance are never correct. By eliminating the answers Joe Bloggs wants to pick, you can improve the odds tremendously.

Joe's Favorite Answers

Joe Bloggs's initial reaction to a difficult Data Sufficiency question is, "I don't know how to do this." This statement doesn't seem to help Joe in answering the question. Therefore on questions he perceives to be difficult, Joe's favorite answer is usually choice (E) (statements (1) and (2) TOGETHER are not sufficient).

His second favorite answer is choice (C) (BOTH statements TOGETHER are sufficient, but neither statement alone is sufficient). Joe likes choice (C) because he assumes that a difficult question like this one will need a lot of information.

Joe's favorite answers on tough Data Sufficiency questions are choices (E) and (C), but that doesn't mean these will never be the answer to difficult questions. We should eliminate choice (E) and/or (C) *only* when they are Joe Bloggs's first or second impulse.

18. If $xy \neq 0$, what is the value of $\dfrac{x^4 y^3 z^2}{y^2 x^2 y^1 z^2}$?

  (1) $x = 3$
  (2) $y = 5$

Here's how to crack it: Joe's *first* impulse here might be to pick answer choice (E). He sees an expression with x's, y's, and z's, but the two statements underneath give values only for x and y.

If Joe thinks for a minute, he might realize that there is a $\{z^2\}$ in the numerator and a $\{z^2\}$ in the denominator. These cancel out, eliminating all the z's in the expression. Joe's *second* impulse might be to pick answer choice (C). He now sees an equation with x's and y's, and assumes he will need values for both in order to answer the question.

Having eliminated Joe's answers, we're down to choices (A), (B), or (D). If that's as far as you have time to get on this problem, guess and move on. You have a one-in-three shot of getting it right—good odds.

The correct answer is answer choice (A). The $\{y^2\}$ and the $\{y^1\}$ in the denominator can be consolidated to form $\{y^3\}$. The y's cancel out.

When Joe Thinks a Tough Question Is Easy

The only time the correct answer to a tough Data Sufficiency question will actually turn out to be (E) or (C) is when Joe is convinced that the question is easy.

19. What was the combined average attendance at
    Memorial Stadium for the months of June and July?

    (1) The average attendance for the month of June
        was 23,100, and the average attendance for
        the month of July was 25,200.
    (2) There were 20 games played in June at the
        stadium and 22 games played in July.

Here's how to crack it: Joe thinks this is an easy one. Statement (1) gives us the average attendance for June and the average attendance for July. Joe probably decides this is sufficient by itself. He thinks you can get the total average of the two months by averaging the two averages. (You—having completed our chapter on arithmetic—know better.) Joe looks at statement (2) and doesn't see any attendance figures at all. He picks answer choice (A).

Because he is convinced that this is an easy question and that the answer is choice (A), Joe Bloggs never even considers his two favorite answers—choices (E) and (C). *This* time he *knows* he's right!

But, of course, he is wrong. The answer to this question is choice (C). An average is the *total* sum of values divided by the total number of values. We need to know the number of games in each month in order to find out the *total* number of people attending.

Putting It All Together

Eliminating Joe Bloggs answers gives you an enormous advantage on Data Sufficiency problems. But by coupling this technique with POE, you can do even better. Remember our Danish question?

12. How tall is Frank?

    (1) Frank is 6'2".
    (2) Frank er en stor mand.

Using POE, and completely ignoring statement (2), we were able to get down to a fifty-fifty choice. Since statement (1) unequivocally answers the question, we knew the answer had to be choice (A) or (D). Now suppose this had been question 25 instead of question 12. We were already down to a fifty-fifty choice. The answer is choice (A) or (D).

Consider for a moment: Which of the two remaining choices does Joe like?

Since Joe doesn't know anything about statement (2), he'll probably choose (A). This is question 25. There's no way Joe's answer could be correct. In that case we'd better pick answer choice (D).

Here's one last example:

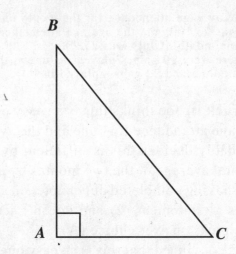

23. If the perimeter of right triangle *ABC* above is 3 + 3 $\sqrt{3}$, what is the area of the triangle?

(1) Side *AC* ≠ side *AB*.
(2) Angle *ABC* = 30 degrees.

Here's how to crack it: The area of a triangle is $\frac{1}{2}$ *base × height*. Joe looks at statements (1) and (2) and sees neither the length of the base nor the length of the height. Joe likes choice (E) a lot on this problem. He doesn't see how he can get the area of the triangle from this information. Joe might also be tempted by choice (C) just because it seems like he is being given an awful lot of information; maybe, he reasons, there's some formula he doesn't know about.

Let's look at the problem seriously now. Cover up statement (2). Statement (1) tells us only that two of the sides of the triangle are not equal. Is there any conceivable way this information could help us find the base and the height of the triangle? No, statement (1) doesn't answer the question. Since statement (1) is not sufficient by itself, we can eliminate answer choices (A) and (D).

We are left with three choices: (B), (C), or (E).

Are any of these choices Joe Bloggs answers? Well, yes. We decided a moment ago that choice (E) was definitely Joe Bloggs and that, in fact, choice (C) might be as well. It therefore seems quite likely that the answer is choice (B).

Here's how ETS wants you to crack it: Statement (2) tells us that the right triangle is a 30-60-90 triangle. If you have already read our chapter on geometry, you know that the dimensions of a 30-60-90 triangle are always in the same proportion: The short side (the side opposite the 30-degree angle) is always equal to half the hypotenuse, and the middle side is always equal to the short side times $\sqrt{3}$. If we call the short side x, then the hypotenuse is $2x$ and the middle side is $x\sqrt{3}$. Thus the formula for the perimeter of a 30-60-90 triangle is $3x + x\sqrt{3}$, where x is the side opposite the 30-degree angle. If we set this equal to the actual perimeter of the triangle, we can solve for x.

$$3x + x\sqrt{3} = 3 + 3\sqrt{3}$$

After a lot of work solving for x, it turns out that $x = \sqrt{3}$. This is equal to the base of our triangle. We can now figure out the height, which would be the short side ($\sqrt{3}$) times $\sqrt{3}$, or 3. If we know the base and the height, we can figure out the area, which means that statement (2) is sufficient, and the answer is choice (B).

Wait a minute! If the base is $\sqrt{3}$ and the height is 3, doesn't this agree with statement (1) that AC $\neq$ AB? Sure, but so what? Just because statement (1) seems to *agree* with statement (2) doesn't mean it says the same thing.

That Was a Lot of Work

This problem was very difficult and took a long time if you actually tried to solve it mathematically, the way ETS wanted you to. You will notice that we got the same answer within only a few seconds by using a combination of POE and the Joe Bloggs technique.

Using our method isn't infallible, but unless you're extremely good at Data Sufficiency, you'll probably do better on the last seven problems by using POE and Joe Bloggs than you will by trying to figure out the answer mathematically.

There just isn't time.

Summary

1. The 25 Data Sufficiency questions are presented in order of difficulty. Numbers 1–8 are relatively easy, 9–17 are medium, 18–25 are very difficult.

2. The instructions for this section are very complicated. Memorize them now. Here is a pared-down checklist:

- If only the first statement answers the question, the answer is choice (A).
- If only the second statement answers the question, the answer is choice (B).
- If you need both statements together to answer the question, the answer is choice (C).
- If both statements individually answer the question, the answer is choice (D).
- If neither statement, together or separately, answers the question, the answer is choice (E).

3. Use the Process of Elimination to narrow down the field. If you *know* that one statement is sufficient, you are already down to a fifty-fifty guess. If you *know* that one statement is *not* sufficient, you are already down to a one-in-three guess.

4. If you are stuck on statement (1), skip it and look at statement (2). POE will be just as helpful.

5. The math content of the Data Sufficiency section is exactly the same as it is on the regular math sections.

6. As you would in the regular math sections, look for the clues that tell you how to solve a particular problem.

7. When a problem asks a "yes or no" question, remember that the answer can be no.

8. In "yes or no" questions, a statement is sufficient if it always gives us the *same* answer: always yes or always no. If the answer is sometimes yes and sometimes no, the statement is insufficient.

9. In the medium and difficult portions of the Data Sufficiency section, you must be on guard against careless assumptions.

10. In the *difficult* portions of the Data Sufficiency section:

- If Joe Bloggs *thinks* the problem is difficult, his favorite answers are choices (E) ("there isn't enough information") or (C) ("this problem needs all the information it can get").
- If Joe Bloggs thinks the problem is easy, he will be drawn to choices (A), (B), or (D).

11. On difficult Data Sufficiency questions, Joe's answer is always wrong.

12. By combining the techniques of POE and Joe Bloggs, you can do some very shrewd guessing on the most difficult problems. If you *know* that one statement is sufficient, you're already down to a fifty-fifty choice. Is Joe Bloggs attracted to either of the two answers that remain? If he is, pick the other one. If you *know* that one statement is not sufficient, you have a one-in-three shot at guessing the right answer. Is Joe attracted to any of these three? If he is, choose among the remaining answers.

PART FOUR

ANSWER KEY TO DRILLS

DRILL 1
(pages 158–59)
1) 77
2) 79
3) 10
4) 16
5) choice (B)

DRILL 2
(pages 159–60)
1) $9 \times 30 = 270$
2) $55 \times 100 = 5500$
3) ab + ac − ad
4) c(ab + xy)
5) $\dfrac{12y - 6y}{y} = \dfrac{y(6)}{y} = 6$

   Choice (B)

DRILL 3
(page 165)

1) $\dfrac{145}{24}$ or $6\dfrac{1}{24}$

2) $\dfrac{1}{5}$

3) $\dfrac{29}{3}$

4) 18
5) choice (C)

DRILL 4
(page 169)
1) 24.66
2) 266.175
3) 6.09
4) 8
5) choice (C)

DRILL 5 (ANGLES AND LENGTHS)
(pages 218–19)
1) $x = 110°$
2) $x = 50°$ $y = 130°$ $z = 130°$
3) $x = 60°$ $y = 120°$ $z = 120°$
4) $\dfrac{3}{4}$

5) choice (D)

DRILL 6 (TRIANGLES)
(pages 224–26)
1) $x = 8$
2) $x = 60$
3) $x = 5$
4) x must be less than 11 and greater than 3
5) $3\sqrt{2}$
6) $2\sqrt{3}$
7) choice (B)

DRILL 7 (CIRCLES)
(page 227)
1) area = 25
   circumference = 10
2) circumference = 12
3) 60°
4) choice (B)

PART FIVE

THE
PRINCETON
REVIEW
GMAT
DIAGNOSTIC

Graduate Management

Admission Test

584

THE
PRINCETON
REVIEW

SECTION 2
Time—30 Minutes
20 Questions

Directions: In this section solve each problem, using any available space on the page for scratchwork. Then indicate the best of the answer choices given.

Numbers: All numbers used are real numbers.

Figures: Figures that accompany problems in the text are intended to provide information useful in solving the problems. They are drawn as accurately as possible EXCEPT when it is stated in a specific problem that its figure is not drawn to scale. All figures lie in a plane unless otherwise indicated.

1. If $(16)(3)^2 = x(2^3)$, then $x =$

(A) 81 (B) 72 (C) 18 (D) 16 (E) 8

2. Starting at 9 a.m. on a certain day, snow began to fall at a rate of $1\frac{1}{4}$ inches every two hours until 3 p.m. If there were already $2\frac{1}{4}$ inches of snow on the ground at 9 a.m., how many inches of snow were on the ground at 3 p.m. that day?

(A) $3\frac{3}{4}$ (B) 6 (C) 7 (D) $7\frac{1}{2}$ (E) $9\frac{3}{4}$

3. $\dfrac{\frac{1}{2}}{\frac{2}{3} - \frac{1}{4}} =$

(A) $\frac{2}{7}$ (B) $\frac{3}{4}$ (C) $\frac{12}{5}$ (D) 5 (E) 12

4. At a Wall Street company, 70 percent of this year's new employees are graduates of business schools and the remainder are graduates of liberal arts colleges. If 550 new employees were hired this year, what is the difference between the number of new business school employees and the number of new liberal arts employees?

(A) 55 (B) 220 (C) 240 (D) 385 (E) 440

GO ON TO THE NEXT PAGE.

Note: Section 1 of this test was the experimental section and has been left out since it did not count toward your score.

5. $(165)^2 - (164)^2 =$

(A) 1
(B) 2
(C) 4
(D) 325
(E) 329

6. The formula $E = \sqrt{\dfrac{a}{6}}$ describes the relationship between the length of the edge E of a cube and the surface area a of the cube. How much longer is the edge of a cube with a surface area of 1350 than the edge of one with a surface area of 600?

(A) 5   (B) 15   (C) 150   (D) 250   (E) 750

7. If y is an odd integer, which of the following must be an even integer?

(A) $y + 2$ (B) $y + 6$ (C) $2y - 1$
(D) $3y$ (E) $3y + 1$

8. If $x = \dfrac{5}{6} + \dfrac{15}{18} - \dfrac{10}{12}$, then $(x - 1)^3 =$

(A) $-\dfrac{1}{216}$ (B) $-\dfrac{1}{6}$ (C) $\dfrac{1}{6}$

(D) $\dfrac{27}{216}$ (E) $\dfrac{125}{216}$

9. There are 240 doctors and nurses at a hospital. If the ratio of doctors to nurses is 5 to 7, how many nurses are at the hospital?

(A) 20   (B) 60   (C) 100   (D) 140   (E) 180

10. A popular book club, which formerly offered five promotional books for $1, now offers four of them for $1. The new price for each book was what percent greater than the old price for each book?

(A) 0.25%
(B) 1%
(C) 5%
(D) 20%
(E) 25%

11. If k is an integer greater than 44 and less than 51, then which of the following could be the product of 11 and k?

(A) 565   (B) 550   (C) 500   (D) 484   (E) 440

GO ON TO THE NEXT PAGE.

12. If the temperature rises 25 percent from *d* degrees to 60 degrees, then 60 − *d* =

    (A) 12   (B) 30   (C) 35   (D) 48   (E) 85

13. A computer is programmed to generate a list of multiples of prime numbers 2, 3 and 5, as shown below:

    _____

    Program 1- *List multiples of 2*
    Program 2- *List multiples of 3*
    Program 3- *List multiples of 5*
    _____

    How many integers less than 100 will appear on all of the lists of programs produced above?

    (A) None
    (B) 1
    (C) 3
    (D) 5
    (E) An infinite number of integers

14. A grocer is storing small cereal boxes in large cartons that measure 25 inches by 42 inches by 60 inches. If the measurement of each small cereal box is 7 inches by 6 inches by 5 inches, then what is the maximum number of small cereal boxes that can be placed in each large carton?

    (A) 25   (B) 210   (C) 252   (D) 300   (E) 420

15. Sue is now 10 years younger than Jane. If in 5 years, Jane will be twice as old as Sue, how old will Sue be in 3 years?

    (A) 6   (B) 8   (C) 11   (D) 14   (E) 18

16. The price for a pair of cuff links is $1. The price for a 5-pair package of cuff links is $3.40. The 5-pair package is what percent cheaper per pair than 5 pairs purchased separately?

    (A) 63%   (B) 62%   (C) 55%
    (D) 32%   (E) 20%

17. If x, y and z are non-zero numbers such that $1 \geq y > x$ and $xy = z$, which of the following cannot be true?

    (A) $y > z$ (B) $y = z$ (C) $z = x$
    (D) $x > z$ (E) $z > 0$

GO ON TO THE NEXT PAGE.

266

18. A company bought a total of 60 computers and 20 printers to modernize billing operations. If the price of each computer was three times the price of each printer, what percent of the total cost of the purchase was the total cost of the printers?

(A) 10% (B) 11% (C) 15% (D) 20% (E) 25%

19. A machine costs m dollars per day to maintain and n cents for each unit it produces. If the machine is operated 7 days a week and produces r units in a week, which of the following is the total cost, in dollars, of operating the machine for a week?

(A) $7m + 100nr$ (B) $\dfrac{700m + nr}{100}$ (C) $m + nr$

(D) $\dfrac{7m + 100nr}{100}$ (E) $700mnr$

20. A shipment of banners contains banners of two different shapes, triangular and square, and two different colors, red and green. In a particular shipment 26% of the banners are square and 35% of the banners are red. If 60% of the red banners in the shipment are square, what is the ratio of red triangular banners to green triangular banners?

(A) $\dfrac{7}{50}$ (B) $\dfrac{3}{13}$ (C) $\dfrac{7}{30}$ (D) $\dfrac{13}{37}$ (E) $\dfrac{35}{26}$

S T O P

IF YOU FINISH BEFORE TIME IS CALLED, YOU MAY CHECK YOUR WORK ON THIS SECTION ONLY.
DO NOT WORK ON ANY OTHER SECTION IN THE TEST.

SECTION 3
Time—30 Minutes
25 Questions

<u>Directions</u>: Each passage in this group is followed by questions based on its content. After reading a passage, choose the best answer to each question and blacken the corresponding space on the answer sheet. Answer all questions following a passage on the basis of what is <u>stated</u> or <u>implied</u> in that passage.

While anti-slavery sentiment eventually dictated policy in both the United States and Great Britain, the course of abolition differed greatly in the two nations. In America, the
(5) institution of slavery was vehemently defended in a debate that ultimately resulted in the Civil War of 1860. In Britain, by contrast, slavery was outlawed by 1807 and barred throughout its colonial possessions by 1833. In analyzing
(10) Britain's course, historians have well documented the influences of economic change, humanitarian protest and reform movement.

One factor that has been largely ignored by scholars, however, is the impetus that was
(15) provided by children's literature. This medium gained great popularity in Britain during the last half of the eighteenth century and provided direct access to young, impressionable minds. Consequently, children's literature constituted the
(20) perfect vehicle for the dissemination of humanitarian ideas and played a vital role in creating anti-slavery concerns.

In 1761, John Newberry's *Tom Telescope* included the first known reference to the slave
(25) trade in children's literature. Tom, the book's protagonist, took issue with a man who doted on his household pet yet, as a slave merchant, thought "nothing of separating the husband from the wife, the parents from the children." Slavery
(30) was not only cruel and oppressive, Tom seemed to be saying, but it was also irrational and contrary to natural law. Written before much of the horrors of the Atlantic slave trade were revealed, *Tom Telescope* contained an implicit message.
(35) Soon afterward, writers and publishers were in a position to be more explicit. One of the leaders in this crusade was the Society of Friends who, in 1787, published *Little Truths*. Passages in this work directly related conditions aboard slave
(40) ships: "children were the steerage, pressed together like herrings in a barrel."

Around the turn of the century, blacks were introduced for the first time as main characters in children's literature. An early example of this

(45) device is found in Thomas Day's immensely popular *The History of Sandford and Merton* (1783-1789), in which a black beggar miraculously rescues Harry Sandford from a raging bull. Significantly, Day says very little
(50) about the institution of slavery itself, but the reader is left with no doubt that it is inhumane and cruel.

While it would be misleading to assume that every children's book published between 1750 and
(55) 1850 contained anti-slavery sentiments, the numbers are significant enough to suggest that they played a vital role in shaping attitudes toward blacks. At the same time, even when the capabilities of blacks were recognized, there was
(60) always a tendency to depict them as different rather than equal. Perhaps unwittingly, children's literature helped to form a stereotype that—while successfully attacking slavery—also strengthened the 19th century Englishmen's sense of racial
(65) superiority.

1. According to the passage, all of the following may have been factors in creating anti-slavery sentiment in the British territories EXCEPT:

(A) children's literature
(B) economic changes
(C) the Civil War of 1860
(D) protest by humanitarian groups
(E) the reform movement

GO ON TO THE NEXT PAGE.

2. It can be inferred from the passage that at the time of the publication of John Newberry's *Tom Telescope* in 1761,

(A) there was no anti-slavery sentiment in England
(B) little was known about the horrors of conditions aboard slave ships
(C) the protagonist of the book, Tom, was already a popular literary character in England
(D) it was generally accepted in England that slavery was irrational and contrary to natural law
(E) it was common practice in England to separate husbands from wives

3. It can be inferred from the passage that John Newberry's book *Tom Telescope* was important for which of the following reasons?

(A) It marked an early example of children's literature that was widely available to the public.
(B) It was the first children's book to explicitly advocate the abolition of slavery.
(C) It compared slaves to household pets, and advocated fair treatment of both.
(D) It advocated compassionate humanitarianism.
(E) It was the first book written for children to imply that slavery was wrong.

4. It can be inferred from the passage that the author believes which of the following to be true about British authors of children's literature in the mid-18th century?

(A) Their writing played a major role in all reforms of the 19th century.
(B) Most were not only talented story writers but accomplished historians.
(C) They believed that blacks were equal rather than different.
(D) Some were more concerned with the treatment of pets than with the treatment of people.
(E) A significant number of these writers were opposed to slavery.

5. Which of the following best describes the organization of the passage?

(A) An observation is made and then some exceptions to it are noted.
(B) A hypothesis is presented and then examples that support and oppose the theory are given.
(C) An idea is first supported, and then evidence is introduced to disprove it.
(D) A theory is presented and then data is introduced to support it.
(E) Current beliefs are challenged and new evidence is presented.

6. The author of this passage states that some 18th-century children's literature in Britain portrayed

(A) children as the ideal audience for humanitarian ideas
(B) miserliness and prejudice as American evils
(C) slave merchants as cruel and irrational
(D) British politicians as slow to initiate humanitarian reform
(E) blacks in the same way as other British citizens

GO ON TO THE NEXT PAGE.

7. According to the passage, John Newberry's *Tom Telescope* was different from Thomas Day's *The History of Sandford and Merton* in that

   (A) Thomas Day's book was more explicit about the conditions aboard slave ships
   (B) John Newberry unwittingly helped to form a cultural stereotype through his writing
   (C) Thomas Day was the first to introduce a black person as a major character in his book
   (D) John Newberry believed in the dissemination of humanitarian ideas
   (E) Thomas Day attacked the institution of slavery itself

8. The primary purpose of the passage is to

   (A) highlight the manner in which the abolition of slavery in Great Britain differed from that in the United States
   (B) emphasize the unnatural oppression inherent in the institution of slavery
   (C) underscore the continued racism in Great Britain despite that country's abolition of slavery
   (D) discuss the influence of 18th-century children's literature on the debate over slavery in Britain
   (E) praise British authors who wrote children's literature during the late 18th century

GO ON TO THE NEXT PAGE.

An important research tool in protecting wildlife involves tracking the journey of a species from its birthplace to its mating site. In the case of the green turtle, which does not start breeding
(5) until the age of 30, this has proven to be a difficult challenge. Researchers have tried to monitor its meanderings by tagging it with metal disks or wires, but the turtle's dramatic growth over the decades—from four inches at infancy to
(10) four feet in adulthood—has stymied efforts to keep the tags in place.

Seeking an alternative tracking method, Brian W. Bowen, an evolutionary geneticist, turned instead to natural markings. Bowen analyzed
(15) mitochondrial DNA from eggs and hatchlings at four green-turtle breeding sites in the Atlantic and the Caribbean. He and his co-workers report that turtles from the four breeding sites tended to differ slightly in genetic sequence. The existence
(20) of variations in DNA among geographically distinct groups has helped scientists sway the balance between different theories of the mating habits of the green turtle.

Their findings, Bowen asserts, lend credence
(25) to the "natal homing" theory proposed in the 1960s. This theory holds that while reptiles born in different regions may share common feeding grounds away from home, the animals part company at breeding time, each swimming
(30) hundreds or thousands of miles to breed and nest at its own birthplace.

At the same time, the new work undercuts a competing theory known as the social facilitation model. This approach contends that virgin female
(35) turtles randomly follow experienced breeders to nesting sites regardless of their birthplace. Bowen concludes that such "social mixing" must be rare in green turtles. Widespread interbreeding of diverse turtle groups, he points out, would have
(40) long ago erased the genetic differences highlighted by the study.

Bowen and his co-workers, however, offer several caveats to the interpretation of their findings. They note that turtles from two of the nesting sites—Florida's Hutchinson Island and
(45) Costa Rica's Tortuguero sanctuary—had indistinguishable mitochondrial DNA sequences. This finding indicates that either some social mixing occurred between these two groups or that the DNA test was not sensitive enough to detect
(50) extremely subtle differences in DNA. In addition, they report that one of eight study turtles from Aves Island, off Venezuela, showed the same genetic pattern as the Tortuguero and Hutchinson turtles in their sample.

(55) Nonetheless, Bowen's study appears to have bolstered the idea that most populations of green turtles are genetically distinct and return to their birthplaces at nesting time.

9. According to the passage, studies of DNA from eggs and hatchlings at four green turtle breeding sites indicate that

(A) virgin female turtles randomly follow experienced breeders to nesting sites
(B) green turtles usually go back to their place of birth during mating time
(C) there is widespread interbreeding among turtle groups from certain nesting sites
(D) there may be subtle differences in DNA sequences that are not detected by currently available tests
(E) green turtles routinely swim hundreds of miles to find fertile feeding grounds

10. The information provided in the passage about Bowen's research can be used to answer conclusively which of the following questions?

(A) Does social mixing occur between turtles from Florida's Hutchinson Island and Costa Rica's Tortuguero sanctuary?
(B) Can DNA always be used to detect genetic differences?
(C) Is there extensive interbreeding among green turtles from different areas?
(D) Does tagging wild animals with metal disks or wires alter their mating habits?
(E) By what mechanism do green turtles find their way back to their birthplace when they are ready to breed?

GO ON TO THE NEXT PAGE.

11. It can be inferred that the geneticist Brian W. Bowen and his co-workers believe each of the following about green turtles EXCEPT

   (A) turtles seldom interbreed with turtles from a different birthplace
   (B) DNA testing does not always reveal genetic differences
   (C) frequent interbreeding can lead to fewer genetic differences among green turtles
   (D) turtles born in separate areas interbreed
   (E) when choosing a breeding partner, a female green turtle disregards the birthplace of the mating prospect

12. According to the passage, which of the following supports the contention that green turtles rarely interbreed?

   (A) The turtles from Florida's Hutchinson Island and Costa Rica's Tortuguero sanctuary had indistinguishable mitochondrial DNA sequences.
   (B) When analyzing the DNA of turtles, scientists found differences in the genetic makeup of turtles from various areas.
   (C) One of eight turtles studied from Aves Island, Venezuela shared a genetic pattern characteristic of turtles from a different breeding ground.
   (D) Bowen's team found a discrete mitochondrial pattern in each turtle they studied.
   (E) Turtles from each nesting ground share common feeding grounds that may be thousands of miles apart.

13. Which of the following best summarizes the primary purpose of the scientists' study?

   (A) to disprove the social facilitation model theory
   (B) to show that interbreeding does not exist among green turtles
   (C) to replace existing tracking methods which have had little success
   (D) to determine whether green turtles return to their place of birth during breeding time
   (E) to establish that there is substantially widespread interbreeding of diverse green turtles

14. Which of the following would most strengthen the "natal homing" theory concerning the genetic differences among green turtles?

   (A) New studies indicate that green turtles can interbreed and their offspring still retain genetic distinctions.
   (B) Recent tests found that there were subtle differences between the mitochondrial DNA sequences found in turtles from Florida's Hutchinson Island and Costa Rica's Tortuguero sanctuary.
   (C) Brian Bowen was recently asked to do further research on genetic differences among green turtles.
   (D) The population of green turtles at Florida's Hutchinson Island and Costa Rica's Tortuguero sanctuary has declined in recent years.
   (E) Research done on DNA testing has shown that DNA is not always a reliable measure of genetic differences.

15. The author regards the validity of the social facilitation model with

   (A) scrupulous impartiality
   (B) hesitant disbelief
   (C) judicious admiration
   (D) censurious disapproval
   (E) reasoned skepticism

GO ON TO THE NEXT PAGE.

In Roman times, defeated enemies were generally put to death as criminals for having offended the emperor of Rome. In the Middle Ages, however, the practice of ransoming, or returning prisoners in exchange for money, became common. Though some saw this custom as a step towards a more humane society, the primary reasons behind it were economic rather than humanitarian.

In those times, rulers had only a limited ability to raise taxes. They could neither force their subjects to fight nor pay them to do so. The promise of material compensation in the form of goods and ransom was therefore the only way of inducing combatants to participate in a war. In the Middle Ages, the predominant incentive for the individual soldier to participate in a war was the expectation of spoils. Although collecting ransom clearly brought financial gain, keeping a prisoner and arranging for his exchange had its costs. Consequently, several procedures were devised to reduce transaction costs.

One such device was a rule asserting that the prisoner had to assess his own value. This compelled the prisoner to establish a value without much distortion; indicating too low a value would increase the captive's chances of being killed, while indicating too high a value would either ruin him financially or create a prohibitively expensive ransom that would also result in death.

A second means of reducing costs was the practice of releasing a prisoner on his word of honor. This procedure was advantageous to both parties since the captor was relieved of the expense of keeping the prisoner while the captive had freedom of movement. The captor also benefited financially by having his captive raise the ransom himself. This "parole" was a viable practice since the released prisoner risked recapture or retaliation against his family. Moreover, in medieval society, breaking one's word had serious consequences. When, for example, King Francois I broke his word to the Emperor Charles V in 1525, his reputation suffered immensely.

A third method of reducing costs was the use of specialized institutions to establish contact between the two parties. Two types of institutions emerged: professional dealers who acted as brokers, and members of religious orders who acted as neutral intermediaries. Dealers advanced money for the ransom and charged interest on the loan. Two of the religious orders that became

(55) intermediaries were the Mercedarians and the Trinitarians, who between them arranged the ransom of nearly one million prisoners.

16. The primary purpose of the passage is to

(A) discuss the economic basis of the medieval practice of exchanging prisoners for ransom
(B) examine the history of the treatment of prisoners of war
(C) emphasize the importance of a warrior's "word of honor" during the Middle Ages
(D) explore three ways of reducing the costs of ransom
(E) demonstrate why warriors of the Middle Ages looked forward to battles

17. It can be inferred from the passage that a medieval soldier

(A) was less likely to kill captured members of opposing armies than was a soldier of the Roman Empire
(B) was similar to a 20th-century terrorist in that he operated on a basically independent level and was motivated solely by economic incentives
(C) had few economic options and chose to fight because it was the only way to earn an adequate living
(D) was motivated to spare prisoners' lives by humanitarian rather than economic ideals
(E) had no respect for his captured enemies since captives were typically regarded as weak

GO ON TO THE NEXT PAGE.

18. Which of the following best describes the change in policy from executing prisoners in Roman times to ransoming prisoners in the Middle Ages?

(A) The emperors of Rome demanded more respect than did medieval rulers, and thus Roman subjects went to greater lengths to defend their nation.
(B) It was a reflection of the lesser degree of direct control medieval rulers had over their subjects.
(C) It became a show of strength and honor for warriors of the Middle Ages to be able to capture and return their enemies.
(D) Medieval soldiers were not as humanitarian as their ransoming practices might have indicated.
(E) Medieval soldiers demonstrated more concern about economic policy than did their Roman counterparts.

19. The author uses the phrase "without much distortion" (line 26) in order

(A) to indicate that prisoners would fairly assess their worth
(B) to emphasize the important role medieval prisoners played in determining whether they should be ransomed
(C) to explain how prisoners often paid more than an appropriate ransom in order to increase their chances for survival
(D) suggest that captors and captives often had understanding relationships
(E) to show that when in prison a soldier's view could become distorted

20. All of the following are mentioned in the passage as actions that were taken to ensure that ransoming prisoners was a profitable operation EXCEPT

(A) each prisoner was made to designate the amount of ransom to be paid for his return
(B) prisoners were released on the condition that they guaranteed that their ransoms would paid
(C) professional intermediaries were employed to facilitate the smooth exchange of prisoner and ransom, at a price to the prisoner
(D) religious orders acted as impartial mediators, arranging the trade-off of ransom and prisoner
(E) medieval rulers promised to aid soldiers in their efforts to collect ransom

21. In the author's opinion, a soldier's decision to spare an adversary's life can be linked historically to

(A) the economic relationship of the warring states
(B) the ease with which a soldier could capture and subsequently imprison his enemy
(C) the economic gain from taking an enemy prisoner rather than killing him in combat
(D) technological advances in weaponry
(E) the desire for soldiers to uphold their word of honor

22. It can be inferred from the passage that the process of arranging ransoms during medieval times was

(A) more lucrative for medieval soldiers and kings than the winning of spoils
(B) a procedure so costly that it was not economically worthwhile for the captors
(C) futile for the captive since he risked recapture even after his ransom was paid
(D) a potential source of income for others aside from the captors of the prisoners
(E) handled only through Mercedarian or Trinitarian intermediaries

GO ON TO THE NEXT PAGE

23. Which of the following best describes the organization of the passage?

    (A) An assertion is made, briefly explained, and then several examples that refute the assertion are given.

    (B) A hypothesis is offered, carefully qualified, and then supporting data is analyzed.

    (C) A generally accepted historical viewpoint is presented in order to introduce discussion of its strengths and limitations.

    (D) A historical analysis is made of a phenomenon and supporting details are offered.

    (E) A historical dispute is introduced, and the case for one side is examined in detail.

STOP

IF YOU FINISH BEFORE TIME IS CALLED, YOU MAY CHECK YOUR WORK ON THIS SECTION ONLY. DO NOT WORK ON ANY OTHER SECTION IN THE TEST.

SECTION 4
Time—30 Minutes
20 Questions

Directions: In this section solve each problem, using any available space on the page for scratchwork. Then indicate the best of the answer choices given.

Numbers: All numbers used are real numbers.

Figures: Figures that accompany problems in the text are intended to provide information useful in solving the problems. They are drawn as accurately as possible EXCEPT when it is stated in a specific problem that its figure is not drawn to scale. All figures lie in a plane unless otherwise indicated.

94.08

A

94.07

1. A portion of a thermometer above is calibrated to show degrees in equal increments. If the temperature indicates a reading at level A, what is the temperature?

(A) 94.069   (B) 94.070   (C) 94.079
(D) 94.080   (E) 94.790

2. The owner of a boutique decides to calculate the percentage of customers who purchase hats. If 40 percent of the store's customers decide to purchase items, and of those customers 15 percent purchase hats, what percent of the store's customers purchase hats?

(A) 4%   (B) 6%   (C) 15%
(D) 24%   (E) 55%

3. The result obtained when x is multiplied by y is equal to ten times the result obtained when y is subtracted from x. If y equals 5, what does x equal?

(A) 50
(B) 25
(C) 15
(D) 10
(E) 5

GO ON TO THE NEXT PAGE.

4. A rectangle with dimensions 24 inches by 42 inches is to be divided into squares of equal size. Which of the following could be a length of a side of the squares?

(A) 4 inches   (B) 6 inches   (C) 7 inches
(D) 8 inches   (E) 10 inches

5. $\left[1-\left(\frac{2}{3}\right)^2\right]^2 =$

(A) $-\frac{1}{3}$ (B) $\frac{1}{27}$ (C) $\frac{125}{729}$ (D) $\frac{25}{81}$ (E) $\frac{5}{9}$

6. After reading $\frac{3}{5}$ of his biology homework on Monday night, Bernie read $\frac{1}{3}$ of his remaining homework on Tuesday night. What fraction of his original homework would Bernie have to read on Wednesday night to complete his biology assignment?

(A) $\frac{1}{15}$ (B) $\frac{2}{15}$ (C) $\frac{4}{15}$ (D) $\frac{2}{5}$ (E) $\frac{4}{5}$

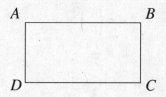

Note: Figure not drawn to scale

7. If the perimeter of rectangle $ABCD$ above is equal to 40, what is the area of $ABCD$?

(A)   19
(B)   20
(C)   75
(D) 100
(E) It cannot be determined from the information given.

8.   For all values of $x \neq 1$, $\dfrac{3x^2 + 6x - 9}{3x - 3} =$

(A) $x + 1$ (B) $x - 1$ (C) $3x + 1$
(D) $x + 3$ (E) $3x + 3$

GO ON TO THE NEXT PAGE.

$$a = \left(\frac{1}{10}\right)^2$$

$$b = \frac{1}{5}$$

$$c = \sqrt{\frac{1}{100}}$$

9. The values of a, b, and c are shown above. Which of the following is correct?

(A) $a < b < c$
(B) $a < c < b$
(C) $b < c < a$
(D) $c < a < b$
(E) $c < b < a$

10. If $\frac{1}{y} = 3\frac{1}{2}$, then $\frac{1}{y+2} =$

(A) $\frac{7}{16}$ (B) $\frac{4}{7}$ (C) $\frac{7}{9}$ (D) $\frac{7}{8}$ (E) $\frac{16}{7}$

11. Laura borrowed $240, interest free, from her parents to pay for her college education. If she pays back $2\frac{1}{2}$ percent of this amount quarterly, and has already paid $42.00, for how many months has she been paying back her loan?

(A) 6 (B) 7 (C) 19 (D) 21 (E) 24

12. If Claire paid $6,885.45 for a car, which included 7 percent sales tax, what was the price of the car excluding the tax?

(A) $6,012.34 (B) $6,335.00 (C) $6,435.00
(D) $7,111.05 (E) $7,367.43

13. The function * is defined by the equation $a * b = \frac{ab}{b-a}$, where $a \neq b$. Which of the following has a value of 3?

(A) 1 * 3 (B) 3 * 0 (C) 2 * 6
(D) 6 * 2 (E) 4 * −1

14. A store raised the price of an item by exactly 10 percent. Which of the following could NOT be the resulting price of the item?

(A) $5.50
(B) $7.60
(C) $11.00
(D) $12.10
(E) $75.90

15. If when a certain integer x is divided by 5 the remainder is 2, then each of the following could also be an integer EXCEPT

(A) $\frac{x}{17}$ (B) $\frac{x}{11}$ (C) $\frac{x}{10}$ (D) $\frac{x}{6}$ (E) $\frac{x}{3}$

16. In a certain flower shop, which stocks four types of flowers, there are $\frac{1}{3}$ as many violets as carnations, and $\frac{1}{2}$ as many tulips as violets. If there are equal numbers of roses and tulips, what percent of the flowers in the shop are carnations?

(A) 10%
(B) 33%
(C) 40%
(D) 50%
(E) 60%

GO ON TO THE NEXT PAGE.

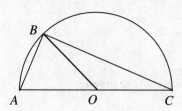

Note: Figure not drawn to scale

17. If triangle *AOB* is equilateral, *O* is the center of the semicircle *ABC,* and the radius of semicircle *ABC* is 6, what is the length of *BC*?

(A) 12   (B) 6√3   (C) 10
(D) 6√2   (E) √42

18. All of the following have the same number of distinct prime factors EXCEPT

(A) 20   (B) 21   (C) 24   (D) 30   (E) 45

19. A car averages 40 miles per hour for the first 6 hours of a trip and averages 60 miles per hour for each additional hour of travel time. If the average speed for the entire trip is 55 miles per hour, how many hours long is the trip?

(A) 8   (B) 12   (C) 16   (D) 18   (E) 24

20. How many integers between 100 and 150, inclusive, can be evenly divided by neither 3 nor 5?

(A) 33
(B) 28
(C) 27
(D) 25
(E) 24

STOP

IF YOU FINISH BEFORE TIME IS CALLED, YOU MAY CHECK YOUR WORK ON THIS SECTION ONLY. DO NOT WORK ON ANY OTHER SECTION IN THE TEST.

SECTION 5
Time—30 Minutes
20 Questions

Directions: For each question in this section, select the best of the answer choices given.

1. A mail order company recently had a big jump in clothing sales after hiring a copywriter and a graphic artist to give its clothing catalog a magazinelike format designed to appeal to a more upscale clientele. The company is now planning to launch a housewares catalog using the same concept.

The company's plan assumes that

(A) other housewares catalogs with magazinelike formats do not already exist
(B) an upscale clientele would be interested in a housewares catalog
(C) the same copywriter and graphic artist could be employed for both the clothing and housewares catalogs
(D) a magazinelike format requires a copywriter and a graphic artist
(E) customers to whom the old clothing catalog appealed would continue to make purchases from catalogs with the new format

2. Civic Leaders: The high cancer rate among our citizens is the result of hazardous material produced at your plant.

Board of Directors: Our statistics show that rates of cancer are high throughout the valley in which the plant is situated because local wells that supply drinking water are polluted, not because of the plant.

Which of the following, if true, most seriously weakens the board's claims?

(A) The statistics do not differentiate between types of cancer.
(B) Nearby communities have not changed the sources of their drinking water.
(C) Cancer-causing chemicals used at the plant are discharged into a nearby river and find their way into local wells.
(D) The plant both uses and produces chemicals that have been shown to cause cancer.
(E) Some of the pollutants cited by the board as contaminating the local wells have been present in the wells for decades.

GO ON TO THE NEXT PAGE.

3. Economies in which a high percentage of resources are invested in research and development show greater growth in the long run than do those in which resources are channeled into consumption. Japanese workers spend a higher percentage of their income investing in research and development than do American workers. To grow as fast as Japan has in the past three decades, the United States must change the tax code in order to encourage savings and investment and discourage debt.

Which of the following, if true, tends to weaken the argument?

(A) Japanese research is more focused on consumers than is research by American firms.
(B) Class mobility, highly valued in American culture, is encouraged by a growing rather than a stagnant economy.
(C) Studies have shown that countries with high consumption rates prosper in the short run.
(D) Proposed changes to the tax code could involve strict limits on the deductability of interest, and increased allowance for research.
(E) Because a decreasing percentage of the United States is under 40, an age when savings are traditionally low, the savings rate will increase without changes to the tax code.

4. Television programing experts maintain that with each 1% increase in the prime-time ratings of a television station there is a 3.5% increase in the number of people who watch its evening news program. However, in the last ten years at Channel NTR, there was only one year of extremely high prime-time ratings—and during that year, fewer people than ever watched Channel NTR's evening news program.

Which of the following conclusions can properly be drawn from the statements above?

(A) When a news program has good ratings, the channel as a whole will have good ratings.
(B) The programming experts neglected to consider daytime news programs.
(C) The year of high ratings at NTR was a result of two hit shows which were subsequently canceled because of contractual problems.
(D) The ten-year period in question is not representative of normal viewing patterns.
(E) Prime-time ratings are not the only factor affecting how many people watch an evening news program.

5. The people who are least likely to be audited by the Internal Revenue Service this year are those who have been audited since 1985 and who were found to have made no mistakes in filing their returns during that audit.

Of the following people, who is MOST likely to be audited by the IRS?

(A) A person who was audited in 1986 but was not found to have made any mistakes in filing his return.
(B) A person who was audited in 1986 and whose lawyer corrected several mistakes in the tax return prior to the filing deadline.
(C) A person whose spouse was convicted of tax fraud in 1987, who was then audited and found to have made no mistakes.
(D) A person who was last audited in 1984, and had no mistakes uncovered by the IRS during that audit.
(E) A person who was audited in each of the past five years, but was found to have made no mistakes in any of the filings.

6. James's grade point average puts him in the top third of the graduating class of college A. Nestor is in the top tenth of the same class. Elizabeth has the same grade point average as Nestor. Nancy has a lower grade point average than Elizabeth.

If the information above is true, which of the following must also be true?

(A) James has a higher grade point average than Elizabeth
(B) James has a higher grade point average than Nancy
(C) Nestor has a higher grade point average than Nancy
(D) Elizabeth and Nancy both have a higher grade point average than James
(E) Nestor and James both have a higher grade point average than Nancy

GO ON TO THE NEXT PAGE.

7. Whenever a major airplane accident occurs, there is a dramatic increase in the number of airplane mishaps reported, a phenomenon that may last for as long as a few months after the accident. Airline officials assert that the publicity given the gruesomeness of major airplane accidents focuses media attention on the airline industry, and the increase in the number of reported accidents is caused by an increase in the number of news sources covering airline accidents, not by an increase in the number of accidents.

Which of the following, if true, would seriously weaken the assertions of the airline officials?

(A) The publicity surrounding airline accidents is largely limited to the country in which the crash occurred.
(B) Airline accidents tend to occur far more often during certain peak travel months.
(C) News organizations do not have any guidelines to help them decide how severe or how close an accident must be for it to receive coverage.
(D) Airplane accidents receive coverage by news sources only when the news sources find it advantageous to do so.
(E) Studies by government regulators show that the number of airplane flight miles remains relatively constant from month to month.

Questions 8-9 are based on the following:

Investing in real estate would be a profitable venture at this time. A survey in *House* magazine revealed that 85% of the magazine's readers are planning to buy a second home over the next few years. A study of the real estate industry, however, revealed that the current supply of homes could only provide for 65% of that demand each year.

8. Which of the following, if true, reveals a weakness in the evidence cited above?

(A) Real estate is a highly labor-intensive business.
(B) Home builders are not evenly distributed across the country.
(C) The number of people who want second homes has been increasing each year for the past ten years.
(D) Readers of *House* magazine are more likely than most people to want second homes.
(E) *House* magazine includes articles about owning a second home as well as articles about building a second home.

9. Which of the following, if true, would undermine the validity of the investment advice in the paragraph above?

(A) Some home owners are satisfied with only one home.
(B) About half of the people who buy homes are investing in their first home.
(C) About half of the people who buy homes have to take out a mortgage to do so.
(D) Only a quarter of the homes that are built are sold within the first two weeks.
(E) Only a quarter of those who claim that they want a second home actually end up purchasing one.

GO ON TO THE NEXT PAGE.

0. Traffic safety experts predict that the installation of newly designed air bags in all cars in the United States would reduce the average number of fatalities per traffic accident by 30 percent. In order to save lives, the Department of Transportation (DOT) is considering requiring automobile manufacturers to install air bags of this design in all cars produced after 1998.

Which of the following, if true, represents the strongest challenge to the DOT's proposal?

(A) Air bags of the new design are more given to being inadvertently triggered, an occurrence that can sometimes result in fatal traffic accidents.

(B) The DOT is planning to require automobile manufacturers to produce these air bags according to very strict specifications.

(C) After installing air bags in new cars, automobile manufacturers will experience an increase in sales.

(D) The proposed air bag installation program will adversely affect the resale of cars manufactured prior to 1998.

(E) As production costs increase, the profits of many domestic automobile dealers show a marked decrease.

11. A private bus company gained greater profits and provided bus service to the area at lower fares by running buses more frequently and stimulating greater ridership. Hoping to continue these financial trends, the company plans to replace all older buses with new, larger buses, including some double-decker buses.

The plan of the bus company as described above assumes all of the following EXCEPT

(A) the demand for bus service in the company's area of service will increase in the future

(B) increased efficiency and revenues will compensate for any new expenses the company incurs

(C) the new buses will be sufficiently reliable to ensure the company a net financial gain once they are in place

(D) driving the new buses will be no more difficult than driving the buses they are to replace

(E) the larger, double-decker buses will not face obstacles such as height and weight restrictions in the bus company's area of service

12. A newly discovered disease is thought to be caused by a certain bacterium. However, recently released data notes that the bacterium thrives in the presence of a certain virus, implying that it is actually the virus that causes the new disease.

Which of the following pieces of evidence would most support the data's implication?

(A) In the absence of the virus, the disease has been observed to follow infection by the bacterium.

(B) The virus has been shown to aid the growth of bacterium, a process which often leads to the onset of the disease.

(C) The virus alone has been observed in many cases of the disease.

(D) In cases where the disease does not develop, infection by the bacterium is usually preceded by infection by the virus.

(E) Onset of the disease usually follows infection by both the virus and the bacterium.

GO ON TO THE NEXT PAGE.

13. A sociologist recently studied two sets of teenagers. The members of one set spent 10 or more hours per week watching violent television programs, and the members of the other set spent 2 hours or less per week watching violent television programs. A significantly greater proportion of the teenagers in the former group exhibited aggressive behavior during the period of the study. The sociologists reasoned that the prolonged exposure to television violence caused the aggressive behavior.

Which of the following, if true of the teenagers in the study, provides the strongest challenge to the sociologist's conclusion?

(A) Some teenagers who watched more than 10 hours of violent television programming per week behaved less aggressively than others in the same group of teenagers.

(B) Some teenagers who watched 2 hours of violent television programming per week did not behave aggressively.

(C) Some teenagers voluntarily stopped watching violent television programs after being victims of violence.

(D) Some teenagers watched violent television programs alone, while others did so in groups.

(E) Many of the teenagers in the first group exhibited aggressive behavior before the study began.

14. Because of a recent drought in Florida during the orange-growing season, the price of oranges this season will be three times the usual price. This will drive up the cost of producing orange juice and thus push up the price of orange juice for the consumer.

Which of the following, if true, most seriously weakens the argument above?

(A) The recent drought was not as severe as scientists predicted.

(B) States other than Florida also supply oranges orange juice manufacturers.

(C) Other ingredients are used in the production o orange juice.

(D) Last year the price of oranges was actually lower than the average price over the past ten years.

(E) The price of oranges will eventually be $0.48 per crate.

GO ON TO THE NEXT PAGE

Questions 15-16 are based on the following:

Local phone companies have monopolies on phone service within their areas. Cable television can be transmitted via the wires that are already in place and owned by the phone companies. Cable television companies argue that if the telephone companies were to offer cable service, these telephone companies would have an unfair advantage, because their cable transmissions could be subsidized by the profits of their monopolies on phone service.

15. Which of the following, if true, would ease the cable companies' fear of unfair competition?

(A) In order to use existing telephone wire, telephone companies would need to modernize their operations, a process so expensive it would virtually wipe out all profit from their monopoly for the foreseeable future.
(B) If a phone company were to offer cable service within a particular area, it would have a monopoly within that area.
(C) The cost of television service, whether provided by cable or telephone companies, scales; that is, the total cost of transmission rises only marginally as more homes are added to the network.
(D) Cable programming that offers more channels is already available through satellite dish, but the initial cost of the dish is extremely high.
(E) Cable television will never be able to compete with the burgeoning video rental industry, especially as more homes now have video cassette recorders than ever did before.

16. On the basis of the information provided in the passage above, which of the following questions can be answered?

(A) Are phone companies as efficient as cable companies in providing reliable and inexpensive service?
(B) If phone companies were allowed to provide cable service, would they want to do so?
(C) Do the cable companies believe that the local phone companies make a profit on phone service?
(D) Are local phone companies forbidden to offer cable service?
(E) Is it expected that phone companies will have a monopoly on cable service?

17. In the past year, there has been a large drop in the number of new cars sold, due to harsh economic conditions in the marketplace and high taxes. At the same time, the average price paid for a new car has risen dramatically.

Which of the following, if true, best explains the increase in the average price of a new car?

(A) The price of used cars has climbed steadily over the past ten years.
(B) There will be a tax reduction later in the year which is expected to aid moderate and low income families.
(C) The market for expensive cars has been unaffected by the current economic conditions.
(D) Economic conditions are expected to get significantly worse before the end of the year.
(E) Low demand for trucks and vans has led to lower production in the factories.

18. Critics of sales seminars run by outside consultants point out that since 1987, revenues of vacuum cleaner companies whose employees attended consultant-led seminars were lower than revenues of vacuum cleaner companies whose employees did not attend such seminars. The critics charge that for vacuum cleaner companies, the sales seminars are ill-conceived and a waste of money.

Which of the following, if true, is the most effective challenge to the critics of sales seminars?

(A) Those vacuum cleaner companies whose sales were highest prior to 1987 are the only companies that did not send employees to the seminars.
(B) Vacuum cleaner companies that have sent employees to sales seminars since 1987 experienced a greater drop in sales than they had prior to 1987.
(C) The cost of vacuum cleaner sales seminars run by outside consultants has risen dramatically since 1987.
(D) The poor design of vacuum cleaner sales seminars is not the only reason for their ineffectiveness.
(E) Since 1987, sales of vacuum cleaners have risen twenty percent.

GO ON TO THE NEXT PAGE.

19. Informed people generally assimilate information from several divergent sources before coming to an opinion. However, most popular news organizations view foreign affairs solely through the eyes of our State Department. In reporting the political crisis in foreign country B, news organizations must endeavor to find alternative sources of information.

Which of the following inferences can be drawn from the argument above?

(A) To the degree that a news source gives an account of another country that mirrors that of our State Department, that reporting is suspect.

(B) To protect their integrity, news media should avoid the influence of State Department releases in their coverage of foreign affairs.

(C) Reporting that is not influenced by the State Department is usually more accurate than are other accounts.

(D) The alternative sources of information mentioned in the passage would probably not share the same views as the State Department.

(E) A report cannot be seen as influenced by the State Department if it accurately depicts the events in a foreign country.

20. A light bulb company produces 2,000 light bulbs per week. The manager wants to ensure that standards of quality remain constant from week to week. The manager, therefore, claims that out of 2,000 light bulbs produced per week, 500 light bulbs are rejected.

Of the following, the best criticism of the manager's plan is that the plan assumes that

(A) light bulb manufacturers cannot accept all light bulbs that are produced

(B) the overall quality of the light bulbs would not be improved if the total number of light bulbs produced were reduced

(C) each light bulb that is reviewed is worthy of being reviewed

(D) it is difficult to judge the quality of a light bulb

(E) the 1,500 light bulbs that are accepted will be of the same quality from week to week

STOP

IF YOU FINISH BEFORE TIME IS CALLED, YOU MAY CHECK YOUR WORK ON THIS SECTION ONLY.
DO NOT WORK ON ANY OTHER SECTION IN THE TEST.

SECTION 6
Time—30 Minutes
25 Questions

<u>Directions</u>: Each of the data sufficiency problems below consists of a question and two statements, labeled (1) an~
(2), in which certain data are given. You have to decide whether the data given in the statements are <u>sufficient</u> for
answering the question. Using the data given in the statements <u>plus</u> your knowledge of mathematics and everyday
facts (such as the number of days in July or the meaning of <u>counterclockwise</u>), you are to blacken space

- A if statement (1) ALONE is sufficient, but statement (2) alone is not sufficient to answer
the question asked;
- B if statement (2) ALONE is sufficient, but statement (1) alone is not sufficient to answer
the question asked;
- C if BOTH statements (1) and (2) TOGETHER are sufficient to answer the question asked,
but NEITHER statement ALONE is sufficient;
- D if EACH statement ALONE is sufficient to answer the question asked;
- E if statements (1) and (2) TOGETHER are NOT sufficient to answer the question asked,
and additional data specific to the problem are needed.

<u>Numbers</u>: All numbers used are real numbers.

<u>Figures</u>: A figure in a data sufficiency problem will conform to the information given in the question, but will
not necessarily conform to the additional information given in statements (1) and (2).

You may assume that lines shown as straight are straight and that angle measures are greater than zero.

You may assume that the positions of points, angles, regions, etc., exist in the order shown.
All figures lie in a plane unless otherwise indicated.

Example:

In $\triangle PQR$, what is the value of x ?

(1) $PQ = PR$
(2) $y = 40$

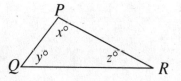

<u>Explanation</u>: According to statement (1), $PQ = PR$; therefore, $\triangle PQR$ is isosceles and $y = z$. Since $x + y + z = 180$,
$x + 2y = 180$. Since statement (1) does not give a value for y, you cannot answer the question using statement (1)
by itself. According to statement (2), $y = 40$; therefore, $x + z = 140$. Since statement (2) does not give a value for
z, you cannot answer the question using statement (2) by itself. Using both statements together, you can find y and
z; therefore, you can find x, and the answer to the problem is C.

GO ON TO THE NEXT PAGE.

A   Statement (1) ALONE is sufficient, but statement (2) alone is not sufficient.
B   Statement (2) ALONE is sufficient, but statement (1) alone is not sufficient.
C   BOTH statements TOGETHER are sufficient, but NEITHER statement ALONE is sufficient.
D   EACH statement ALONE is sufficient.
E   Statements (1) and (2) TOGETHER are NOT sufficient.

1. What is the area of triangular region T?

(1) The base of triangle T is 12.

(2) The ratio of the height of T to the base of T is 3:1.

2. Bob purchased 18 cans of soda, some of which contained diet soda. How many of the cans did not contain diet soda?

(1) Of the cans Bob purchased, the number containing diet soda is equal to the number not containing diet soda.

(2) Of the cans Bob purchased, the number containing diet soda is odd.

3. In 1988, was the number of people in City X greater than three times the number of people in City Y?

(1) In 1988, there were approximately 1.1 million more people in City X than in City Y.

(2) In 1988, the 300,000 Mormons in City X made up 20 percent of its population, and the 141,000 Buddhists in City Y made up 30 percent of its population.

4. If point X is directly north of point Y and directly west of point Z, what is the distance from point X to point Z?

(1) The distance from Y to Z is 20.

(2) The distance from X to Y is equal to half the distance from Y to Z.

GO ON TO THE NEXT PAGE.

A Statement (1) ALONE is sufficient, but statement (2) alone is not sufficient.
B Statement (2) ALONE is sufficient, but statement (1) alone is not sufficient.
C BOTH statements TOGETHER are sufficient, but NEITHER statement ALONE is sufficient.
D EACH statement ALONE is sufficient.
E Statements (1) and (2) TOGETHER are NOT sufficient.

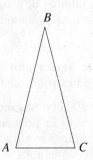

5. What is the area of the isosceles triangle ABC above?

   (1) The perimeter of ABC is 30.

   (2) AB = BC = 12

6. Is v equal to the average (arithmetic mean) of s, t, and u?

   (1) $s + t + u = 3v$

   (2) $\dfrac{s + t + u}{6} = \dfrac{v}{2}$

7. What is the maximum capacity in cups of a pail that contains only sand and is filled to three-fourths of its capacity?

   (1) If one cup of sand were added to the pail, it would be filled to seven-eighths of its capacity.

   (2) If two cups were removed from the pail, it would be filled to one-half of its capacity.

8. What is the value of x?

   (1) $x^2 = 4x$

   (2) x is an even integer.

9. Marc has to get information from either the library or the University Center. Which of these two buildings is a greater distance from his home?

   (1) It takes Marc an average of 20 minutes to ride his bike from his home to the library.

   (2) It takes Marc an average of 20 minutes to ride his bike from the library to the University Center.

GO ON TO THE NEXT PAGE

A Statement (1) ALONE is sufficient, but statement (2) alone is not sufficient.
B Statement (2) ALONE is sufficient, but statement (1) alone is not sufficient.
C BOTH statements TOGETHER are sufficient, but NEITHER statement ALONE is sufficient.
D EACH statement ALONE is sufficient.
E Statements (1) and (2) TOGETHER are NOT sufficient.

10. Is x^3 equal to 125?

 (1) $x > 4$

 (2) $x < 6$

11. A circular peg is to be placed in a square hole. What is the perimeter of the hole?

 (1) The radius of the peg is 4 centimeters.

 (2) Each edge of the hole is tangent to the peg.

12. Over a seven-week period a company monitored the output of two of its branches, C and D. Each week the company calculated how many units were produced in each branch. The branch that produced the greatest number of units for four or more of the seven weeks was considered the more efficient branch. Which office was deemed the more efficient?

 (1) Over the seven-week period Branch C produced twice as many units as Branch D.

 (2) The branch that was more efficient was known by the fifth week.

13. All of the tickets for two real estate seminars, F and G, were either purchased or given away, and the ratio of F tickets to G tickets was 2 to 1. Of the total number of F tickets and G tickets, what percentage was purchased?

 (1) The total number of F tickets and G tickets is 240.

 (2) Of the F tickets, exactly 60 percent were purchased, and of the G tickets, exactly 80 percent were purchased.

14. What is the greatest common factor of positive integers x and y?

 (1) The greatest common factor of $\frac{x}{2}$ and $\frac{y}{2}$ is 5.

 (2) x and y are even.

GO ON TO THE NEXT PAGE.

A   Statement (1) ALONE is sufficient, but statement (2) alone is not sufficient.
B   Statement (2) ALONE is sufficient, but statement (1) alone is not sufficient.
C   BOTH statements TOGETHER are sufficient, but NEITHER statement ALONE is sufficient.
D   EACH statement ALONE is sufficient.
E   Statements (1) and (2) TOGETHER are NOT sufficient.

15. If x and y are positive integers, is $x + 4y$ odd?

(1) y is odd.

(2) x is odd.

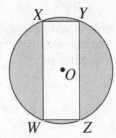

16. Rectangle $WXYZ$ is inscribed in a circle with center O as shown above. If the diameter of the circle is equal to 16, then what is the area of the shaded region?

(1) $WZ = OW$

(2) $XW < XY$

17. A rectangle with dimensions 75 inches by 100 inches is divided into 20 smaller rectangles. If each new rectangle has equal dimensions, how many inches of lines are needed to divide the original rectangle?

(1) One of the dimensions of each of the rectangles is 15 inches.

(2) One of the dimensions of each of the rectangles is 25 inches.

18. Is rectangular block B a cube?

(1) At least two faces of rectangular block B are square.

(2) The volume of rectangular block B is 64.

19. Is the statement $0 < y < 1$ true?

(1) $0 < \sqrt{y} < 1$

(2) $y^2 = \frac{1}{4}$

GO ON TO THE NEXT PAGE.

A Statement (1) ALONE is sufficient, but statement (2) alone is not sufficient.
B Statement (2) ALONE is sufficient, but statement (1) alone is not sufficient.
C BOTH statements TOGETHER are sufficient, but NEITHER statement ALONE is sufficient.
D EACH statement ALONE is sufficient.
E Statements (1) and (2) TOGETHER are NOT sufficient.

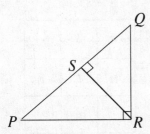

0. In the figure above, what is the length of *PQ* times the length of *RS*?

(1) The length of *PQ* is 5.

(2) The length of *QR* times the length of *PR* is equal to 12.

21. Vanda's Butcher Shop sells packages of ground turkey and ground beef. Is the price for a pound of ground turkey less than that for a pound of ground beef?

(1) The price for a package of ground turkey is 30 percent greater than the price for a package of ground beef.

(2) A package of ground turkey weighs 25 percent more than a package of ground beef.

22. If *P* is a set of integers and 3 is in *P*, is every positive multiple of 3 in *P*?

(1) If *x* is in *P*, then *x* + 3 is in *P*.

(2) If *x* is in *P*, then *x* − 3 is in *P*.

GO ON TO THE NEXT PAGE.

A   Statement (1) ALONE is sufficient, but statement (2) alone is not sufficient.
B   Statement (2) ALONE is sufficient, but statement (1) alone is not sufficient.
C   BOTH statements TOGETHER are sufficient, but NEITHER statement ALONE is sufficient.
D   EACH statement ALONE is sufficient.
E   Statements (1) and (2) TOGETHER are NOT sufficient.

23. If t is a multiple of prime number s, is t a multiple of s^2?

(1) $s < 4$

(2) $t = 18$

	s	
u	t	8
	4	

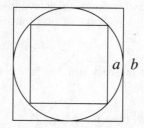

24. In the figure above, a circle is inscribed in a square with side b and a square with side a is inscribed in the circle. What is the area of the square with side b?

(1) $a = 4$

(2) The radius of the circle is $2\sqrt{2}$.

25. A computer generates non-zero numbers for the figure above so that the product of the numbers along any vertical column is equal to the product of the numbers in any horizontal row. What number does s represent?

(1) u equals 6.

(2) t equals 2.

STOP

IF YOU FINISH BEFORE TIME IS CALLED, YOU MAY CHECK YOUR WORK ON THIS SECTION ONLY.
DO NOT WORK ON ANY OTHER SECTION IN THE TEST.

SECTION 7
Time—30 Minutes
27 Questions

Directions: In each of the following sentences, some part of the sentence or the entire sentence is underlined. Beneath each sentence you will find five ways of phrasing the underlined part. The first of these repeats the original; the other four are different. If you think the original is better than any of the alternatives, choose answer A; otherwise choose one of the others. Select the best version and blacken the corresponding space on your answer sheet.

This is a test of correctness and effectiveness of expression. In choosing answers, follow the requirements of standard written English; that is, pay attention to grammar, choice of words, and sentence construction. Choose the answer that expresses most effectively what is presented in the original sentence; this answer should be clear and exact, without awkwardness, ambiguity, or redundancy.

1. Violence in the stands at soccer matches has gotten so pronounced in several European countries that some stadiums have adopted new rules that aim to identify fans of visiting teams and that seat them in a separate area.

   (A) to identify fans of visiting teams and that seat them
   (B) to identify fans of visiting teams and seat them
   (C) to identify fans of visiting teams for seating
   (D) at identifying fans of visiting teams so as to seat them
   (E) at identifying fans of visiting teams and that seat them

2. Despite the recent election of a woman to the office of prime minister, the status of women in Pakistan is little changed from how it was in the last century.

   (A) is little changed from how it was
   (B) is a little changed from how it was
   (C) has changed little
   (D) has changed little from how it has been
   (E) is little changed from the way it was

GO ON TO THE NEXT PAGE.

. Not since Galileo suffered the "scurvy humor" of the Inquisition <u>has a religious organization so effectively curbed the ability of a major scientist that he could pursue</u> a theory.

(A) has a religious organization so effectively curbed the ability of a major scientist that he could pursue

(B) did a religious organization so effectively curb the ability of a major scientist that he could pursue

(C) has a religious organization so effectively curbed the ability of a major scientist to pursue

(D) did a religious organization so effectively curb the ability of a major scientist to pursue

(E) has a religious organization so effectively curbed whether a major scientist had the ability that he could be pursuing

. In the last twenty years, despite the chauvinism of European connoisseurs, California wines <u>are respected</u> throughout the world.

(A) are respected

(B) are becoming better respected

(C) which have gained respect

(D) have gained respect

(E) have since become respected

5. Recently there has been increased debate <u>over if a budget surplus should go towards lower taxes or increased spending</u> on social programs.

(A) over if a budget surplus should go towards lower taxes or increased spending

(B) over whether a budget surplus should go towards lowering taxes or increasing spending

(C) about a budget surplus going towards lower taxes or increasing spending

(D) about if lower taxes should come from a budget surplus or spending increases

(E) concerning a budget surplus and its going towards lower taxes or increased spending

6. Chicago, <u>where industrial growth in the nineteenth century was more rapid than any other American city</u>, was plagued by labor troubles like the Pullman Strikes of 1894.

(A) where industrial growth in the nineteenth century was more rapid than any other American city

(B) which had industrial growth in the nineteenth century more rapid than that of other American cities

(C) which had growth industrially more rapid than any other American city in the nineteenth century

(D) whose industrial growth in the nineteenth century was more rapid than any other American city

(E) whose industrial growth in the nineteenth century was more rapid than that of any other American city

GO ON TO THE NEXT PAGE.

7. With total sales of less than three hundred thousand dollars and fewer new subscribers than last year, the New England Theatre Company is in danger of losing its building.

(A) of less than three hundred thousand dollars and fewer
(B) lower than three hundred thousand dollars and less
(C) lesser than three hundred thousand dollars and fewer
(D) fewer than three hundred thousand dollars and less
(E) of fewer than three hundred thousand dollars and of fewer

8. A recent *New York Times* editorial criticized the city's election board for, first of all, failing to replace outmoded voting machines prone to breakdowns, and secondarily, for their failure to investigate allegations of corruption involving board members.

(A) secondarily, for their failure to
(B) secondly, for their failure to
(C) secondly, that they failed and did not
(D) second, that they failed to
(E) second, for failing to

9. Two week notice being given to employers before leaving a job is the generally accepted protocol.

(A) Two week notice being given to employers before leaving
(B) Giving notice to employers of two weeks before having to leave
(C) Two week's notice to give to employers before leaving
(D) Giving notice to employers two weeks before leaving
(E) To give two weeks' worth of notice before having to leave

10. More than ever, paper is expected to be recycled this year, due to new mandatory recycling laws in municipalities across the nation.

(A) More than ever, paper is expected to be recycled this year
(B) It is expected that more paper than ever will be recycled this year than previously and that is
(C) The paper expected to be recycled this year is more than ever
(D) The amount of paper that will be recycled this year is expected to be greater than ever
(E) A great increase in the amount of paper that will be recycled this year is

11. Upset by the recent downturn in production numbers during the first half of the year, the possibility of adding worker incentives was raised by the board of directors at its quarterly meeting.

(A) the possibility of adding worker incentives was raised by the board of directors at its quarterly meeting
(B) the addition of worker incentives was raised as a possibility by the board of directors at its quarterly meeting
(C) added worker incentives was raised by the board of directors at its quarterly meeting as a possibility
(D) the board of directors raised at its quarterly meeting the possibility of worker incentives being added
(E) the board of directors, at its quarterly meeting, raised the possibility of adding worker incentives

GO ON TO THE NEXT PAGE.

12. IRS provision 354-B requires that an S corporation with assets of greater than $200,000 send W-2 forms to their full- and part-time employees on or before Jan. 31.

(A) that an S corporation with assets of greater than $200,000 send W-2 forms to their full- and part-time employees on or before Jan. 31

(B) an S corporation with assets of greater than $200,000 send W-2 forms to their full- and part-time employees on or before Jan. 31

(C) that an S corporation with assets of greater than $200,000 send W-2 forms to its full- and part-time employees on or before Jan. 31

(D) an S corporation with assets of greater than $200,000 to send W-2 forms to their full- and part-time employees on Jan. 31 or before

(E) an S corporation with assets of greater than $200,000 send W-2 forms to its full- and part-time employees on or before Jan. 31

13. Just as the European countries of the early eighteenth century sought to exploit the resources of our continent, so too are we now attempting to extract energy and minerals from the ocean bed.

(A) Just as the European countries of the early eighteenth century sought to exploit the resources of our continent, so too

(B) The European countries of the early eighteenth century sought to exploit the resources of our continent, and in a similar way

(C) Like the case of the European countries of the early eighteenth century who sought to exploit the resources of our continent, so too

(D) As in the exploitation of the resources of our continent by European countries of the early eighteenth century,

(E) Similar to the European countries which sought in the early eighteenth century to exploit the resources of our continent

14. Physics professors, the Arnmore Laboratories and Arnmore Research Facilities were founded by Leo and Fontove Arnmore in 1989 after ten years of fundraising.

(A) the Arnmore Laboratories and Arnmore Research Facilities were founded by Leo and Fontove Arnmore in 1989 after ten years of fundraising

(B) Leo and Fontove Arnmore founded the Arnmore Laboratories and Arnmore Research Facilities in 1989, after ten years of fundraising

(C) after ten years of fundraising, the Arnmore Laboratories and Arnmore Research Facilities were founded by Leo and Fontove Arnmore in 1989

(D) the Arnmore Laboratories and Arnmore Research Facilities were founded in 1989 by Leo and Fontove Arnmore after ten years of fundraising

(E) Leo and Fontove Arnmore founded after ten years of fundraising the Arnmore Laboratories and Arnmore Research Facilities in 1989

15. In 1978 a national study found that not only had many contractors licensed by a self-policing private guild failed to pass qualifying exams, they in addition falsified their references.

(A) they in addition falsified their references
(B) they had their references falsified in addition
(C) but they had also falsified their references
(D) they had also falsified their references
(E) but their references were falsified as well

GO ON TO THE NEXT PAGE.

16. An attempt to ratify the Equal Rights Amendment, begun almost two decades ago, has been unsuccessful despite efforts by many important groups, including the National Organization for Women.

    (A) to ratify the Equal Rights Amendment, begun almost two decades ago,
    (B) begun almost two decades ago, for ratifying the Equal Rights Amendment
    (C) begun for ratifying the Equal Rights Amendment almost two decades ago
    (D) at ratifying the Equal Rights Amendment, begun almost two decades ago,
    (E) that has begun almost two decades ago to ratify the Equal Rights Amendment

17. When evidence of financial wrongdoing by an elected official surfaces, it is the electorate who must decide whether the evidence warrants censuring him or ousting him from office.

    (A) whether the evidence warrants censuring him or ousting him
    (B) if there is evidence that warrants a censure or an ousting of him
    (C) whether or not the evidence warrants the censuring or ousting of him
    (D) if there is evidence that warrants censuring him or his ousting
    (E) if the evidence would warrant that he be censured or that he be ousted

18. Because the enemy's new ship is the quietest and it is therefore the most elusive submarine, it is being increasingly viewed by the military as a threat to security.
    (A) and it is therefore the most elusive submarine, it is being increasingly viewed
    (B) it is therefore the most elusive of submarines, and it has increased the view
    (C) and therefore the most elusive submarine, it is being increasingly viewed
    (D) and therefore it is the most elusive of submarines, there is an increasing view
    (E) therefore being the most elusive of submarines, it is increasingly viewed

19. The economic forces which may affect the new public offering of stock include sudden downturns in the market, hedging and other investor strategies for preventing losses, loosening the interest rates in Washington, and fearing that the company may still be undercapitalized.

    (A) loosening the interest rates in Washington, and fearing that the company may still be undercapitalized
    (B) loosening the interest rates in Washington, and a fear of the company still being undercapitalized
    (C) a loosening of the interest rates in Washington, and fearing that the company may still be undercapitalized
    (D) a loosening of the interest rates in Washington, and a fear of the still undercapitalized company
    (E) a loosening of the interest rates in Washington, and a fear that the company may still be undercapitalized

20. Like the government that came before it, which set new records for growth, laissez-faire capitalism is the cornerstone of the new government.

    (A) laissez-faire capitalism is the cornerstone of the new government
    (B) the cornerstone of the new government is laissez-faire capitalism
    (C) laissez-faire capitalism is the new government's cornerstone
    (D) the new government has made laissez-faire capitalism its cornerstone
    (E) the new government has a laissez-faire cornerstone of capitalism

GO ON TO THE NEXT PAGE.

21. To compare the lightning-fast genius of playwright Tom Stoppard with the pedestrian efforts of some of his contemporaries is to compare the exquisite bouquet of a fine wine with that of ordinary grape juice.

(A) To compare the lightning-fast genius of playwright Tom Stoppard with the pedestrian efforts of some of his contemporaries is to compare the exquisite bouquet of a fine wine with that of ordinary grape juice.

(B) To compare the lightning-fast genius of playwright Tom Stoppard with the pedestrian efforts of some of his contemporaries is comparing the exquisite bouquet of a fine wine with that of ordinary grape juice.

(C) Comparing the lightning-fast genius of playwright Tom Stoppard with the pedestrian efforts of some of his contemporaries is to compare the exquisite bouquet of a fine wine with ordinary grape juice.

(D) Comparing the lightning-fast genius of playwright Tom Stoppard with the pedestrian efforts of some of his contemporaries is like comparing the exquisite bouquet of a fine wine with ordinary grape juice.

(E) To compare the lightning-fast genius of playwright Tom Stoppard with the pedestrian efforts of some of his contemporaries is to compare a fine wine's bouquet with ordinary grape juice's bouquet.

22. During the 1980s it became clear that soliciting private funds was far more efficient for environmentalists who sought financial aid than to go to state or federal agencies.

(A) that soliciting private funds was far more efficient for environmentalists who sought financial aid

(B) that for environmentalists who sought financial aid, it was far more efficient to solicit private funds

(C) that for environmentalists seeking financial aid, private organizations were far more efficient to go to

(D) for environmentalists seeking financial aid, going to private organizations was far more efficient

(E) for environmentalists who sought financial aid, private organizations were far more efficient

23. The major areas of medicine in which lasers are effective is in the cutting and closing of blood vessels, and in the destruction of tumors.

(A) is in the cutting and closing of blood vessels, and in the destruction

(B) are the cutting and closing of blood vessels, and also the case of destroying

(C) are the cutting, closing of blood vessels, and in the destroying

(D) are the cutting and closing of blood vessels, and the destruction

(E) is in the cutting and closing of blood vessels, and the destroying

GO ON TO THE NEXT PAGE.

24. Since the movie was released seventeen UFOs have been sighted in the state, <u>which is more than had been sighted</u> in the past ten years together.

    (A) which is more than had been sighted
    (B) more than had been sighted
    (C) more than they had sighted
    (D) more than had reported sightings
    (E) which is more than had reported sightings

25. Ignoring the admonitions of his staff, the chief financial officer accepted the advice of the consulting company because <u>he believed that the standardized accounting procedures would prove not only inexpensive but</u> reliable indicators of economic performance.

    (A) he believed that the standardized accounting procedures would prove not only inexpensive but
    (B) the standardized accounting procedures will prove both inexpensive and also
    (C) he believed the standardized accounting procedures would prove themselves to be both inexpensive and
    (D) he believed that the standardized accounting procedures would prove to be both inexpensive and
    (E) standardized accounting procedures will prove his belief that they are both inexpensive and

26. A large rise in the number of housing starts in the coming year should boost new construction dollars by several billion dollars, <u>making the construction industry's economic health much more robust than five years ago</u>.

    (A) making the construction industry's economic health much more robust than five years ago
    (B) and make the construction industry's economic health much more robust than five years ago
    (C) making the construction industry's economic health much more robust than it was five years ago
    (D) to make the construction industry's economic health much more robust than five years ago
    (E) in making the construction industry's economic health much more robust than it was five years ago

27. <u>The rules that govern political contributions are less stringent in local elections than they are in national elections because they typically involve smaller amounts of money and present less opportunity for abuse.</u>

    (A) The rules that govern political contributions are less stringent in local elections than they are in national elections because they typically involve smaller amounts of money and present less opportunity for abuse.
    (B) Because they typically involve smaller amount of money and present less opportunity for abuse, the rules that govern political contributions are less stringent in local elections than the rules are in national elections.
    (C) The rules that govern political contributions are less stringent in local elections than national elections because they typically involve smaller amounts of money and present less opportunity for abuse.
    (D) Because local elections typically involve smaller amounts of money and present less opportunity for abuse than national elections the rules that govern local political contributions are less stringent than national contributions.
    (E) The rules that govern political contributions are less stringent in local elections than they are in national elections because local elections typically involve smaller amounts of money and present less opportunity for abuse.

STOP

IF YOU FINISH BEFORE TIME IS CALLED, YOU MAY CHECK YOUR WORK ON THIS SECTION ONLY.
DO NOT WORK ON ANY OTHER SECTION IN THE TEST.

Correct Answers for Graduate Management Admissions Test
Diagnostic 584

Section 2	Section 3	Section 4	Section 5	Section 6	Section 7
1. C	1. C	1. C	1. B	1. C	1. B
2. B	2. B	2. B	2. C	2. A	2. C
3. C	3. E	3. D	3. E	3. B	3. C
4. B	4. E	4. B	4. E	4. C	4. D
5. E	5. D	5. D	5. D	5. C	5. B
6. A	6. C	6. C	6. C	6. D	6. E
7. E	7. C	7. E	7. B	7. D	7. A
8. A	8. D	8. D	8. D	8. E	8. E
9. D	9. B	9. B	9. E	9. E	9. D
10. E	10. C	10. A	10. A	10. E	10. D
11. B	11. E	11. D	11. D	11. C	11. E
12. A	12. B	12. C	12. C	12. E	12. C
13. C	13. D	13. C	13. E	13. B	13. A
14. D	14. B	14. B	14. B	14. A	14. B
15. B	15. E	15. C	15. A	15. B	15. C
16. D	16. A	16. E	16. C	16. A	16. A
17. B	17. A	17. B	17. C	17. D	17. A
18. A	18. B	18. D	18. A	18. E	18. C
19. B	19. A	19. E	19. D	19. A	19. E
20. C	20. E	20. C	20. E	20. B	20. D
	21. C			21. C	21. A
	22. D			22. A	22. B
	23. D			23. E	23. D
				24. D	24. B
				25. A	25. D
					26. C
					27. E

Princeton Review Techniques
as they applied to this test:

PROBLEM SOLVING (SECTIONS 2 AND 4)
Ballparking:
    section 2— #2 cross off A, #8 cross off A and B
    section 4— #5 cross off A and B, #12 cross off D and E

Working backward:
    section 2— #12,15
    section 4— #12,14,19

Plugging In:
    section 2— #7,17,18,19
    section 4— #2, 8, 16

Joe Bloggs answers:
    section 2— #15E, 18D, 20E

Translation:
    section 4— #3

Quadratic formulas:
    section 2— #5
    section 4— #8

READING COMPREHENSION (SECTION 3)
Which passages were structural—The first and the third
Minority passage— #1
Disputable answer choices— #2A, 3B, 4A, 13B
WOC— #2D, 7B, 7E, 22E
Wally wouldn't like these answers— #3C, 4D, 6B, 8C, 15D, 22E
structures—
passage one: (minority passage) children's literature changes England's
                attitude toward slavery
    paragraph one: discusses causes of a cultural shift
    paragraph two: a new cause is presented by the author
    paragraphs three and four: supporting evidence for this new cause
passage two: mating habits of the green turtle
    paragraph one: introduction of a scientific problem
    paragraph two: a solution to the problem
    paragraph three: this solution supports one theory...
    paragraph four: ...and refutes another
    paragraph five: qualifications are given
    paragraph six: reiteration of solution
passage three: economic reasons for ransoming of medieval hostages
    paragraph one: an idea is proposed
    paragraph two: supporting evidence is given
    paragraph three: first of three procedures
    paragraph four: second of three procedures
    paragraph five: third of three procedures

CRITICAL REASONING (SECTION 5)

Causal argument— #2, 4, 12, 13, 18
Analogy arguments— #1, 3
Statistical arguments— #7, 8
All-some-most argument— #6

DATA SUFFICIENCY (SECTION 6)

Yes or no problems—#3, 6, 10, 15 (answer is "no"), 18, 19, 21, 22, 23
Careless Assumption answers— #8A, 9C,13D
True but irrelevant problems— #14 statement 2
Joe Bloggs answers— #18A or C, 19B or D, 20C, 21A, 22D,
23C, 24C or E, 25D

SENTENCE CORRECTION (SECTION 7)

Misplaced modifier— #11, 14, 20
Pronoun— #12, 24, 27
Parallel construction— #1, 8, 18, 19
Idiom— #2, 3, 5, 15, 25
Apples and oranges— #6, 26
Subject-verb agreement— #23

CONVERSION TABLE FOR TOTAL SCORES
Graduate Management Admission Test

Corrected Raw Score	Total Scaled Score	Corrected Raw Score	Total Scaled Score	Corrected Raw Score	Total Scaled Score	Corrected Raw Score	Total Scaled Score
134 & Up	800	97	630	60	470	23	310
133	790	96	630	59	460	22	300
132	780	95	620	58	460	21	300
131	780	94	620	57	460	20	290
130	770	93	610	56	450	19	290
129	770	92	610	55	450	18	290
128	770	91	600	54	440	17	280
127	760	90	600	53	440	16	280
126	760	89	600	52	430	15	270
125	750	88	590	51	430	14	270
124	750	87	590	50	430	13	260
123	740	86	580	49	420	12	260
122	740	85	580	48	420	11	260
121	730	84	570	47	410	10	250
120	730	83	570	46	410	9	250
119	730	82	560	45	400	8	240
118	720	81	560	44	400	7	240
117	720	80	560	43	390	6	230
116	710	79	550	42	390	5	230
115	710	78	550	41	390	4	230
114	700	77	540	40	380	3	220
113	700	76	540	39	380	2	220
112	700	75	530	38	370	1	210
111	690	74	530	37	370	0	200
110	690	73	530	36	360		
109	680	72	520	35	360		
108	680	71	520	34	360		
107	670	70	510	33	350		
106	670	69	510	32	350		
105	670	68	500	31	340		
104	660	67	500	30	340		
103	660	66	500	29	330		
102	650	65	490	28	330		
101	650	64	490	27	330		
100	640	63	480	26	320		
99	640	62	480	25	320		
98	630	61	470	24	310		

AFTERWORD

About the Princeton Review Course

The Princeton Review GMAT Course is a six-week course to prepare students for the GMAT.

Students are assigned to small classes (no more than twelve students) grouped by ability. Everyone in your math class is scoring at your math level; everyone in your verbal class is scoring at your verbal level. This enables your teacher to focus each lesson on your problems because everybody else in your class has precisely the same problems.

Each week you will cover one math area and one verbal area. If you don't understand a particular topic thoroughly, some courses expect you to listen to audiocassettes.

Not so with The Princeton Review.

If you want more work on a topic, you can come to an extra-help session later in the week. If after coming to an extra-help class you want still more practice, you can request free private tutoring with your instructor.

Four times during the course you will take a diagnostic test that is computer-evaluated. Each diagnostic test is constructed according to the statistical design of actual GMATs. The computer evaluation of your diagnostic tests is used to assign you to your class, as well as to measure your progress. The computer evaluation tells you what specific areas you need to concentrate on. We know how busy you are. We don't ask you to spend time on topics you already understand.

Princeton Review instructors undergo a strict selection process and a rigorous training period. All of them have done exceedingly well on standardized tests like the GMAT, and most of them have gone to highly competitive colleges. All Princeton Review instructors are chosen because we believe they can make the course enjoyable as well as instructive.

Our materials are updated each year to reflect changes in the test design and improved techniques.

Are Your Books Just Like Your Courses?

Since our SAT book first came out in 1986, many students and teachers have asked us, "Are your books just like your courses?"

No.

We like to think that this book is fun, informative, and well written, but no book can capture the rigor and advantages of our course structure, or the magic of our instructors. It isn't easy to raise GMAT scores. Our course is spread over six weeks and requires class participation, diagnostic exams, and some homework.

Moreover, this book cannot contain all of the techniques we teach in our course for a number of reasons. Some of our techniques are too difficult to explain, without a trained Princeton Review teacher to describe and demonstrate them. Also, this book is written for the average student. Classes in our course are grouped by ability so that we can gear our techniques to each student's level. A 500-level Princeton Review student learns different techniques from those learned by a 400- or 600-level Princeton Review student.

If You'd Like More Information

The Princeton Review offers courses in hundreds of cities around the country and around the world. For the office nearest you, call 1-800-995-5585.

About Computerized Testing

Introduction to Computerized Testing:
ETS, CBT, CAT, GRE—What Does It All Mean?

In 1990, Howard Wainer, an official of the Educational Testing Service, published a book called *Computer Adaptive Testing: A Primer*, in which he wrote, "There are . . . several aspects of computerized and adaptive testing that raise new issues in the consideration of validity," and went on to admit, "There is, as yet, very little information available about the validity of computerized adaptive tests." The book was co-written by four other ETS functionaries and includes a foreword by ETS Vice President C. Victor Bunderson.

In 1991, despite these reservations, ETS began offering the computer-based GRE. Baffling, isn't it?

Anyway, the world is now graced with two forms of the GRE: the pencil-and-paper (standard) test and the CBT (computer-based test). The CBT has the same format as the standard GRE, except it's on a computer. However, along with its regular (linear) sections, the CBT includes a computer-*adaptive* test (CAT) which, depending on the individual tester's performance, can be used at the program's discretion as either the scored or the experimental section. "Computer adaptive" means that the computer program molds itself to the individual test-taker's performance level. For example, if you answer an easy question correctly, the test will give you a harder one. If you miss a medium question, you'll get an easy one next. Supposedly, this process enables the computer to pinpoint your scoring level more quickly and accurately than a paper-and-pencil test could.

ETS has stated that they plan to eliminate the computer-based test (CBTs) once they are confident of the validity of their computer-adaptive tests. As of November 17, 1993, in fact, all sections of the GRE—math, verbal, and analytic—will be offered in CAT format. However, ETS is not confident enough in its CAT analytic section to let it stand alone; therefore, immediately following the CAT section, there will be two computer-*based* analytic sections. Just in case. Whichever analytic section you score best on will be the one that counts.

While ETS has not yet made any formal announcement about offering other tests in CBT or CAT format, they do have a tendency to keep their tests uniform. Considering this history of homogeneity, it is highly likely that ETS will, at some time in the near future, come up with a CAT option for its other admissions tests.

Enter RevieWare

It looks like we're in for a major CAT proliferation, folks. And we at The Princeton Review feel that the only effective way of dealing with this crisis is to help people start preparing now. That's why we developed the RevieWare Computer Diagnostic, our version of ETS's CBT/CAT, and included it in this book. We have attempted to duplicate precisely the format, style, appearance, and workings of the ETS CBT and CAT tests. Aesthetically, ETS's program is rather unattractive, and it's a bit hard to move around in. So is ours. In mirroring the GRE test's look and feel, we made the decision that an accurate test would be more helpful as an instructive and evaluative tool than a fun, attractive test that bore little resemblance to the barren moonscape that is the GRE. They're bland, so we're bland.

But a discussion of the philosophy behind RevieWare isn't really meaningful without an understanding of exactly what computerized testing means to ETS, and what it means to you as a test taker.

What's In It for Them: Cash and Convenience

The big question is, if ETS itself questions the validity of these tests, why do they offer the CBT, let alone a fully adaptive CAT?

For one thing, convenience. The standard paper-and-pencil exams are administered five times per year. For each administration, ETS must rent thousands of rooms worldwide, hire proctors, transport materials, and register and collect fees from walk-in testers. In the case of the CBT/CAT, all ETS needs is a room in one of their or Sylvan Learning Centers' (Sylvan) offices equipped with a couple of computers, and an employee to deal with testers. This room can be open for testing at ETS/Sylvan's discretion, thus eliminating almost all of the hassle associated with administering the paper-and-pencil exam.

Another plus, for ETS and Sylvan, is dollars. The fee for the CBT/CAT is $45 *more* than the fee for the paper-and-pencil exam. At this rate, the expenditure for computer hardware and software will be paid back in very little time. After that, it's straight profit. Or should we say "non-profit"? That ETS might have financial concerns is often overlooked. Most people assume that ETS is some kind of government organ. Actually, ETS is a non-profit association of academic organizations, which means that they're not supposed to make a profit. But if they do, well, oops! It's called an "overage," and can be spent on anything from incredibly high salaries and perks to one of the tennis courts or swimming pools in ETS's Princeton, NJ, compound. Sylvan, on the other hand, is a good old-fashioned corporation. They are in business for the bucks, plain and simple.

What's In It for You:
Bias, Eyestrain, Tears, and Sweat

What seem to be the advantages to the test taker? For one, he or she can take the exam virtually any day of the work week. Also, a computerized test can often take far less time than its paper-and-pencil counterpart. That's what ETS would like you to believe, anyway. Now, let's look at these "advantages" and see how they really play out.

First, fourteen states do not have a single test center that offers the CBT/CAT, and ten others have only one. Also, a sampling of test centers showed that none offers testing on the weekends, so anyone interested would have to be in a position to take a day off if he or she wanted to take the CBT/CAT. This means that if you don't live near a test center or if you go to school or work during the week— situations that apply to a large portion of the country—the first "advantage" does not apply.

Second, who in his or her right mind would not use every minute allotted? If you are told, as you are for the GRE CBT, that you have thirty-two minutes per section, then you are going to use thirty-two minutes. In addition, according to our friend from ETS, Mr. Wainer, ". . . a CAT makes much more stringent demands on its component items than does its paper-and-pencil counterpart. Because the CAT tends to be much shorter . . . each item is more critical. If an item is flawed, its impact on the . . . examinee's proficiency is doubled. Additionally, because not everyone gets the same set of items, a flawed item can affect some examinees and not others. Hence, test fairness, in addition to test validity, can be compromised." So much for the second "advantage."

The difficulties described above begin to bring to light some of the other serious problems with computerized testing. For example, what about the simple, undeniable fact that this test is *on a computer*? Think about the people you know who own and/or spend lots of time with computers and/or video games. Are most of these people members of one gender? Are most of these people members of a specific socioeconomic class? Probably. As Wainer puts it, "It is conceivable that a CAT may be more vulnerable to problems of [bias] than are conventional paper-and-pencil tests, due to the possibility that differences between ethnic groups or genders in familiarity with computers in general may affect scores on computerized tests." In fact, the question of general bias is perhaps the most profound problem facing ETS in creating and administering the CBT/CAT.

For its part, ETS has steadfastly denied that any of its tests exhibit a bias for or against any gender, ethnicity, or race. But for something that doesn't exist, the subject sure does get a lot of attention. In fact, the standardized test-writing community is so worried about bias that its members don't even use the word "bias," opting instead for more comfortable euphemisms. Recently, the term *differential item functioning (dif)* has replaced *item bias* as a less evaluative label. Item bias refers to a specific question that exhibits a bias against a specific group or groups.

Computerized tests, especially computer-adaptive tests like the one that ETS wants to replace the CBT with, are at far greater risk of showing bias than are paper-and-pencil tests. Wainer explains, "Adaptive tests may be more vulnerable to the effects of *dif* on validity than fixed tests. A fixed test may contain items with counter-balancing *dif* that can 'cancel each other out'; however, in an adaptive testing situation, the presence of such [biased] items in the test pool permits the possibility that an unlucky examinee could be administered several items biased against him or her. The resulting test score would not provide a good indication of proficiency." Basically, a paper-and-pencil test is an equal-opportunity bigot, while a CAT can tailor itself to discriminate against you specifically. (See the diagram below for a description of the adaptive flow.)

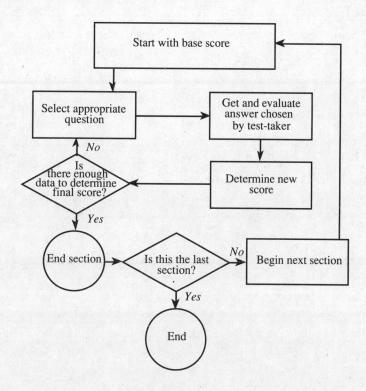

Get It Before It Gets You

You've been taking multiple-choice, paper-and-pencil, fill-in-the-bubble tests your whole life. So while the prospect of taking another one may not be pleasant, at least it's familiar. But imagine walking into something as completely unfamiliar as a computer-adaptive test. You've never seen anything like it before. You've never practiced on it. You feel like Captain Kirk in that *Star Trek* episode where he has to dress up in a really short toga and act like some live pawn in a game these super-intelligent aliens are playing, but he doesn't know any of the rules.

Well, you don't have to feel that way. RevieWare Computer Diagnostics are here to help. Because adaptive testing is the future, if you don't get familiar with it, you'll regret it. Maybe not today, maybe not tomorrow, but soon, and for the rest of your life. Okay, okay, probably not for the rest of your life. But since you have the option, why not use RevieWare Computer Diagnostics to beat ETS at its own game? Happy testing and good luck!

Installation

HOW TO INSTALL YOUR REVIEWARE™ COMPUTER DIAGNOSTIC DISK

This book includes RevieWare Computer Diagnostics. These tests will allow you to practice your test-taking skills by taking full, timed tests in the privacy of your own home. The package is made up of four tests designed and tested to read and score just like the real thing.

The disk within is a 3 1/2" floppy for Windows™-compatible systems. If you need a Macintosh™ or a 5 1/4" disk, please call the Random House customer-service line toll-free, at 1-800-726-0600. They'll be happy to help you. For any technical or content-related questions, call The Princeton Review at 1-212-874-8282. If your question is of a technical nature, ask for the Operations Department. For questions about test items, please ask for the Research and Development Department.

This version of the RevieWare Computer Diagnostic has the following hardware requirements:

1. An IBM or IBM-compatible computer.
2. At least 4 megabytes of RAM.
3. At least 3 megabytes of free disk space.
4. The Windows™ operating system, version 3.1 or better.
5. A mouse.

In order to install the testing program, please follow the steps listed below:

1. Place program disk into your A: or B: drive.
2. From the Windows™ Program Manager, go into the File menu and select Run. Type A:SETUP or B:SETUP, depending on which floppy drive you are using, and press Enter.
3. The program will then search your hard drive for a previous installation of RevieWare Computer Diagnostics. If no previous installation is found, the program will create a directory on your hard drive named TPR1 and install RevieWare Computer Diagnostics to that directory. If a previous installation is found, the directory containing the prior installation will be used as the default setting for the current installation.
4. The Installation Options dialogue will appear next. You can now change the installation directory from step 3 and choose which portions of the RevieWare Computer Diagnostic to install. After you have set up the options for this installation, select Install, or press Enter, to begin the installation.
5. When Setup has finished copying the files to your hard disk, a Program Manager group will be created, including icons you will choose for tester activation.

RevieWare Instructions

WHAT ARE REVIEWARE COMPUTER DIAGNOSTIC TESTS™?

Sitting down and working through assorted standardized test questions will certainly help you to get a feel for each individual question. But how can you experience a full test, short of shelling out the money and taking one?

That's where Revieware comes in. The RevieWare Computer Diagnostics present you with complete, timed exams developed by The Princeton Review. These tests each underwent a lengthy process of modeling, testing, rewriting, and retesting to ensure that RevieWare reads, tests, and scores just like an actual ETS computer-based test. Add to that the fact that you can take our tests at your convenience, in the privacy of your own home, and you've got the next best thing to spending a Saturday morning sitting through an actual test administration!

RevieWare Computer Diagnostics also have a special feature for those of you who want to practice, but occasionally may not have time to work through an entire test: a computer-adaptive test. An adaptive test allows you to receive a score in less time than a regular, or "linear," test would take. The program accomplishes this by using your performance on one question to determine what question follows, thus zeroing in on your score in far less time than would normally be required. This process is explained in depth later.

STARTING YOUR ENGINES: RUNNING REVIEWARE COMPUTER DIAGNOSTICS

To get started, just open the Program Manager group called RevieWare. Then, all you have to do is double click on the RevieWare icon (picture). For those of you who may be icon-impaired, you also have the option of "launching" RevieWare Computer Diagnostics from the File menu. First, choose the Run line. Then type in the path to the RevieWare program (the file name is Setup.exe), and press either the OK button or Enter.

If you have any questions about RevieWare Computer Diagnostics, please call The Princeton Review at (212) 874-8282. If your question is of a technical nature, ask for the Operations Department. For questions about test items, please ask for the Research and Development Department.

THE GUIDED TOUR

The RevieWare Computer Diagnostic menu bar contains three items: File, Score, and Help. The File menu has three options: Start New Exam, Resume Suspended Exam, and Exit.

- Start New Exam: This is how you start an exam. When you choose Start New Exam, a window listing all available exams will open. To take one, just select the exam desired and press the OK button or Enter. The first time you run a RevieWare Computer Diagnostic, you will be asked to authorize your copy of the software. You will need to do this only once. A box will appear asking you to enter a code which corresponds to the pair of icons appearing in the dialogue box. Refer to the copy protection code sheet (located on the next-to-last page of this book) and enter the numeric code that corresponds to the icons presented. Once the exam has been authorized and loaded, you will have the option of taking a short tutorial on topics with which you will need to be familiar when taking the exams. Please note that the tutorial is presented automatically the first time you use RevieWare. After that, you have the option to go directly to an exam.

- Resume Suspended Exam: It's Thursday night at 8:00 and you're in the middle of a test. Of course, you're such a dedicated student that you'll forget about "The Simpsons" and finish the test. Wrong! RevieWare gives you the option of suspending an exam in progress. Of course, you cannot do this in a real test so *it is a bad thing to do when not absolutely necessary!* But since this is practice, we make it available for emergencies like "The Simpsons".

To resume a suspended exam, select the Resume Suspended Exam function from the File menu. A list of suspended exams will appear. Pick the one you want to resume and press OK or Enter. The test will restart where you left off. This option is available only for linear exams. Adaptive tests cannot be exited and resumed. If you quit an adaptive test, it's over for good. Be aware that a test can only be suspended once. When you restart a previously suspended exam, the file holding the information from the first session is deleted from the record and is replaced with the current session of the exam.

- Exit: Choosing Exit will end your testing session.

The Score Menu has four options: Load Score, Print Score, Review Score, and Close Score Window.

- Load Score: Before you are able to use the Print Score or Review Score functions, you must first use Load Score to place a previously taken exam into the program's Score folder. After you select Load Score, a window will open listing all previous exams. Select the exam(s) whose score(s) you wish to Print or Review and it/they will be loaded into memory.

- Print Score: This will give you a printout of your score, including a breakdown by category and question type, for any previously Loaded exam.

- Review Score: The Review Score function allows you to go over any previously Loaded exam, section by section and/or question by question. The first window to appear will list the sections of the test. Selecting a section will open a Section Review screen showing you a listing of the section, question by question. This listing will tell you whether a question was answered correctly, incorrectly, left unanswered, or not seen. Then, by selecting a question and hitting the Go to Question button, you can review a specific question. The program will show you the question and mark your answer and, if you chose an incorrect answer, place a check mark by the correct answer. Hitting the Review button returns you to the Section Review screen.

- Close Score Window: Choose this option to exit the Score window.

WHAT DO I DO NOW?: TAKING A TEST

As soon as you begin a session with the Computer Diagnostic, push your keyboard as far out of the way as you can. Give yourself plenty of room for your scratch paper, mouse, mouse pad, and elbows.

Once you begin your first testing session, you'll work your way through a computer tutorial intended to teach you how to take the test. You should know the tutorial material cold before you begin the test. Doing so will give you a chance to familiarize yourself with the look of the screen, the responsiveness of the mouse, and the speed of the computer as it runs the program.

The tutorial contains lessons on the following topics:
- How to Use a Mouse
- How to Select an Answer
- How to Use the Testing Tools
- How to Scroll

You should spend as much time as you need with the tutorial. Once you have left the tutorial, you may not return to it during your testing session. Be sure to take whatever amount of time is needed to accustom yourself to the program and the hardware (the computer and the mouse).

The most important lesson in the tutorial is the one called Testing Tools. These tools are **NEXT, PREV, MARK, REVIEW, TIME, EXIT SECTION, QUIT TEST, HELP,** and **CONFIRM.** When you take a test, the tools will appear as buttons along the bottom of your screen. You activate each one by pointing at it with your mouse and clicking. You use the tools to navigate through the test, so understanding them thoroughly is very important.

Here are the tools and what they do:

NEXT moves you to the next question. It's the tool you'll use most often. You click it when you've answered (or decided to skip) one question and are ready for the next.

PREV moves you back to the previous question. You use it if you suddenly change your mind, or if the current question gives you an insight into the previous one.

MARK flags a question to remind you that the question requires further attention. Marking a question is not the same as answering it; marking a question has no effect on your score. You can unmark a question by clicking the **MARK** tool a second time, so that the little check mark disappears. Unmarking a question will not erase your answer.

REVIEW lets you return to any question in the current section. When you click **REVIEW**, you are shown a screen in which questions from the current section are listed in order and described by question type. The status of each question—Answered, Not Answered, or Not Seen—is noted beside it. Any question that you marked earlier using the **MARK** tool will have a small check beside its status designation. To return to one of these questions, click on it with the mouse to select it, then click on the Go to Question button on the right side of the screen. To return to the place in the test where you were when you clicked **REVIEW**, click on the Return to Where I Was button, also on the right side of the screen.

TIME hides and displays a small digital timer in the upper-left-hand corner of the screen. The timer shows you how much time you have left to work on the current section. When five minutes are left, the timer will flash and begin counting seconds as well, and you will no longer be able to hide it.

EXIT gives you the option of exiting the current section to proceed to the next one, or suspending the exam for later resumption by using the Resume Suspended Exam selection in the File menu.

QUIT works similarly to **EXIT**, but **QUIT** will throw you out of the test entirely if you choose not to use the Suspend Exam function.

HELP reviews directions. Basically, it lists the tools and, when you click on one, allows you to remind yourself of how the selected tool works. **HELP** does not give you any information that is not provided in the Tutorial.

SCROLL BAR will appear occasionally on the right side of a passage, chart, or diagram that is too big to fit on the screen all at once. If you aren't already familiar with scroll bars from other computer applications, spend plenty of time practicing during the tutorial.

COMPUTER-ADAPTIVE TESTING: A BRAVE NEW WORLD

Let's say that before you begin preparing for a test, you want a rough idea of what scoring range you fall into. Basically, you have to sit down and take a full test, right? Right, unless you use RevieWare Computer Diagnostics, which include computer-adaptive tests that allow you to determine a score in far less time than in a linear, or standard, format test. This is done by assigning each individual question on the adaptive test a difficulty rating. Unlike a normal test, in which there is a set number of questions that tend to get more and more difficult as the test goes on, in adaptive testing the difficulty of one question is determined by whether or not you picked the correct response for the previous question. So if you choose the correct response for a question, the next one will be harder. But if you select an incorrect response, then the next question will be easier. This method allows the program to zero in on your score, saving you the angst of having to deal with questions that are either so easy that they are patronizing or so difficult that you want to reconsider your life goals.

Answering questions on an adaptive test is somewhat different than answering questions on a linear test. On a linear test, you just click on your answer, mumble a short prayer to the deity of your choice, and go on to another question. On the adaptive test, however, choosing an answer is a two-part task. First, you click on your answer. Then, since *you can neither go back to prior work nor skip questions* on an adaptive test, you must push the **CONFIRM** button after you push the **NEXT** button. You will notice that until you push **NEXT**, **CONFIRM** will be gray, and thus inactive. After you push **NEXT**, it will become gray until you either change your answer or press **CONFIRM**. Once you confirm an answer, the question is locked, and you may not go back to review this question. Therefore, the **MARK** and **REVIEW** buttons that are available as features in taking linear exams will not be available in the adaptive test.

Since a question becomes unavailable after it has been confirmed, an adaptive section is completed once the computer determines your level of proficiency, or when the time allotted has run out. On average, about 30–35 questions are needed before the program's formula, or algorithm, is able to arrive at an accurate score.

NOTES

NOTES

NOTES

NOTES

NOTES

NOTES

NOTES

NOTES

About the Authors

Geoff Martz was born in 1956. He attended Dartmouth College and Columbia University, joining The Princeton Review in 1985 as a teacher and writer. Martz headed the development team which designed the Review's GMAT course. He is the author or co-author of *Cracking the ACT, Paying for College,* and *How to Survive Without Your Parents' Money.*

Adam Robinson was born in 1955. He graduated from Wharton before earning a law degree at Oxford University in England. Robinson, a rated chess master, devised and perfected the now-famous "Joe Bloggs" approach to beating standardized tests in 1980, as well as numerous other core Princeton Review techniques. A freelance author of many books, Robinson has collaborated with The Princeton Review to develop a number of its courses.

John Katzman was born in 1959. He graduated from Princeton University in 1980. After working briefly on Wall Street, he founded The Princeton Review in 1981. Having begun with nineteen high school students in his parents' apartment, Katzman now oversees courses that prepare tens of thousands of high school and college students annually for tests, including the SAT, GRE, GMAT, and LSAT.

All three authors live in New York City.

The Princeton Review
Diagnostic Test Form ○ Side 1

1.

YOUR NAME: _____
(Print) Last   First   M.I.

SIGNATURE: _____ DATE: ___ / ___ / ___

HOME ADDRESS: _____
(Print)   Number and Street

_____
City   State   Zip Code

PHONE NO.: _____
(Print)

IMPORTANT: Please fill in these boxes exactly as shown on the back cover of your test book.

2. TEST FORM

_____

3. TEST CODE

4. REGISTRATION NUMBER

5. YOUR NAME

First 4 letters of last name				FIRST INIT	MID INIT

(bubbles A through Z)

6. DATE OF BIRTH

MONTH	DAY	YEAR
○ JAN		
○ FEB		
○ MAR		
○ APR		
○ MAY		
○ JUN		
○ JUL		
○ AUG		
○ SEP		
○ OCT		
○ NOV		
○ DEC		

7. SEX
○ MALE
○ FEMALE

Begin with number 1 for each new section of the test. Leave blank any extra answer spaces.

SECTION 1

1 Ⓐ Ⓑ Ⓒ Ⓓ Ⓔ	11 Ⓐ Ⓑ Ⓒ Ⓓ Ⓔ	21 Ⓐ Ⓑ Ⓒ Ⓓ Ⓔ	31 Ⓐ Ⓑ Ⓒ Ⓓ Ⓔ
2 Ⓐ Ⓑ Ⓒ Ⓓ Ⓔ	12 Ⓐ Ⓑ Ⓒ Ⓓ Ⓔ	22 Ⓐ Ⓑ Ⓒ Ⓓ Ⓔ	32 Ⓐ Ⓑ Ⓒ Ⓓ Ⓔ
3 Ⓐ Ⓑ Ⓒ Ⓓ Ⓔ	13 Ⓐ Ⓑ Ⓒ Ⓓ Ⓔ	23 Ⓐ Ⓑ Ⓒ Ⓓ Ⓔ	33 Ⓐ Ⓑ Ⓒ Ⓓ Ⓔ
4 Ⓐ Ⓑ Ⓒ Ⓓ Ⓔ	14 Ⓐ Ⓑ Ⓒ Ⓓ Ⓔ	24 Ⓐ Ⓑ Ⓒ Ⓓ Ⓔ	34 Ⓐ Ⓑ Ⓒ Ⓓ Ⓔ
5 Ⓐ Ⓑ Ⓒ Ⓓ Ⓔ	15 Ⓐ Ⓑ Ⓒ Ⓓ Ⓔ	25 Ⓐ Ⓑ Ⓒ Ⓓ Ⓔ	35 Ⓐ Ⓑ Ⓒ Ⓓ Ⓔ
6 Ⓐ Ⓑ Ⓒ Ⓓ Ⓔ	16 Ⓐ Ⓑ Ⓒ Ⓓ Ⓔ	26 Ⓐ Ⓑ Ⓒ Ⓓ Ⓔ	36 Ⓐ Ⓑ Ⓒ Ⓓ Ⓔ
7 Ⓐ Ⓑ Ⓒ Ⓓ Ⓔ	17 Ⓐ Ⓑ Ⓒ Ⓓ Ⓔ	27 Ⓐ Ⓑ Ⓒ Ⓓ Ⓔ	37 Ⓐ Ⓑ Ⓒ Ⓓ Ⓔ
8 Ⓐ Ⓑ Ⓒ Ⓓ Ⓔ	18 Ⓐ Ⓑ Ⓒ Ⓓ Ⓔ	28 Ⓐ Ⓑ Ⓒ Ⓓ Ⓔ	38 Ⓐ Ⓑ Ⓒ Ⓓ Ⓔ
9 Ⓐ Ⓑ Ⓒ Ⓓ Ⓔ	19 Ⓐ Ⓑ Ⓒ Ⓓ Ⓔ	29 Ⓐ Ⓑ Ⓒ Ⓓ Ⓔ	39 Ⓐ Ⓑ Ⓒ Ⓓ Ⓔ
10 Ⓐ Ⓑ Ⓒ Ⓓ Ⓔ	20 Ⓐ Ⓑ Ⓒ Ⓓ Ⓔ	30 Ⓐ Ⓑ Ⓒ Ⓓ Ⓔ	40 Ⓐ Ⓑ Ⓒ Ⓓ Ⓔ

SECTION 2

1 Ⓐ Ⓑ Ⓒ Ⓓ Ⓔ	11 Ⓐ Ⓑ Ⓒ Ⓓ Ⓔ	21 Ⓐ Ⓑ Ⓒ Ⓓ Ⓔ	31 Ⓐ Ⓑ Ⓒ Ⓓ Ⓔ
2 Ⓐ Ⓑ Ⓒ Ⓓ Ⓔ	12 Ⓐ Ⓑ Ⓒ Ⓓ Ⓔ	22 Ⓐ Ⓑ Ⓒ Ⓓ Ⓔ	32 Ⓐ Ⓑ Ⓒ Ⓓ Ⓔ
3 Ⓐ Ⓑ Ⓒ Ⓓ Ⓔ	13 Ⓐ Ⓑ Ⓒ Ⓓ Ⓔ	23 Ⓐ Ⓑ Ⓒ Ⓓ Ⓔ	33 Ⓐ Ⓑ Ⓒ Ⓓ Ⓔ
4 Ⓐ Ⓑ Ⓒ Ⓓ Ⓔ	14 Ⓐ Ⓑ Ⓒ Ⓓ Ⓔ	24 Ⓐ Ⓑ Ⓒ Ⓓ Ⓔ	34 Ⓐ Ⓑ Ⓒ Ⓓ Ⓔ
5 Ⓐ Ⓑ Ⓒ Ⓓ Ⓔ	15 Ⓐ Ⓑ Ⓒ Ⓓ Ⓔ	25 Ⓐ Ⓑ Ⓒ Ⓓ Ⓔ	35 Ⓐ Ⓑ Ⓒ Ⓓ Ⓔ
6 Ⓐ Ⓑ Ⓒ Ⓓ Ⓔ	16 Ⓐ Ⓑ Ⓒ Ⓓ Ⓔ	26 Ⓐ Ⓑ Ⓒ Ⓓ Ⓔ	36 Ⓐ Ⓑ Ⓒ Ⓓ Ⓔ
7 Ⓐ Ⓑ Ⓒ Ⓓ Ⓔ	17 Ⓐ Ⓑ Ⓒ Ⓓ Ⓔ	27 Ⓐ Ⓑ Ⓒ Ⓓ Ⓔ	37 Ⓐ Ⓑ Ⓒ Ⓓ Ⓔ
8 Ⓐ Ⓑ Ⓒ Ⓓ Ⓔ	18 Ⓐ Ⓑ Ⓒ Ⓓ Ⓔ	28 Ⓐ Ⓑ Ⓒ Ⓓ Ⓔ	38 Ⓐ Ⓑ Ⓒ Ⓓ Ⓔ
9 Ⓐ Ⓑ Ⓒ Ⓓ Ⓔ	19 Ⓐ Ⓑ Ⓒ Ⓓ Ⓔ	29 Ⓐ Ⓑ Ⓒ Ⓓ Ⓔ	39 Ⓐ Ⓑ Ⓒ Ⓓ Ⓔ
0 Ⓐ Ⓑ Ⓒ Ⓓ Ⓔ	20 Ⓐ Ⓑ Ⓒ Ⓓ Ⓔ	30 Ⓐ Ⓑ Ⓒ Ⓓ Ⓔ	40 Ⓐ Ⓑ Ⓒ Ⓓ Ⓔ

The Princeton Review Diagnostic Test Form ○ Side 2

Begin with number 1 for each new section of the test. Leave blank any extra answer spaces.

SECTION 3

1 Ⓐ Ⓑ Ⓒ Ⓓ Ⓔ	11 Ⓐ Ⓑ Ⓒ Ⓓ Ⓔ	21 Ⓐ Ⓑ Ⓒ Ⓓ Ⓔ	31 Ⓐ Ⓑ Ⓒ Ⓓ Ⓔ
2 Ⓐ Ⓑ Ⓒ Ⓓ Ⓔ	12 Ⓐ Ⓑ Ⓒ Ⓓ Ⓔ	22 Ⓐ Ⓑ Ⓒ Ⓓ Ⓔ	32 Ⓐ Ⓑ Ⓒ Ⓓ Ⓔ
3 Ⓐ Ⓑ Ⓒ Ⓓ Ⓔ	13 Ⓐ Ⓑ Ⓒ Ⓓ Ⓔ	23 Ⓐ Ⓑ Ⓒ Ⓓ Ⓔ	33 Ⓐ Ⓑ Ⓒ Ⓓ Ⓔ
4 Ⓐ Ⓑ Ⓒ Ⓓ Ⓔ	14 Ⓐ Ⓑ Ⓒ Ⓓ Ⓔ	24 Ⓐ Ⓑ Ⓒ Ⓓ Ⓔ	34 Ⓐ Ⓑ Ⓒ Ⓓ Ⓔ
5 Ⓐ Ⓑ Ⓒ Ⓓ Ⓔ	15 Ⓐ Ⓑ Ⓒ Ⓓ Ⓔ	25 Ⓐ Ⓑ Ⓒ Ⓓ Ⓔ	35 Ⓐ Ⓑ Ⓒ Ⓓ Ⓔ
6 Ⓐ Ⓑ Ⓒ Ⓓ Ⓔ	16 Ⓐ Ⓑ Ⓒ Ⓓ Ⓔ	26 Ⓐ Ⓑ Ⓒ Ⓓ Ⓔ	36 Ⓐ Ⓑ Ⓒ Ⓓ Ⓔ
7 Ⓐ Ⓑ Ⓒ Ⓓ Ⓔ	17 Ⓐ Ⓑ Ⓒ Ⓓ Ⓔ	27 Ⓐ Ⓑ Ⓒ Ⓓ Ⓔ	37 Ⓐ Ⓑ Ⓒ Ⓓ Ⓔ
8 Ⓐ Ⓑ Ⓒ Ⓓ Ⓔ	18 Ⓐ Ⓑ Ⓒ Ⓓ Ⓔ	28 Ⓐ Ⓑ Ⓒ Ⓓ Ⓔ	38 Ⓐ Ⓑ Ⓒ Ⓓ Ⓔ
9 Ⓐ Ⓑ Ⓒ Ⓓ Ⓔ	19 Ⓐ Ⓑ Ⓒ Ⓓ Ⓔ	29 Ⓐ Ⓑ Ⓒ Ⓓ Ⓔ	39 Ⓐ Ⓑ Ⓒ Ⓓ Ⓔ
10 Ⓐ Ⓑ Ⓒ Ⓓ Ⓔ	20 Ⓐ Ⓑ Ⓒ Ⓓ Ⓔ	30 Ⓐ Ⓑ Ⓒ Ⓓ Ⓔ	40 Ⓐ Ⓑ Ⓒ Ⓓ Ⓔ

SECTION 4

1 Ⓐ Ⓑ Ⓒ Ⓓ Ⓔ	11 Ⓐ Ⓑ Ⓒ Ⓓ Ⓔ	21 Ⓐ Ⓑ Ⓒ Ⓓ Ⓔ	31 Ⓐ Ⓑ Ⓒ Ⓓ Ⓔ
2 Ⓐ Ⓑ Ⓒ Ⓓ Ⓔ	12 Ⓐ Ⓑ Ⓒ Ⓓ Ⓔ	22 Ⓐ Ⓑ Ⓒ Ⓓ Ⓔ	32 Ⓐ Ⓑ Ⓒ Ⓓ Ⓔ
3 Ⓐ Ⓑ Ⓒ Ⓓ Ⓔ	13 Ⓐ Ⓑ Ⓒ Ⓓ Ⓔ	23 Ⓐ Ⓑ Ⓒ Ⓓ Ⓔ	33 Ⓐ Ⓑ Ⓒ Ⓓ Ⓔ
4 Ⓐ Ⓑ Ⓒ Ⓓ Ⓔ	14 Ⓐ Ⓑ Ⓒ Ⓓ Ⓔ	24 Ⓐ Ⓑ Ⓒ Ⓓ Ⓔ	34 Ⓐ Ⓑ Ⓒ Ⓓ Ⓔ
5 Ⓐ Ⓑ Ⓒ Ⓓ Ⓔ	15 Ⓐ Ⓑ Ⓒ Ⓓ Ⓔ	25 Ⓐ Ⓑ Ⓒ Ⓓ Ⓔ	35 Ⓐ Ⓑ Ⓒ Ⓓ Ⓔ
6 Ⓐ Ⓑ Ⓒ Ⓓ Ⓔ	16 Ⓐ Ⓑ Ⓒ Ⓓ Ⓔ	26 Ⓐ Ⓑ Ⓒ Ⓓ Ⓔ	36 Ⓐ Ⓑ Ⓒ Ⓓ Ⓔ
7 Ⓐ Ⓑ Ⓒ Ⓓ Ⓔ	17 Ⓐ Ⓑ Ⓒ Ⓓ Ⓔ	27 Ⓐ Ⓑ Ⓒ Ⓓ Ⓔ	37 Ⓐ Ⓑ Ⓒ Ⓓ Ⓔ
8 Ⓐ Ⓑ Ⓒ Ⓓ Ⓔ	18 Ⓐ Ⓑ Ⓒ Ⓓ Ⓔ	28 Ⓐ Ⓑ Ⓒ Ⓓ Ⓔ	38 Ⓐ Ⓑ Ⓒ Ⓓ Ⓔ
9 Ⓐ Ⓑ Ⓒ Ⓓ Ⓔ	19 Ⓐ Ⓑ Ⓒ Ⓓ Ⓔ	29 Ⓐ Ⓑ Ⓒ Ⓓ Ⓔ	39 Ⓐ Ⓑ Ⓒ Ⓓ Ⓔ
10 Ⓐ Ⓑ Ⓒ Ⓓ Ⓔ	20 Ⓐ Ⓑ Ⓒ Ⓓ Ⓔ	30 Ⓐ Ⓑ Ⓒ Ⓓ Ⓔ	40 Ⓐ Ⓑ Ⓒ Ⓓ Ⓔ

SECTION 5

1 Ⓐ Ⓑ Ⓒ Ⓓ Ⓔ	11 Ⓐ Ⓑ Ⓒ Ⓓ Ⓔ	21 Ⓐ Ⓑ Ⓒ Ⓓ Ⓔ	31 Ⓐ Ⓑ Ⓒ Ⓓ Ⓔ
2 Ⓐ Ⓑ Ⓒ Ⓓ Ⓔ	12 Ⓐ Ⓑ Ⓒ Ⓓ Ⓔ	22 Ⓐ Ⓑ Ⓒ Ⓓ Ⓔ	32 Ⓐ Ⓑ Ⓒ Ⓓ Ⓔ
3 Ⓐ Ⓑ Ⓒ Ⓓ Ⓔ	13 Ⓐ Ⓑ Ⓒ Ⓓ Ⓔ	23 Ⓐ Ⓑ Ⓒ Ⓓ Ⓔ	33 Ⓐ Ⓑ Ⓒ Ⓓ Ⓔ
4 Ⓐ Ⓑ Ⓒ Ⓓ Ⓔ	14 Ⓐ Ⓑ Ⓒ Ⓓ Ⓔ	24 Ⓐ Ⓑ Ⓒ Ⓓ Ⓔ	34 Ⓐ Ⓑ Ⓒ Ⓓ Ⓔ
5 Ⓐ Ⓑ Ⓒ Ⓓ Ⓔ	15 Ⓐ Ⓑ Ⓒ Ⓓ Ⓔ	25 Ⓐ Ⓑ Ⓒ Ⓓ Ⓔ	35 Ⓐ Ⓑ Ⓒ Ⓓ Ⓔ
6 Ⓐ Ⓑ Ⓒ Ⓓ Ⓔ	16 Ⓐ Ⓑ Ⓒ Ⓓ Ⓔ	26 Ⓐ Ⓑ Ⓒ Ⓓ Ⓔ	36 Ⓐ Ⓑ Ⓒ Ⓓ Ⓔ
7 Ⓐ Ⓑ Ⓒ Ⓓ Ⓔ	17 Ⓐ Ⓑ Ⓒ Ⓓ Ⓔ	27 Ⓐ Ⓑ Ⓒ Ⓓ Ⓔ	37 Ⓐ Ⓑ Ⓒ Ⓓ Ⓔ
8 Ⓐ Ⓑ Ⓒ Ⓓ Ⓔ	18 Ⓐ Ⓑ Ⓒ Ⓓ Ⓔ	28 Ⓐ Ⓑ Ⓒ Ⓓ Ⓔ	38 Ⓐ Ⓑ Ⓒ Ⓓ Ⓔ
9 Ⓐ Ⓑ Ⓒ Ⓓ Ⓔ	19 Ⓐ Ⓑ Ⓒ Ⓓ Ⓔ	29 Ⓐ Ⓑ Ⓒ Ⓓ Ⓔ	39 Ⓐ Ⓑ Ⓒ Ⓓ Ⓔ
10 Ⓐ Ⓑ Ⓒ Ⓓ Ⓔ	20 Ⓐ Ⓑ Ⓒ Ⓓ Ⓔ	30 Ⓐ Ⓑ Ⓒ Ⓓ Ⓔ	40 Ⓐ Ⓑ Ⓒ Ⓓ Ⓔ

SECTION 6

1 Ⓐ Ⓑ Ⓒ Ⓓ Ⓔ	11 Ⓐ Ⓑ Ⓒ Ⓓ Ⓔ	21 Ⓐ Ⓑ Ⓒ Ⓓ Ⓔ	31 Ⓐ Ⓑ Ⓒ Ⓓ Ⓔ
2 Ⓐ Ⓑ Ⓒ Ⓓ Ⓔ	12 Ⓐ Ⓑ Ⓒ Ⓓ Ⓔ	22 Ⓐ Ⓑ Ⓒ Ⓓ Ⓔ	32 Ⓐ Ⓑ Ⓒ Ⓓ Ⓔ
3 Ⓐ Ⓑ Ⓒ Ⓓ Ⓔ	13 Ⓐ Ⓑ Ⓒ Ⓓ Ⓔ	23 Ⓐ Ⓑ Ⓒ Ⓓ Ⓔ	33 Ⓐ Ⓑ Ⓒ Ⓓ Ⓔ
4 Ⓐ Ⓑ Ⓒ Ⓓ Ⓔ	14 Ⓐ Ⓑ Ⓒ Ⓓ Ⓔ	24 Ⓐ Ⓑ Ⓒ Ⓓ Ⓔ	34 Ⓐ Ⓑ Ⓒ Ⓓ Ⓔ
5 Ⓐ Ⓑ Ⓒ Ⓓ Ⓔ	15 Ⓐ Ⓑ Ⓒ Ⓓ Ⓔ	25 Ⓐ Ⓑ Ⓒ Ⓓ Ⓔ	35 Ⓐ Ⓑ Ⓒ Ⓓ Ⓔ
6 Ⓐ Ⓑ Ⓒ Ⓓ Ⓔ	16 Ⓐ Ⓑ Ⓒ Ⓓ Ⓔ	26 Ⓐ Ⓑ Ⓒ Ⓓ Ⓔ	36 Ⓐ Ⓑ Ⓒ Ⓓ Ⓔ
7 Ⓐ Ⓑ Ⓒ Ⓓ Ⓔ	17 Ⓐ Ⓑ Ⓒ Ⓓ Ⓔ	27 Ⓐ Ⓑ Ⓒ Ⓓ Ⓔ	37 Ⓐ Ⓑ Ⓒ Ⓓ Ⓔ
8 Ⓐ Ⓑ Ⓒ Ⓓ Ⓔ	18 Ⓐ Ⓑ Ⓒ Ⓓ Ⓔ	28 Ⓐ Ⓑ Ⓒ Ⓓ Ⓔ	38 Ⓐ Ⓑ Ⓒ Ⓓ Ⓔ
9 Ⓐ Ⓑ Ⓒ Ⓓ Ⓔ	19 Ⓐ Ⓑ Ⓒ Ⓓ Ⓔ	29 Ⓐ Ⓑ Ⓒ Ⓓ Ⓔ	39 Ⓐ Ⓑ Ⓒ Ⓓ Ⓔ
10 Ⓐ Ⓑ Ⓒ Ⓓ Ⓔ	20 Ⓐ Ⓑ Ⓒ Ⓓ Ⓔ	30 Ⓐ Ⓑ Ⓒ Ⓓ Ⓔ	40 Ⓐ Ⓑ Ⓒ Ⓓ Ⓔ

SECTION 7

1 Ⓐ Ⓑ Ⓒ Ⓓ Ⓔ	11 Ⓐ Ⓑ Ⓒ Ⓓ Ⓔ	21 Ⓐ Ⓑ Ⓒ Ⓓ Ⓔ	31 Ⓐ Ⓑ Ⓒ Ⓓ Ⓔ
2 Ⓐ Ⓑ Ⓒ Ⓓ Ⓔ	12 Ⓐ Ⓑ Ⓒ Ⓓ Ⓔ	22 Ⓐ Ⓑ Ⓒ Ⓓ Ⓔ	32 Ⓐ Ⓑ Ⓒ Ⓓ Ⓔ
3 Ⓐ Ⓑ Ⓒ Ⓓ Ⓔ	13 Ⓐ Ⓑ Ⓒ Ⓓ Ⓔ	23 Ⓐ Ⓑ Ⓒ Ⓓ Ⓔ	33 Ⓐ Ⓑ Ⓒ Ⓓ Ⓔ
4 Ⓐ Ⓑ Ⓒ Ⓓ Ⓔ	14 Ⓐ Ⓑ Ⓒ Ⓓ Ⓔ	24 Ⓐ Ⓑ Ⓒ Ⓓ Ⓔ	34 Ⓐ Ⓑ Ⓒ Ⓓ Ⓔ
5 Ⓐ Ⓑ Ⓒ Ⓓ Ⓔ	15 Ⓐ Ⓑ Ⓒ Ⓓ Ⓔ	25 Ⓐ Ⓑ Ⓒ Ⓓ Ⓔ	35 Ⓐ Ⓑ Ⓒ Ⓓ Ⓔ
6 Ⓐ Ⓑ Ⓒ Ⓓ Ⓔ	16 Ⓐ Ⓑ Ⓒ Ⓓ Ⓔ	26 Ⓐ Ⓑ Ⓒ Ⓓ Ⓔ	36 Ⓐ Ⓑ Ⓒ Ⓓ Ⓔ
7 Ⓐ Ⓑ Ⓒ Ⓓ Ⓔ	17 Ⓐ Ⓑ Ⓒ Ⓓ Ⓔ	27 Ⓐ Ⓑ Ⓒ Ⓓ Ⓔ	37 Ⓐ Ⓑ Ⓒ Ⓓ Ⓔ
8 Ⓐ Ⓑ Ⓒ Ⓓ Ⓔ	18 Ⓐ Ⓑ Ⓒ Ⓓ Ⓔ	28 Ⓐ Ⓑ Ⓒ Ⓓ Ⓔ	38 Ⓐ Ⓑ Ⓒ Ⓓ Ⓔ
9 Ⓐ Ⓑ Ⓒ Ⓓ Ⓔ	19 Ⓐ Ⓑ Ⓒ Ⓓ Ⓔ	29 Ⓐ Ⓑ Ⓒ Ⓓ Ⓔ	39 Ⓐ Ⓑ Ⓒ Ⓓ Ⓔ
10 Ⓐ Ⓑ Ⓒ Ⓓ Ⓔ	20 Ⓐ Ⓑ Ⓒ Ⓓ Ⓔ	30 Ⓐ Ⓑ Ⓒ Ⓓ Ⓔ	40 Ⓐ Ⓑ Ⓒ Ⓓ Ⓔ

REVIEWWARE™ Code Sheet for Volume #102

🔺	⛵	33707	🙂	⛵	29108	☎	⛵	11852
🔺	✛	26663	🙂	✛	16788	☎	✛	32736
🔺	🙂	7217	🙂	🙂	8768	☎	🙂	30866
🔺	♀	32074	🙂	♀	25148	☎	♀	32112
🔺	☎	37116	🙂	☎	7184	☎	☎	34407
🔺	⬜	21424	🙂	⬜	8310	☎	⬜	17530
🔺	💡	8651	🙂	💡	30026	☎	💡	4692
🔺	◎	17546	🙂	◎	9978	☎	◎	26573
🔺	🦈	30579	🙂	🦈	30038	☎	🦈	1046
🔺	🐜	15924	🙂	🐜	5659	☎	🐜	33316
✛	⛵	9634	♀	⛵	15934	⬜	⛵	18960
✛	✛	3172	♀	✛	8632	⬜	✛	11335
✛	🙂	4932	♀	🙂	1550	⬜	🙂	2312
✛	♀	30005	♀	♀	6895	⬜	♀	39286
✛	☎	5329	♀	☎	20680	⬜	☎	9628
✛	⬜	27723	♀	⬜	5234	⬜	⬜	14598
✛	💡	14287	♀	💡	11223	⬜	💡	25745
✛	◎	3503	♀	◎	2161	⬜	◎	24125
✛	🦈	26364	♀	🦈	27461	⬜	🦈	1715
✛	🐜	752	♀	🐜	24958	⬜	🐜	31037

SOFTWARE LICENSE

This License Agreement is your proof of license. Please treat it as valuable property.

RevieWare License Agreement

This is a legal agreement between you (either an individual or an entity), the end user, and The Princeton Review Publishing Corporation Inc., ("TPRP"). If you do not agree to its terms, promptly return the disk package and accompanying items (including written materials and binders or other containers) to the place you obtained them for a full refund.

REVIEWARE SOFTWARE LICENSE

1. GRANT OF LICENSE. This RevieWare License Agreement ("License") permits you to use one copy of the specified version of the RevieWare software product identified above ("SOFTWARE") on any single computer, provided the SOFTWARE is in use on only one computer at any time. If you have multiple Licenses for the SOFTWARE, then at any time you may have as many copies of the SOFTWARE in use as you have Licenses. The SOFTWARE is "in use" on a computer when it is loaded into the temporary memory (i.e., RAM) or installed into the permanent memory (e.g., hard disk, CD-ROM, or other storage device) of that computer, except that a copy installed on a network server for the sole purpose of distribution to other computers is not "in use." If the anticipated number of users of the SOFTWARE will exceed the number of applicable Licenses, then you must have a reasonable mechanism or process in place to assure that the number of persons using the SOFTWARE concurrently does not exceed the number of Licenses. If the SOFTWARE is permanently installed on the hard disk or other storage device of a computer (other than a network server) and one person uses that computer more than 80% of the time it is in use, then that person may also use the SOFTWARE on a portable or home computer.

2. COPYRIGHT. The SOFTWARE is owned by TPRP or its suppliers and is protected by United States copyright laws and international treaty provisions. Therefore, you must treat the SOFTWARE like any other copyrighted material (e.g., a book or musical recording) <u>except</u> that you may either (a) make one copy of the SOFTWARE solely for backup or archival purposes, or (b) transfer the SOFTWARE to a single hard disk provided you keep the original solely for backup or archival purposes. You may not copy the written materials accompanying the SOFTWARE.

3. OTHER RESTRICTIONS. This RevieWare License Agreement is your proof of license to Licenses the rights granted herein and must be retained by you. You may not rent or lease the SOFTWARE, but you may transfer your rights under this RevieWare License Agreement on a permanent basis provided you transfer this License Agreement, the SOFTWARE, and all accompanying written materials and retain no copies, and the recipient agrees to the terms of this Agreement. You may not reverse engineer, decompile, or disassemble the SOFTWARE. Any transfer of the SOFTWARE must include the most recent update and all prior versions.

LIMITED WARRANTY

LIMITED WARRANTY. TPRP warrants that (a) the SOFTWARE will perform substantially in accordance with the accompanying written materials for a period of ninety (90) days from the date of receipt; and (b) any hardware accompanying the SOFTWARE will be free from defects in materials and workmanship under normal use and service for a period of one (1) year from the date of receipt. Any implied warranties on the SOFTWARE and hardware are limited to ninety (90) days and one (1) year, respectively. Some states do not allow limitations on duration of an implied warranty so the above limitation may not apply to you.

CUSTOMER REMEDIES. TPRP's entire liability and your exclusive remedy shall be at TPRP's option, either (a) return of the price paid or (b) repair or replacement of the SOFTWARE or hardware that does not meet TPRP Limited Warranty and that is returned to TPRP with a copy of your receipt. This Limited Warranty is void if failure of the SOFTWARE or hardware has resulted from accident, abuse, or misapplication. Any replacement SOFTWARE will be warranted for the remainder of the original warranty period or thirty (30) days, whichever is longer. **These remedies are not available outside the United States of America.**

<u>NO OTHER WARRANTIES.</u> **TPRP disdains all other warranties, either express or implied, including but not limited to implied warranties of merchantability and fitness for a particular purpose with respect to the SOFTWARE, the accompanying written materials,** and any accompanying hardware. This limited warranty gives you specific legal rights. You may have others, which vary from state to state.

<u>NO LIABILITY FOR CONSEQUENTIAL DAMAGES.</u> **In no event shall TPRP or its suppliers be liable for any damages whatsoever (including, without limitation, damages for loss of business profits, business interruption, loss of business information, or other pecuniary loss) arising out of the use or inability to use this TPRP product, even if TPRP has been advised of the possibility of such damages. Because some states do not allow the exclusion or limitation of liability for consequential or incidental damages, the above limitation may not apply to you.**

U.S. GOVERNMENT RESTRICTED RIGHTS

The SOFTWARE and documentation are provided with RESTRICTED RIGHTS. Use, duplication, or disclosure by the Government is subject to restrictions as set forth in subparagraph (c)(I)(ii) of the Rights in Technical Data and Computer Software clause at DFARS 252.227-7013 or subparagraphs (c)(1) and (2) of the Commercial Computer Software—Restricted Rights at 48 CFR 52.227-19, as applicable. Contractor manufacturer is TPRP/2315 Broadway/New York, 10024.

This Agreement is governed by the laws of the State of New York.

For more information about TPRP's licensing policies, please call RevieWare Customer Service at (212) 874-8282, or write: RevieWare Customer Sales and Service/2315 Broadway/New York, NY 10024.